THE
TOYOTA
KATA
PRACTICE
GUIDE

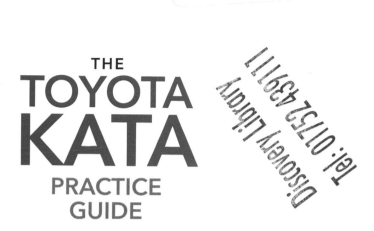

THE
TOYOTA
KATA
PRACTICE
GUIDE

PRACTICING SCIENTIFIC
THINKING SKILLS FOR
SUPERIOR RESULTS IN
20 MINUTES A DAY

MIKE
ROTHER

ILLUSTRATIONS BY LIBBY WAGNER

Mc
Graw
Hill
Education

NEW YORK   CHICAGO   SAN FRANCISCO   ATHENS
LONDON   MADRID   MEXICO CITY   MILAN
NEW DELHI   SINGAPORE   SYDNEY   TORONTO

1 2 3 4 5 6 7 8 9   LCR   22 21 20 19 18 17

ISBN 978-1-259-86102-4
MHID   1-259-86102-3

e-ISBN 978-1-259-86103-1
e-MHID   1-259-86103-1

Cover art figures created by Grace Rother, inspired by *Toyota Kata* "doll figures" designed by Paola Bulcao/ Grupo A.
Design by Mauna Eichner and Lee Fukui
Illustrations by Libby Wagner, MPS North America

McGraw-Hill Education books are available at special quantity discounts to use as premiums and sales promotions or for use in corporate training programs. To contact a representative, please visit the Contact Us pages at www.mhprofessional.com.

CONTENTS

ACKNOWLEDGMENTS

Since the publication of *Toyota Kata* in 2009 I've heard from and learned from hundreds of persons in organizations around the world who are experimenting with and applying the findings described in that book. I thank them as a group!

I also want to highlight and thank the wonderful colleagues and friends listed on the next page, with whom I've been working and learning. It's been a pleasure to test ideas and share what we learn through speaking, slideshares, videos, articles, workshops, and posting online the evolving material that finally became this book. Thank you for 10 years of fruitful experimenting, dialogue, and challenging one another. This book stands on many shoulders. (I apologize to anyone I've accidentally overlooked.)

Most authors have an editor, but at McGraw-Hill I've been fortunate to work with four able editors on the Toyota Kata books and the expanding Toyota Kata topic area. Thank you, Mary Glenn, Knox Huston, Donya Dickerson, and Noah Schwarrzberg. Thank you also to Mauna Eichner and Lee Fukui.

A special thank you to my friend and Kata colleague Mark Rosenthal, who generously rolled up his sleeves and gave me lots of editing feedback and support.

Thank you to my wife Liz and our daughters Grace and Olivia, who've lived with a "Kata" track running in the back of my mind 24/7. They gave me valuable advice on endless texts and artwork, and incorporated more scientific thinking into their own lives—which is really the main point of practicing the Improvement Kata and Coaching Kata.

This book is dedicated to young people, who are the future.

Thank you to these Kata colleagues:

Jens Albat
Katie Anderson
Pia Anhede
Gerd Aulinger
Jennifer Ayers
Toni Benner
Dan Bergeron
Joakim Bjurström
Barb Bouché
Pat Boutier
Bill Boyd
Brandon Brown
Tom Burke
Sam Carlson
Rhonda Carpenter
Beth Carrington
Michael Casten
Bill Costantino
Hank Czarnecki
Joe Dager
Andrea Darabos
Jeremiah Davis and Family
Tracy Defoe
Professor Jochen Deuse
Stéphane Dubreuil
Bob Elliot
Professor Lutz Engel
Dan Ezekiel
Norman Faull
Tyler Fife
Eamon Fitzmaurice
Rick Fleming
Håkan Forss
Brad Frank
Jim Franz
Lean Frontiers
    Jim Huntzinger
    Dwayne Butcher
    Amanda Day-Ott
    Jaclyn Molewyk
Jeff Fuchs
Professor Kai Furmans
Dennis Gawlik

Dale Gehring
Betty Gratopp
Bruce Hamilton
David Harry
Chris Hayes
Sabine Hempen
Doug Hendren
Joakim Hillberg
Hiroshi Hiromoto
Dave Hogg
Jez Humble
Kathy Iberle
Kimio Inagaki
Tom Ingram
Todd Jacobi
Susan Janus
Marco Kamberg
Britta Kammel
Craig Kennedy
Gene Kim
Carsten Klages
Professor Jim Knight
Jeff Kopenitz
Bill Kraus
Daniela Kudernatsch
Brian Lagas
Eduardo Lander
Professor Sylvain Landry
Diane Landsiedel
Jean-Marc Legentil
Adam Light
Professor Jeffrey Liker
Drew Locher
Michael Lombard
Jim Manley
Dan Markovitz
Dana Markunas
Professor Constantin May
Michele McLaughlin
Steve Medland
Janina Meier
Amy Mervak
Wayne Meyer

Bernd Mittelhuber
Yvonne Muir
Pierre Nadeau
Barry O'Reilly
Francisco Ocejo
Tyson Ortiz
Gary Perkerwicz
Melissa Perri
Marek Piatkowski
Anna Possio
Giorgio Possio
Tadas Puksta
Mike Radtke
Ram Ramamurthy
David Rau
Ralph Richter
Andreas Ritzenhoff
Oscar Roche
Mark Rosenthal
Mark Rosenthal
Karyn Ross
Meryl Runion
Jason Schulist
Tilo Schwarz
Julie Simmons and NWHPEC
Scott Simmons
Jenny Snow-Boscolo
Dwayne Soisson
Conrad Soltero
Dario Spinola
Skip Steward
Craig Stritar
Teemu Toivonen
Connie Tolman
Jeff Uitenbroek
Emiel van Est
Jennifer VanHorssen
Dan Vermeesch
Karl Wadensten
Whitney Walters
John Willis
Ralph Winkler

EXCERPT FROM *TOYOTA KATA*

There are perhaps only three things we can and need to know with certainty: where we are, where we want to be, and by what *means* we should maneuver the unclear territory between here and there. And the rest is supposed to be somewhat unclear, because we cannot see into the future! The way from where we are to where we want to be next is a gray zone full of unforeseeable obstacles, problems, and issues that we can only discover along the way. The best we can do is to know the approach, the means, we can utilize for dealing with the unclear path to a new desired condition, not what the content and steps of our actions—the solutions—will be.

—*Toyota Kata* (2009), page 8

A WAY TO LEARN AND TEACH SCIENTIFIC THINKING

Kata are simple, structured routines that you practice deliberately, especially at the beginning, so their pattern becomes a habit and leaves you with new abilities. The word comes from the martial arts, where Kata are used to train combatants in basic building-block moves. But the idea of practicing Kata can be applied in a much broader sense. This practice guide is about practicing a scientific way of working, and, ultimately, thinking, in order to achieve superior results.

No one knows what the world will look like in the future, so one of the most valuable skills you can have is the ability to adapt. *Scientific thinking* is exactly that. It involves a running comparison between what you predict will happen next, seeing what actually happens, and adjusting based on what you learn from the difference. Scientific thinking may be the best way we have of navigating through unpredictable territory to achieve challenging goals. Practiced deliberately for even just 20 minutes a day, scientific thinking can make anyone more adaptive, creative, and successful in the face of uncertainty.

Perhaps the greatest thing about scientific thinking is that it is a life skill that's useful for developing solutions in any situation. We tend to equate creativity with the arts, but scientific thinking *is* creative thinking, and practicing it is at the root of creative capability and mindset. The purpose of this book is to share what we've learned about using the practice routines of the Improvement Kata and Coaching Kata to teach and learn scientific thinking.

You'll find that scientific thinking is not difficult, it's just not our default mode. Practicing the Improvement Kata and Coaching Kata forms habits that help you solve problems, achieve goals, and reframe how you look at and deal with the world. But it is not about learning problem solving. It's about learning a mindset that makes you *better* at problem solving.

How do we modify our way of thinking, and how do you do that across a team or an entire organization?

Many of our thinking patterns live in a self-perpetuating loop. Simply put, every time we think or do something, we are more likely to do it again (Figure I.1). Every time we think or do something, we're adding more pavement to the roadways in our brain, turning them into highways and increasing the likelihood that we'll use those same roads again. They're our habits.

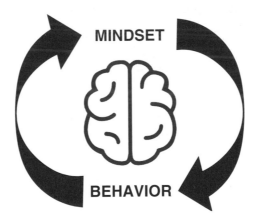

MINDSET

BEHAVIOR

Figure I.1. Every time you think or do something, you are more likely to do it again.

The good news is that habits are essential to our survival. The even better news is that many of our thinking patterns can be modified, through a process that resembles skill development in sports and music. You deliberately practice a new behavior pattern, every day, and over time, and with the right set of emotions, that creates new neural pathways and reshapes your thinking.

However, shifting to a new, life-changing habit all at once is probably impossible, since the strength of our existing neural pathways, our existing habits, tends to pull us back. It's usually more effective to start small, by introducing a few new routines into your daily activity and building on them as your abilities and confidence start to grow.

That's where Kata come in. Or, as I like to call them, "Starter Kata." These are structured practice routines that put you on the road to successfully developing new patterns of thinking (Figure I.2). Practicing Starter Kata modifies the mindsets that drive our behavior, increases the velocity of learning, and is particularly helpful when you want to create a shared way of thinking and acting in a group of people, because everyone starts with the same basics.

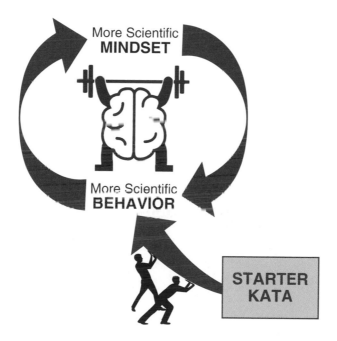

Figure I.2. Practicing Starter Kata helps you develop new thinking by introducing new behaviors.

The Toyota Kata Practice Guide is an instruction manual and reference book for a set of Starter Kata that are utilized to develop scientific thinking. It's designed for two users who work together as a pair:

- **The Learner:** Anyone who wants to become proficient, through practice, in the practical scientific working and thinking pattern described by the Improvement Kata.

- **The Coach:** Anyone who wants to become proficient at providing coaching support to the Improvement Kata learners by practicing the Coaching Kata.

The Toyota Kata Practice Guide gives you an approach for mobilizing the creative capacity of anyone and any team in any organization. Begin by practicing the Starter Kata presented in this book, and then, as you gain greater scientific thinking skill and understanding, build upon them to fit your situation and develop your own way. The Starter Kata are not the end game—they put you on the road to new skills.

A Way of Managing Suitable for Our Time

We may be exiting a business period when the main challenges revolved around maximizing efficiency and reducing cost, and entering a time when challenges are more diverse and paths more unpredictable. Yesterday's solutions may not fit tomorrow's problems. But there is no cause for concern—we're well equipped to meet challenges of all sorts, as long as we practice an effective way of doing that. The most important thing for managers to focus on may not be the content of what their people are working on, but the patterns of thinking and acting we utilize as we strive for goals. What we are talking about here is developing the capability and confidence of people in the organization as a main aspect (and possibly *the* main aspect) of a manager's job.

The management methods we've been practicing over the last few decades were arguably intended to reduce uncertainty, but the management methods of the future may be as much about being effective and comfortable working within unavoidable uncertainty. Practicing the Improvement Kata and Coaching Kata is not going to make you and your team more certain about how to reach a particular goal. It makes you more certain about how to *go about reaching any goal*.

Although learning new skills involves a certain amount of discomfort, it's quite amazing what you can achieve through practicing a practical form of scientific thinking. The more scientific thinking capability you develop in your teams, the more you can empower them to meet challenges that you may have once considered impossible. Managers play a key role in this, because it is their job to create the creators. *The Toyota Kata Practice Guide* is a handbook for how to do that. Look around you. The workplace may be the largest classroom of all, and its managers are the teachers.

Mike Rother
March 2017
Ann Arbor, USA

The Toyota Kata Backstory

The original Toyota Kata research my colleagues and I did ran from 2004 to 2009 and is summarized in the book *Toyota Kata*.[1] It was driven by these two questions:

1. What are the unseen managerial routines and thinking that lie behind Toyota's success with continuous improvement and adaption?

2. How can other companies develop similar routines and thinking in their organizations?

We knew something different was going on at Toyota, and we believed it lay in Toyota's management approach. But that system was not visible to visitors. My colleague, Professor Jeffrey Liker, put it well during a 2010 interview on the National Public Radio program *This American Life* about the Toyota-led NUMMI joint venture between Toyota and General Motors:

> There was no vocabulary, even, to explain it. So I remember, one of the GM managers was ordered, from a very senior level—it came from a vice president—to make a GM plant look like NUMMI. And he said, "I want you to go there with cameras and take a picture of every square inch. And whatever you take a picture of, I want it to look like that in our plant. There should be no excuse for why we're different than NUMMI, why our quality is lower, why our productivity isn't as high, because you're going to copy everything you see."
>
> Immediately, this guy knew that was crazy. We can't copy employee motivation, we can't copy good relationships between the union and management. That's not something you can copy, and you can't even take a photograph of it.[2]

We know from long experience in the Lean community that "copy the artifacts" approaches have a poor record for generating the kind of continuous improvement we see at Toyota. The Toyota Kata research was an attempt to better understand the *culture of improvement* that lay below the surface.

My colleagues and I began by interviewing Toyota people, but it quickly became apparent that they had difficulty articulating and explaining the patterns of their thinking and routines. I believe this is because such patterns represent the customary, habitual way of doing

(continues)

---

1 Rother, Mike, *Toyota Kata, Managing People for Improvement, Adaptiveness, and Superior Results,* 2009 McGraw-Hill.

2 Professor Jeffrey Liker, excerpt from Episode 403, "NUMMI," *This American Life,* aired March 26, 2010.

things in an organization, and are thus somewhat invisible to those carrying them out. This may be true for managers in any management system.

We had to figure it out ourselves by experimenting in factory and managerial settings. Five companies agreed to provide long-term test sites, and several additional companies became sites for shorter, specific trials. The experimenting involved applying technical and managerial Toyota practices and paying particular attention to what *did not* work as intended, investigating why, adjusting, and trying again. During that six-year investigation I also periodically met with Toyota-group sites, Toyota suppliers, and Toyota employees, to observe them and to discuss our interim findings. These discussions would often influence the character of our next trials.

Part of the research challenge was that each Toyota manager has his or her own style. Coaching at Toyota is not prestructured and is not necessarily daily. There is no formal coaching protocol and no protocol for daily practice, though that frequency is desired. Yet when you study what various Toyota managers do long enough, a common pattern of thinking and acting does emerge, which is taught at all levels inside Toyota. The content of what people work on naturally differs from area to area and level to level, as can each manager's approach, but the basic thinking pattern the managers are teaching is the same. After numerous tests and observations, we began to see a pattern of thinking and behavior in the way that Toyota managers work with their people, which is different from traditional Western command-and-control management routines.

We came to see that Toyota's management approach involves teaching all organization members a scientific approach and mindset that can be applied to an infinite number of challenges and objectives. Toyota wants its people to work scientifically, instead of jumping to conclusions. The teaching happens through coached application practice (currently called "on-the-job development" at Toyota) in the course of normal daily work, which creates a deliberate, shared way of working throughout the organization.

Seeing what's behind Toyota's management approach helps explain why simply reverse engineering the visible Lean techniques at Toyota doesn't work. Those practices happen to be solutions Toyota is using at this moment in time. What is more important is how Toyota develops its people to arrive at this moment and begin preparing for tomorrow. The learned scientific way of thinking and working is the invisible context within which Toyota's visible solutions are developed, function, and evolve. We would do well to adopt a similar way of working, rather than just trying to copy Toyota's tools and solutions.

Researchers usually try to represent the phenomenon they are studying with a model. I depicted the pattern of thinking and behavior that Toyota teaches with a four-step behavior model that I called the "Improvement Kata." I gave it this name because of the connection between Toyota's management approach and the concept of Kata—meaning a *way of doing things* and *practice routines*—in Japanese culture.

Focusing on Question 2

We now had a model of what Toyota does. While this addressed the first research question, *What are the unseen managerial routines and thinking that lie behind Toyota's success with continuous improvement and adaptation?* it did not address the second: *How can other companies develop similar routines and thinking in their organizations?* It didn't take long to realize that just sharing the four-step Improvement Kata model, even in great detail, does not generate new ways of thinking and acting. As a result, since publication of the book *Toyota Kata* in 2009, we have focused almost exclusively on that second research question.

We had seen that at Toyota the choreography of the desired scientific thinking pattern lies inside the heads of Toyota's seasoned coaches: its managers. Most other organizations do not have that. Toyota is working to *preserve* its culture and has many experienced coaches among its managers. Other organizations need to *modify* their culture and do not yet have managers with experience in coaching the scientific-thinking way. It's another example of how you can't just copy Toyota. Teams and organizations, even inside Toyota, will require coached practice to build those skills. And effective practice often starts with some simple routines.

Based on the details of what we observed Toyota managers doing, we have been evolving a set of practice routines—called "Starter Kata"—to systematize the practice that is handled implicitly inside Toyota's culture. These Starter Kata make the process explicit, teachable, and transferable to compensate for the fact that most organizations do not yet have a strong surrounding organizational culture of scientific thinking.

The set of practice routines in this book has evolved through trials and daily use at hundreds of different organizations, growing into a popular, non-Toyota-specific approach. It's no longer about copying Toyota, but about emulating the intention and developing our own way.

PART I

BRINGING TOGETHER SCIENTIFIC THINKING AND PRACTICE

CHAPTER **1**

SCIENTIFIC THINKING FOR EVERYONE

How many times has this happened to you? You notice something out of the corner of your eye, but when you turn to look it's not what you thought. That cat is actually just a crumpled-up jacket on a chair. The car on your left is only passing you, not actually entering your lane.

What's interesting about this effect is that our brain didn't react with, *"Not sure what that is . . . need more information . . . please wait."* Instead, it swiftly and without telling us crossed what I call the "threshold of knowledge." That knowledge threshold is the line at which we no longer have facts and data and start speculating. The unconscious part of our brain takes bits of surface information, extrapolates to fill in blanks, and gives us a sense that we know what's going on (Figure 1.1). But we actually know a lot less than we think we do.

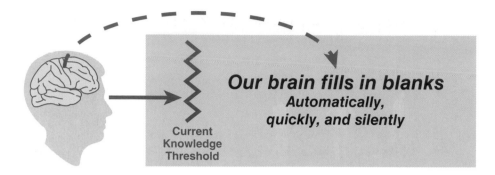

Figure 1.1. We tend to cross over knowledge thresholds.
The brain creates instant judgments using the inputs it receives.

That last paragraph may sound like I'm being critical of the brain's tendency to cross over knowledge thresholds and jump to conclusions, but the story isn't so simple. This cognitive mechanism, or *cognitive bias*, is actually essential for getting us through the day. It's an energy-saving, better-safe-than-sorry approach that's beneficial when fast reaction is more valuable than deep understanding. Imagine trying to navigate situations while your brain says, *"Please wait until I get more information."* We probably wouldn't be here today. It's theorized that we inherited some of our genetic programming from ancestors who quickly ran away from a rustling in the bushes, not from those who turned and said, *"Hey, I wonder what that is."*

Yet this useful cognitive mechanism, our intuition or "flying on anecdote," can also cause a lot of problems. It means we frequently don't notice our knowledge thresholds—a trap we fall into all the time. It's a daily balancing act whereby we tend to unconsciously err on the side of jumping to conclusions and living within the parameters of the stories we tell ourselves.[1] This is useful for navigating rush-hour traffic, but can also be harmful in our work, society, and personal lives. The ability to stop and think, *"Hey, I wonder what that is,"* is also essential to our survival and progress as humans, because it is a way of learning.

Scientific Thinking

Fortunately there is a ready countermeasure for our jump-to-conclusions nature. It's called scientific thinking. That may sound like something complicated and exclusive to professional scientists, but anyone can be a scientist in daily life, including you and me.

---

1 This catchphrase is by Professor Ralph Williams, University of Michigan.

Scientific thinking is not difficult, it just isn't our default mode. With a bit of practice anyone can do it, which is what this practice guide is about.

For the purposes of this book we'll define **scientific thinking** as *a process of deliberately engaging reality with the intent of learning.* At the core of scientific thinking is continuous curiosity about a world we will never fully understand, but we want to take the next step to understand a little better. **It is a continuous comparison between what we *predict* will happen next, seeing what *actually happens*, and adjusting our understanding and actions based on what we learn from the difference (Figure 1.2).**

Figure 1.2. Here's the basic pattern of scientific thinking. You make a prediction, reality happens, and if there's a difference you learn from it.

Scientific thinking is the best way we have to avoid being fooled by our perceptions. You can use scientific thinking yourself, in your team, and throughout your organization to help you achieve goals even though the exact path can't be fully known ahead of time. You *iterate* your way forward—always adding to knowledge as you take steps—instead of trying to decide your way forward.

Conditions around us are complex and dynamic, and today's "benchmark solutions" probably won't fit tomorrow's problems. Given these conditions, the best bet for you and your team is to develop a universal "meta skill" for developing solutions in any situation. This is exactly what scientific thinking does, and it may be the most effective means currently known for navigating through unpredictable and complex territory toward our goals (Figure 1.3).

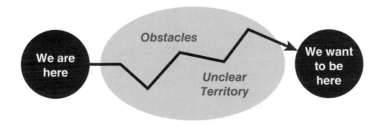

Figure 1.3. Scientific thinking helps us navigate complex, unpredictable territory.

Scientific Thinking Is Especially Useful Because It Is a Meta Skill

Skills are often domain-specific. You don't learn to play baseball by practicing soccer. But scientific thinking is a way of working toward any objective. The basic pattern is always the same, regardless of your goal, business sector, or strategy. That makes it a meta skill.

To understand this, separate *what* you're working on from *how* you're working on it. Meta skills define the how-to, not the what-to. Meta skills tell us how to proceed, but not the content of solutions, and can thus be applied to an infinite variety of situations. Scientists don't change *how* they work with each new research topic. The trick is to develop well-worn mental circuits not for solutions, but for a *means of developing solutions*. This is just like training in sports, where to prepare for unpredictable contests the focus of the training is practicing how to play. That's meta!

Since meta skills are transferable across different situations, including ones you've never experienced before, they can be more valuable than knowledge of a single situation or problem. No one knows what goals and problems your organization will face in the future, so teaching today's known solutions is not enough. Instead, scientific thinking endows you with skills that can be applied to all sorts of issues and problems you can't even see yet, over a lifetime.

Born with, or Learned?

Is scientific thinking a talent that some people naturally have, or is it a learned skill? You've probably noticed that small children do explore somewhat in the manner of scientists. During that early part of life our brain is highly plastic and is shaping itself through our encounters with the physical and social aspects of our environment.

However, by early adulthood our brain has built up an elaborate web of neural pathways, and it now takes conscious effort to counteract them. As small children we use what we learn from sensory input—from experiments!—to build up our internal structures. As adults, we use those established internal structures to navigate, and we tend to seek out situations that match our internal structures or try to alter our environment to make it match them.[2] The child's mind is learning, and the adult mind is performing.[3]

---

2 For more on this subject, read the Introduction to the book *Brain and Culture* by Bruce E. Wexler (2006, MIT Press).

3 This saying is from our colleague Jeremiah Davis.

In short, once we hit early adulthood we are notoriously bad at scientific thinking, due to the neural library of experiences we've constructed that allows us to navigate the world in a way that children cannot. This is both a strength and a weakness for adults. For anyone who has acquired the skills to be able to read this sentence, exploratory scientific thinking is no longer a routine you do naturally. Instead, it's something we do deliberately in order to check our assumptions and compensate for our biases. Adults learn scientific thinking through intentional practice.

The Improvement Kata—The Four-Step Scientific Pattern We're Trying to Learn

If you're going to practice, then you need something *to* practice.

A model is a representation that helps us understand and communicate how something functions in reality. The Improvement Kata pattern is a four-step model of a practical,[4] everyday scientific way of thinking and working. It represents the human creative process, which has probably been around for as long as humans have been around. Scientists and entrepreneurs follow something like this pattern every day. The four steps are illustrated in Figures 1.4 and 1.5 on the next page. **Let's take a quick look at each of the four steps of the Improvement Kata.**

The Planning Phase

Traditionally we want to jump straight to implementing our ideas, because our brains are already filling in the gaps of knowledge and we often feel certain we know what to do. This is a point, though, where we do want to slow down and say, "*Not sure what is going on here . . . need more information.*" Taking the time to more thoroughly understand where you are now and establish where you are trying to go will pay off in the long run. The insight and perspective gained in the first three "planning" steps of the Improvement Kata provide the frame or context for effective iteration and discovery in the "executing" phase. There are three steps here:

- Understand the direction or challenge.

- Grasp the current condition.

- Establish the next target condition.

---

4 I use the word *practical* because a traditional scientist experiments in order to understand, whereas an Improvement Kata practitioner experiments to move toward a goal.

The Improvement Kata Model

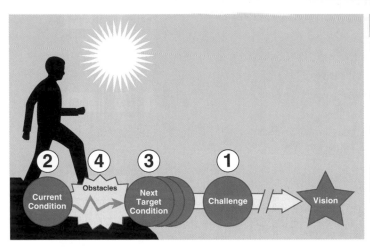

Planning Phase

① Start by considering the overall direction or **Challenge**.

② Get a firsthand grasp of the **Current Condition**.

③ Establish the **Next Target Condition** on the way to the challenge.

Executing Phase

④ Move toward the target condition with **Experiments**, which uncovers obstacles that you need to work on.

Figure 1.4. The four steps of the Improvement Kata model.

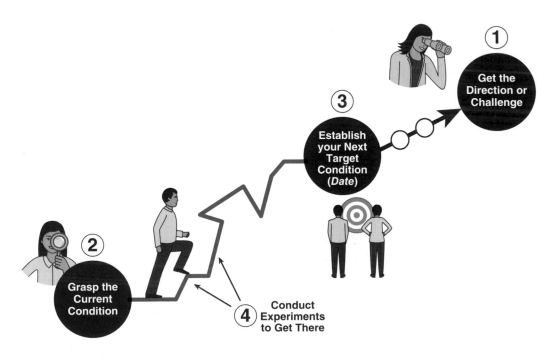

Figure 1.5. A graphic depiction of the Improvement Kata model.

STEP 1: Understand the Direction or Challenge. Step one defines the purpose for improvement. It's generally a longer-range goal that will differentiate you from your competitors, typically something customer-focused and strategic that you can't yet do today. You don't know how you are going to reach that challenge, and at first it may seem impossible and even a little scary. An overall challenge is typically set at the organization or business unit (value stream) level and gets broken into successively smaller challenges as you move down into the organization.

STEP 2: Grasp the Current Condition. *Where are we now?* Once the direction coming from the level above you is understood, go to your own focus process and study its current operating patterns in measurable detail. The results of this observation and analysis represent your current knowledge threshold about that process, and are an input into defining the next target condition for it.

STEP 3: Establish the Next Target Condition. *Where do we want to be next?* Studying the current condition gives you the facts and data you need to establish an appropriate, descriptive, and measurable next target condition for your focus process, in the direction of the larger challenge. A target condition is your *next* goal and has a much closer time frame than the challenge, usually with an achieve-by date between one week and three months out. You don't know exactly how you are going to get there, and it may be difficult, but it doesn't feel impossible. A target condition usually has the following three elements:

1. An achieve-by date.

2. The desired outcome performance of the process—an outcome metric.

3. A verifiable description of the desired operating pattern (how you want the focus process to be operating on the achieve-by date) that you predict will produce the desired outcome performance. This includes a process metric.

While achieving the longer-term challenge can feel overwhelming, having a short-term target condition narrows your focus to the specific obstacles to achieving that nearer condition. Those obstacles are what you will experiment against in step four of the Improvement Kata.

It takes a series of target conditions to reach the challenge, as illustrated by the successive circles in Figures 1.4 and 1.5. Note, however, that those target conditions are defined one after another, not all at once. They are not a predetermined list of milestones or action items. When you reach one target condition or its achieve-by date, the focus process will have a new current condition, you will know more, and then you'll be in a position to establish an appropriate next, further target condition in the direction of the challenge.

You can't tell in advance exactly what the chain of necessary target conditions will be, due to your threshold of knowledge, which moves. Making an initial plan may be valuable, of course, but expect it to change as you learn.

The Executing Phase

Having laid your groundwork in the planning phase, you are now ready to execute, fast and focused, with learning and adjusting as you go.

STEP 4: Experiment Toward the Target Condition. Once you understand the current condition and have a next target condition, there is a gray zone, or learning zone, between them. If your target condition achieve-by date is more than a week or two away, you probably need to do some planning. Nonetheless, you still cannot foresee and plan the exact path to a target condition.[5] The obstacles you encounter on the way will show you what you *need* to work on to get there, and you find your path by conducting daily or frequent experiments against those obstacles. You don't need to work on every conceivable obstacle, only those obstacles that you actually find are preventing your focus process from operating in a way consistent with the next target condition. This is advantageous because you minimize wasting your time, capacity, and resources trying to fix everything. In fact, you'll learn the discipline of ignoring some problems.

The path to the target condition will not be a straight line. You're in a mode of rapid learning and discovery to progressively learn how to get to the target condition. From each experiment you may gain new information and adjust your next step accordingly. Be ready to accept that the path may be different from what you expected, and don't waste time arguing about who has the best solution. Argue instead about what may be the best next experiment for learning more and seeing further as quickly as possible.

When you reach the target condition achieve-by date, you're in a new position. There is a new current condition, and the four steps of the Improvement Kata now are repeated.

The Overall Pattern

The Improvement Kata model can also be depicted linearly, as shown in Figure 1.6. In the linear representation the planning phase and executing phase become visible.

---

5 Making a detailed project plan doesn't eliminate uncertainty, it only provides an illusion of certainty. If you go to business school and learn an analysis and planning process, that's only half of the matter. You should also learn a good iteration process.

Based on the descriptions of the three planning steps, you should notice that "planning" in the Improvement Kata is different from the traditional leap to making an action plan. A common mistake is trying to get into the executing phase too soon—rushing into implementation based on preconceptions. Instead, you take some time to analyze and learn more about the situation. Compared to a traditional businessperson who may be in a hurry to lay out an action plan, a scientific thinker might say that *a problem clearly defined is half solved.*

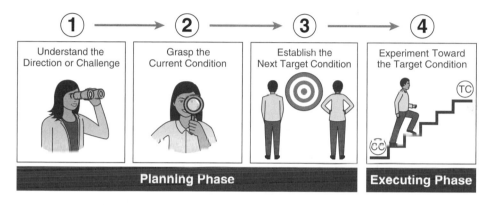

Figure 1.6. A linear depiction of the Improvement Kata model.

As you use this book, always keep in mind that the Improvement Kata pattern is not a problem-solving method, but a mindset; a way of thinking in problem solving. There are many good problem-solving methodologies, and practicing the Improvement Kata supports them all. Notice that no matter what kind of problem solving you are doing, you're going to have these conditions:

- A goal that you have not yet reached

- Obstacles to that goal

- Solutions that don't yet exist (otherwise you would have already implemented them)

- A need to test your ideas

The Improvement Kata pattern doesn't replace your improvement methods. Its purpose is to build the foundational scientific thinking skills that make you even better at whatever problem-solving or improvement methodology you are using. Practicing the Improvement Kata integrates well with existing methods and approaches because it is about the underlying thinking.

What Are Kata?

Here are two slightly different definitions for the Japanese word *Kata*. We'll use both. Notice how definition 1 (a pattern) without definition 2 (practice routines) is unlikely to change behavior and mindset:

1. One definition of *Kata* is a suffix meaning "way of doing." For instance, the Japanese word *kakikata* means "way of writing" or "how to write." This definition pertains to the four-step Improvement Kata model or pattern, which is a *way of improving*. Think of this as the "macro" definition.

2. Another definition of *Kata* is a "structured practice routine or drill." This is the "micro" definition.

That second definition of *Kata* refers to small, predefined practice routines, or drills, of fundamentals that help get us started in adopting a new way of acting and thinking. For clarity's sake, let's differentiate that definition by calling them "Starter Kata," meaning they are the first basic practice routines you begin with. **You practice Starter Kata (micro) in order to learn the scientific way of thinking depicted by the Improvement Kata model (macro).**

Practicing Starter Kata has been utilized for centuries as a way of preserving effective skillsets, transmitting them from person to person, and building effective teamwork. Having a set of Starter Kata is particularly useful when you want to create a shared way of thinking and acting, a deliberate culture, among a group of people, because everyone begins with practicing the same fundamentals.

Starter Kata are stepping-stones for acquiring new habits of thinking and acting, but practicing them does not mean becoming permanently rigid. The intent of formally practicing some structured Starter Kata is not to hem you in, but to help set you on a new path (Figure 1.7). The goal is to internalize each Starter Kata's fundamental pattern so you can then build on and adapt that pattern under a variety of circumstances as a reflex, with little thought or hesitation. For example, as a musician you wouldn't stick with playing a musical scale forever, but you wouldn't change that Starter Kata either. You go beyond it by building on what you learned from practicing it. The next learner who comes along begins with the same Starter Kata. Of course, over time each organization can fine-tune its own set of Starter Kata, which it finds work best for its particular environment and culture. This book gives you the starting point.

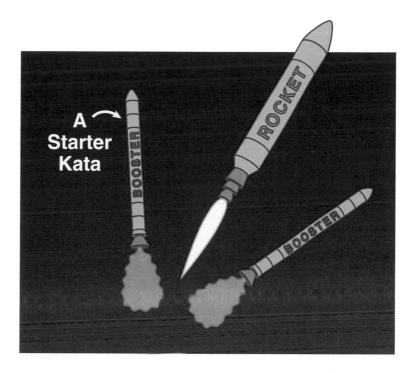

Figure 1.7. Starter Kata (micro definition) are like booster rockets. They're practice routines that help you along in developing new ways of thinking and acting.

The process is like the way you probably learned to handle an automobile. After practicing the basics of the automobile's controls for a while, perhaps in a parking lot, you no longer had to purposely think about how to operate them. Today you can apply your finite cognitive resources to navigating the real road outside of the automobile because you have learned to handle the basic controls inside the automobile more unconsciously as a habit. Mastering fundamentals—making them automatic—frees our brain to focus its limited resources on the less repetitive situational aspects that do require conscious attention.

Many of us dislike structured starter routines and would like to improvise immediately, but that's a mistake that can leave you a permanent beginner. By initially restricting practice improvisation the learner acquires a sense for the essence, which the learner can then apply in increasingly diverse situations. Ultimately, then, the Starter Kata are not the important thing. What are important are the skills and mindset that practicing them imparts, which you can then build upon.

Summary: Benefits of Practicing Starter Kata

- They help beginners start to acquire a new skill by providing simple predefined, step-by-step practice routines for internalizing fundamentals.

- They give the coach a point of comparison for gauging the learner's performance and providing corrective feedback and suggestions.

- They help to develop a shared mode of thinking and acting across a team or organization by providing common routines for everyone's initial practice.

- Perhaps most important, Starter Kata help bridge a gap by translating theoretical principles and concepts into something real and teachable (Figure 1.8).

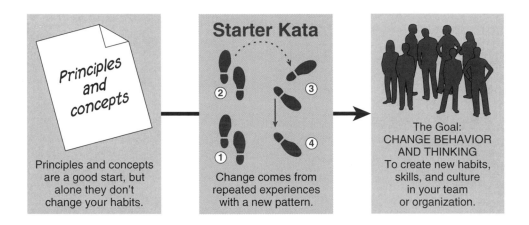

Figure 1.8. Starter Kata help you turn concepts into something real.

Practice Develops New Habits

Attempting to generate a different behavior in someone by explaining it, demonstrating it, or trying to convince a person about the need for it usually doesn't work. We don't think and behave unscientifically because we lack information about the pattern of scientific thinking, but rather because unscientific thinking is our habit.

The brain strongly prefers our established neural pathways, and trying to counteract them with logic or inspiriation usually doesn't work. The learner will almost always automatically stick with or revert back to an old way of thinking, especially when stressed or under pressure. Not because he or she is being hostile, but because it's physiological.

Consider this: The four-step Improvement Kata model is similar to other models of the creative scientific process such as Creative Thinking (1920s), Learning Organization (1970s), Critical Thinking (1980s), Design Thinking (1980s), Solution Focused Practice (1980s), Systems Thinking (starting in the 1990s), Preferred Futuring (1990s), and Evidence-Based Learning (1990s).[6] These and other models have been promoted in the business world for decades, yet they have had little impact on the way most businesses are led and managed. Despite countless books, articles, presentations, and courses, surprisingly few organizations have operationalized these concepts and principles. For most people, a model alone—like the Improvement Kata model—is not enough. The issue is how to change our behavior and mindset to what the model depicts.

What we know can work for learning new ways is to *deliberately practice* a new routine. With the right kind of practice, It is possible to build new habits (new neural pathways) that eventually replace the old ones and shift how we think and act—even as adults. As brain scientists like to say, *"Every time you do something you are more likely to do it again."* Or, to put it another way, *"We are all much more likely to act our way into a new way of thinking than to think our way into a new way of acting."*[7]

However, don't expect to be an expert on your first try with a new way! When you set out to learn a new skill, you are going to be a beginner for a while (though only in that particular area), and you start by working on some basics. This is where the Improvement Kata goes further. Each step of the Improvement Kata model also comes with structured practice routines—Starter Kata—that help individuals, teams, and organizations operationalize its scientific thinking pattern (Figure 1.9).

The Starter Kata practice routines for the four steps of the Improvement Kata model make up Part II of this book.

---

6 If you squint, all these models look about the same. There's a good reason for that: all of them are about human striving.

7 Richard T. Pascale, Mark Millemann, and Linda Gioja, "Changing the Way We Change," *Harvard Business Review*, November–December 1997.

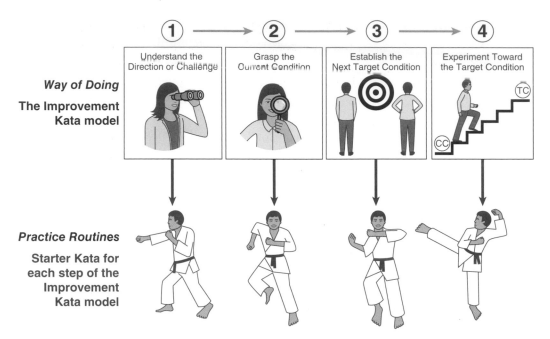

Figure 1.9. There are Starter Kata practice routines for each step of the Improvement Kata model.

Keep in mind that Starter Kata are a skill-development approach. There is no such thing as "implementing a Kata," only "practicing a Kata." The Starter Kata in this book are learning mechanisms that are used to teach and acquire a scientific way of thinking and acting, and in the long term to help modify the culture of an organization as its members develop a new set of shared beliefs and habits.

Stages in Practicing a Starter Kata

When you practice a particular Starter Kata, it can help your initial discipline if you keep the following progression of three stages in mind. In reality, of course, Kata practice won't have quite such distinct and linear phases. Even experts move back and forth between the stages, returning to following a particular Kata in order to refresh some basics. The stages will also intermingle, since a learner will probably have different skill levels with the different Starter Kata. Nonetheless, they are a useful way to help you understand what you are trying to do when you practice a Starter Kata.[8]

---

8 In the martial arts these stages of practice are called *Shu-Ha-Ri*.

Starter Kata Stage 1: FOLLOW. The first phase is to mimic the Kata—to repeat the specific practice routine exactly as described without modification. Initial practice of any new pattern uses your slower conscious mind, like the first time you tried to use the rearview mirror in an automobile. This can make the practice seem awkward and forced, but resist the temptation to deviate from it at this point. That uncomfortable feeling is a normal part of learning something new, and is actually what you should be feeling at this stage. It's a sign that you are building new neural pathways. To experience this feeling right now, try crossing your arms opposite the way you normally do, or signing your name with your nondominant hand.

What would happen if you practiced crossing your arms or signing your name this new way every day for a couple of months? Even if you don't agree with or don't understand something, you can still do it. You'll understand later. Accept doing it, and once the Starter Kata's pattern enters your unconscious and becomes more habitual it will get faster, smoother, and easier. Think of the "follow" practice stage as *going slow to get fast*.

Starter Kata Stage 2: FLUENCY. In the second phase, the pattern of the Starter Kata becomes natural and you don't have to think about it as much. As your proficiency grows, you come to understand the purpose behind the practice routine. Your decisions and actions become more unconscious, and your brain's resources are freer to focus on the situation. You'll start to add your own maneuvers to this element of scientific thinking and automatically begin to apply it to several aspects of work and life.

Starter Kata Stage 3: DETACH. You enter the third phase when you can break away from the formal Starter Kata while sticking to its underlying principles, because you have internalized them. In this phase you use the knowledge you've acquired to create your own approaches and develop your own style.

A great thing about practicing Starter Kata is that it is "learning with the body."[9] If you try to *convince* someone to adopt a different managerial or work practice, you are trying to fight the existing neural highways that make up their established habits. Instead, you begin by getting the learner to just do it, in a structured, prescribed fashion at the start. Its a way to make scientific thinking more natural, because in learning with your body you engage a whole set of experiences, senses, and emotions. When you learn a skill with the body it builds new habits that become hard to forget, like riding a bicycle.

---

9 Thank you to our colleague Pierre Nadeau for introducing us to the phrase "learning with the body."

Two Common Error Modes in Practicing with Starter Kata

1. **The Permanent Beginner.** This error arises when we think we are too skilled to learn and are unwilling to practice things that feel awkward to us. Suppose you have already practiced an improvement approach that now comes naturally to you. You might feel an aversion to mimicking predefined, structured starter routines and immediately want the freedom to improvise—to change the pattern of a Starter Kata before you've taken the time to learn the basics it imparts. Without first resigning our ego to practicing some basics, we're destined to remain a beginner in that area.

2. **The Implementer.** This error arises when we think of a Starter Kata as a method to be implemented and thus permanently stick with its structured routine, rather than seeing it as an initial step in the process of developing new skills. As mentioned, you can't implement a Kata, you can only practice it.

How Long Do You Practice a Starter Kata Before You Achieve Some Fluency and Can Start to Vary Its Routine?

This question sometimes comes up, but cannot be answered precisely because it depends on each learner's progress. The idea is for the learner to reach some proficiency before deviating much from the prescribed Starter Kata routine. Generally speaking it might take about 15 hours of deliberate practice, *with correction*, to shift from being a beginner to basic fluency in the new skill element. (Note that basic fluency does not yet get you to the detach stage.) If you practice 20 minutes every day at work, this could take about two months of practicing a particular Starter Kata. Of course, you'll be practicing more than one Starter Kata at a time.

With regard to learning the overall four-step Improvement Kata pattern, one practical guideline is that a learner should work on at least three successive target conditions at one focus process (three passes through the entire four-step Improvement Kata pattern) and have conducted at least 25 experimenting cycles in step four of the Improvement Kata. This number of coached repetitions—assuming more or less daily coaching cycles[10]—may be enough to begin developing the Improvement Kata pattern as a new habit.

---

10 Coaching cycles are introduced in the next chapter.

What Comes After the Starter Kata?

As you advance to proficiency with the patterns embedded in the Starter Kata, they should become part of how you normally think and work, in a natural, automatic, habitual way. By developing deeper and unconscious understanding, you'll apply the Improvement Kata pattern more on autopilot.

Once you internalize the Starter Kata, you'll develop a growing and delightful ability to quickly sense what is now most important—in other words, what is the next step—in a situation.

You'll be able to recombine and build on skill elements in ways that suit the characteristics of a particular situation, and even develop your own style, all while keeping the essential patterns of the Starter Kata intact.

This does not mean that learning ends. You've begun a lifetime of practice that keeps on deepening your skills. Learning the core skills and underlying purpose is the basis for applying them in situations that are more complex or different from what you are accustomed to and that defy rote application. The Starter Kata are explicit knowledge, and now you work on developing the tacit knowledge that comes with experience. Your repertoire increases when you do this, and you may even enjoy flexing your skills in diverse or difficult areas that are new to you.

You'll be working on your coaching skills and even coaching other coaches by taking on the second coach role. It may surprise you to learn that coaching others will deepen your own scientific thinking skills further and even faster.

Don't be surprised if you find yourself spontaneously expanding the application of scientific thinking to other aspects of your life. This can lead to feeling critical of others when they jump to conclusions rather than thinking scientifically—although, from your own practice of the Starter Kata, you know it does not come naturally, and you know how one can change that!

Summary

We've introduced the idea that you need to practice in order to develop greater scientific thinking in yourself, your team, and your organization. In the next chapter, we'll look at some of the elements and characteristics of effective practice.

Kata and Creativity
by Jeff Liker

Some people believe that practicing predefined routines disables creativity and limits our potential. That's an unfortunate misunderstanding.

For example, music is full of standards. Scales are standards. There are standard chords. There are standard times—3/4, 4/4. You learn these standard techniques and practice them until they become a habit. They're Starter Kata!

The creative music you hear and enjoy is built on standards. The reason that jazz musicians can come together and improvise is because they have learned so many standard patterns to build on. They start with the key, and then there are many standard chord patterns that they can mix and match in a practically infinite number of ways to get different combinations of sounds.

As in martial arts and other complex skills, you begin by practicing Kata until they become routine, then you can begin to break away from the Kata, and then you can leave the Kata behind and focus on the sound of the music. Professionals have learned the basic routines to the point that they are second nature, freeing them to focus on interpretation, in the case of classical music, and developing new combinations of sounds, in the case of jazz and rock. Expert composers and jazz musicians may even break some rules, and when they do it with success it becomes the basis for new standards that others will adopt in their music.

CHAPTER **2**

GUIDELINES FOR GOOD PRACTICE

How well you master the Improvement Kata pattern depends to a considerable degree on *how* you practice. It involves more than just repeating the Starter Kata a large number of times.

This Is About Something Called "Deliberate Practice"

Deliberate practice is practice that is designed to improve performance through a cycle of Doing → Feedback → Adjustment (Figure 2.1). Deliberate practice involves identifying your weaknesses and inventing practice tasks to improve those deficiencies, rather than repeatedly doing what you already know how to do. You get better by correcting your errors. In other words, if you are practicing at a level where you don't make mistakes, then you are probably not improving your skills.

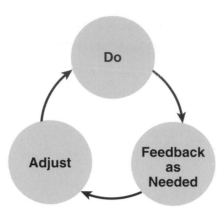

Figure 2.1. Deliberate practice is designed to improve your performance over time by working on mistakes.

Hopefully you can see that deliberate practice is not just repetition. You should be practicing outside your comfort zone and in your *learning zone*, where you will struggle and naturally make some mistakes. This is what grows your brain. As shown in Figure 2.2, your learning zone is comprised of skills and abilities—patterns—that lie just beyond your current abilities. No real learning takes place when you practice activities in your comfort zone, since those are patterns you've already mastered and are easy for you. Similarly, attempting to practice skills too far out, in the fear zone, is unproductive because you haven't yet acquired the prerequisites for those skills. As your skill increases, you keep revising your practice in order to keep stretching yourself by staying in your evolving learning zone.

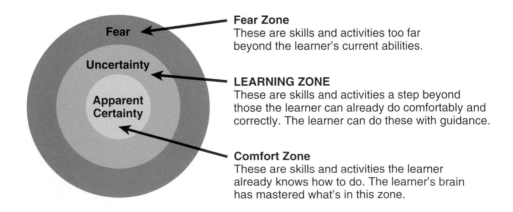

Figure 2.2. To increase skill, practice in your learning zone.

At this point in the story you can probably tell that having someone observe and give feedback on your current performance is critical to understanding what exactly you need to work on next in practicing a new skill. Without feedback, you can get really proficient at doing something badly. This means that deliberate practice is a type of practice that requires a coach.

You're Going to Need a Coach

The learner needs a coach for at least two reasons. One is that by ourselves we automatically and unconsciously default back to exercising our existing habits, rather than those still-weak new neural pathways we're trying to build up. The pattern of the Improvement Kata isn't complicated, but it can be difficult to practice because we're not used to it and unconsciously tend to revert to the familiar. The other reason we need a coach is that we can't see and feel what exactly we are doing wrong; we can't observe ourselves. Perhaps you have had the experience of attempting a new routine again and again and not succeeding until a passerby points out something, which you adjust and then you improve almost immediately. Unfortunately, if you practice the wrong pattern over and over you run the risk of reinforcing weaknesses and making them even harder to change.

Without coaching input, we all too easily lose our way and don't practice the right pattern, or we practice ineffectively. Without coaching, a change in our mindset—in our brain's wiring—is less likely to occur. And, as any accomplished musician or athlete can tell you, even as your skills become advanced checkups with a coach will still be helpful for your continued progress.

The Coaching Kata

If practicing the Improvement Kata pattern requires a coach, then where do these coaches come from? We need to develop them!

Coaching the scientific pattern of the Improvement Kata is a way for managers to develop their team's bench strength for achieving the organization's goals, but coaching is a skill that takes practice like any other. The Coaching Kata is a set of Starter Kata with which managers and supervisors can develop their skill for teaching the Improvement Kata. It's not a general coaching routine, but a set of practice routines specifically for teaching the Improvement Kata pattern (Figure 2.3). This means that coaches-to-be should first have personal experience in using the Improvement Kata, before they start to coach others, so they are able to evaluate and give feedback on their learners'

Improvement Kata practice.[1] But there's no need to wait to master the Improvement Kata. As soon as you internalize the basics of how to apply the Improvement Kata, you should also start practicing the Coaching Kata and teach others, because doing that deepens your own learning even further.

The Starter Kata practice routines for the Coaching Kata make up Part III of this book.

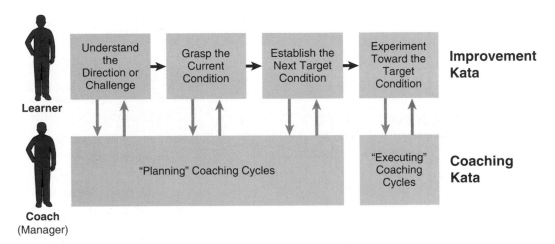

Figure 2.3. The Improvement Kata and Coaching Kata work together.

In a nutshell, with the Coaching Kata every learner is assigned a coach, who in short, daily "coaching cycles" provides feedback and suggestions on the learner's effort to apply the Improvement Kata pattern and routines to a real work process. This coaching is done *one-on-one*. A coach can have more than one learner, but for Improvement Kata practice the coach works with only one learner at a time, because each learner has different weaknesses and practice needs. This coaching is done as *part of normal daily work*, which means that the coach is probably going to be the learner's supervisor or manager. Coaching the Improvement Kata is in fact a way of managing. There is no extra staff and no delay before the learner starts to apply the Improvement Kata pattern, which means it is free training. A beauty of the IK/CK approach is that it is relatively easy to apply for immediate benefit, while being rich enough that it takes time to truly master.

---

1 The coach is someone who has *been there, done that* vis-à-vis the steps and routines of the Improvement Kata.

In sports and music, practice and performance are usually separated, but that's generally not workable in the business world. Here the learner practices the pattern of the Improvement Kata in actual work, and thereby ends up dealing with a healthy mix of real information and problems (Figure 2.4). Practicing as part of daily work means the learner will be applying the Improvement Kata pattern to a real process with real goals. That's good, because practice is more likely to generate mindset change when the learner focuses on something meaningful—in which the learner has a personal stake—and his or her emotions are involved.

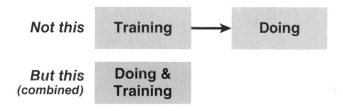

Figure 2.4. Practicing the Improvement Kata on something real is effective for learning.

What the Coach Does for the Learner

The main responsibility of an Improvement Kata coach is to sense what the learner is ready for next, and to give feedback regarding the learner's next practice accordingly. Specifically, the coach's task is to determine whether or not the learner is operating within the "corridor" of scientific thinking and acting specified by the Improvement Kata and its practice routines, and, if not, to introduce procedural adjustments as quickly as possible to get the learner back into that corridor (Figure 2.5).

Note, however, that getting out of the corridor is not bad; it's useful, because wherever we struggle we also learn—improving through errors and correction. The coach expects the learner to get out of the corridor and make mistakes in applying the Improvement Kata, and it is in particular at these "teachable moments" that the coach can give constructive feedback and the learner can advance his or her practice. A lot of us may not enjoy making errors and receiving a corrective input from another person, but that's actually how you move forward in skill development. In fact, the more you practice the Improvement Kata or Coaching Kata, the more you may feel the urge to say, *"Will someone please help me see what I'm doing wrong!"* which is a good sign of your growing expertise.

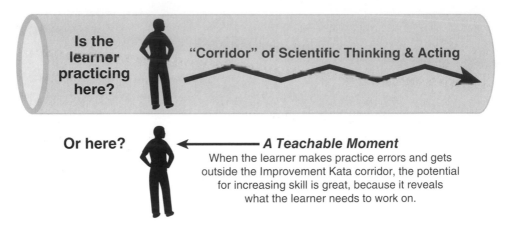

Figure 2.5. The coach guides the learner back into practicing the desired patterns of thinking and acting.

To the untrained eye this may sometimes look like the coach is being directive and telling the learner what to do, but the coach is actually only teaching the learner *how* to go about striving for goals and solving problems, not solving problems for the learner. This is what we mean by "creating capability." If managers tell their people *what* to do, then the capability of the organization is limited to what a few managers know, and they can't know everything nor be everywhere at once. When managers instead coach their people in an effective, scientific way of handling situations, then the brainpower of the organization is greater.

Coaching Cycles, with the Five Coaching Kata Questions and the Learner's Storyboard

Let's take a quick closer look at the Coaching Kata, which is covered in detail in Part III.

In order to formulate appropriate feedback, an Improvement Kata coach has to first gain some understanding of how the learner is currently thinking. How can the coach get that insight? In sports and music, the learner's current skill level is something a coach can readily see or hear. However, the Improvement Kata is about a scientific way of *thinking*, and thinking is invisible and silent! The Improvement Kata coach discerns how the learner is thinking by asking a set of questions and listening to the learner's responses, during a structured daily interaction called a "Coaching Cycle."

A **coaching cycle** is one of the coach's Starter Kata. It's the coach's main forum and routine for teaching the Improvement Kata pattern.[2] A coaching cycle is a short, regularly scheduled, structured face-to-face dialogue between the coach and the learner that is conducted at least once daily, taking 20 minutes or less. The purpose is to frequently review the learner's approach (their practice) and give feedback as necessary to ensure that it proceeds scientifically. Coaching cycles are used to guide and give immediate feedback and suggestions to the learner as the learner goes through all four steps of the Improvement Kata. These frequent exchanges give managers a way to both develop Improvement Kata skill in their learners and to practice and improve their own coaching skills. They also help ensure that improvement efforts remain focused on the organization's objectives. Coaching cycles are the "20 minutes" to which this book's subtitle refers.

The 20-minute coaching cycles are a routine and forum for addressing several issues:

- **Assessing the current status of the learner's thinking.** The coach asks questions and listens, to help him or her formulate appropriate feedback.

- **Identifying the current knowledge threshold** and making sure the learner plans an appropriate next step that will advance learning. (In the Improvement Kata we like to say that *every step is an experiment*.)

- **Giving procedural feedback** to the learner, to help the learner internalize the Improvement Kata pattern by guiding him or her in applying it to a real work process.

- **Understanding the current status of the focus process,** which may be changing as the learner conducts experiments.

- Finally, the daily scheduled coaching cycles are a cue for the coach and learner to practice their respective behavior patterns (Figure 2.6).

Coaching Kata · **Improvement Kata**

Figure 2.6. The Improvement Kata (learner) and Coaching Kata (coach) are two sides of the same coin, and they come together in the coaching cycles.

---

2 As with any Starter Kata, as skills develop your organization can build on this to suit the characteristics of your environment and culture, as long as the basic pattern and principles remain.

A coaching cycle is a pause where the coach and learner reflect on the learner's last step and what has been learned, review the plan for the next step, and introduce adjustments as needed. Problems in the focus process are not solved during coaching cycles. That occurs through the learner's experiments, which are done in between coaching cycles. Outside of the coaching cycles, the learner may typically spend about an hour a day working on their next step, in preparation for the next coaching cycle. On an as-needed basis the coach may also choose to accompany, observe, and assist the learner during that time, especially with beginner learners.

Each coaching cycle is built around a set of questions called the **five Coaching Kata questions** (Figure 2.7), which is another Starter Kata practiced by the coach. The five Coaching Kata questions are the main headings in a coaching cycle and provide its structure. The sequence of questions mirrors the Improvement Kata pattern and gives both coach and learner a way to help make that pattern second nature. The five questions are easy to learn, and each time you go through them it reinforces the scientific thinking pattern.

However, the main purpose of the five Coaching Kata question format is more than just a reinforcement technique. These structured questions are used by the coach as prompts to help make the learner's current thinking visible, so the coach can then give feedback that's tailored to the learner. The main-heading questions are scripted, but the coach's additional questions and feedback are not. They depend on what the coach discerns about the learner's thinking. Here's how it works. In each coaching cycle the coach:

1. Asks the learner the five questions, plus any clarifying questions between the five questions. (This is explained in detail in Part III.)

2. Listens to the learner's responses to get a sense for the learner's thinking and identify the current point or points of weakness.

3. Gives specific feedback, as needed, as a corrective input for this particular learner at this particular time.

Since the questions are prompts, simply reading them is not the core skill. Asking the five questions is like a golf coach saying, *"Please swing the golf club a few times so I can see what you are doing,"* or a music teacher saying, *"Please play a bit so I can hear what you are doing."* Since the Improvement Kata pattern is about an invisible mental process, the approach here is: *"I'm going to ask you these questions, and how you respond will*

COACHING KATA

The Five Questions

① What is the **Target Condition**?

② What is the **Actual Condition** now?

--------(*Turn Card Over*)------------->

③ What **Obstacles** do you think are preventing you from reaching the target condition?
Which *one* are you addressing now?

④ What is your **Next Step**? (Next experiment)
What do you expect?

⑤ How quickly can we go and see what we **Have Learned** from taking that step?

*You'll often work on the same obstacle with several experiments

The card is turned over to reflect on the learner's last step

Reflect on the Last Step Taken

Because you don't actually know what the result of a step will be!

① What did you plan as your **Last Step**?

② What did you **Expect**?

③ What **Actually Happened**?

④ What did you **Learn**?

------------------------------->
Return to question 3

Figure 2.7. The coach's five question card. These questions are the main headings for a coaching cycle (following the scientific pattern of the Improvement Kata) and prompts to help reveal how the learner is thinking (so the coach can give appropriate feedback).

help me to determine how you are thinking. Then I can give you feedback specific to your situation, so that your next practice is as effective as possible." That feedback should be specific and purposeful. *"You need to draw better block diagrams,"* is poor feedback. *"Please redraw your block diagram to show the steps and flow of work, not the physical layout of the process,"* is good feedback.

After a few coaching cycles, the learner should see that he or she doesn't need to be anxious about these interactions, because both learner and coach share the same objective: improve the focus process while also increasing the learner's and coach's skills.

Traditionally the most feared words an employee might say in response to his boss are: *"I don't know."* In a coaching cycle words like these are actually something the coach is listening for, because they help identify the current threshold of knowledge and where the learner's next experiment should take place. Scientific thinking involves recognizing and calmly acknowledging what you don't know, and conducting experiments to find out.

Notice that a coaching cycle is not a "gotcha" exercise, nor a freewheeling ad hoc conversation. The learner already knows what basic questions are going to be asked and prepares her responses in writing before the coaching cycle, in the corresponding fields of a structured, preformatted learner's storyboard.[3] Having the learner do this in advance of the coaching cycle, in writing, also helps the coach understand how the learner is currently thinking.

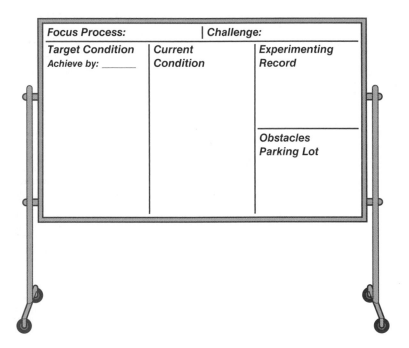

Figure 2.8. This is the Starter Kata layout for the learner's storyboard.

---

3 The certainty of knowing the basic questions that will be asked helps the learner better deal with the uncertainty inherent in the scientific approach they are practicing.

The **learner's storyboard** is another Starter Kata (Figure 2.8), which is used by the learner in the coaching cycles. The storyboard consolidates information from each step of the Improvement Kata in a structured layout that correlates, from left to right, with the pattern of the five Coaching Kata questions (Figure 2.9). Having the learner prepare, refer to, and actively point to information on their storyboard helps reinforce the Improvement Kata pattern and makes the learner's thinking process more apparent.

In the planning phase of the Improvement Kata the learner builds up the information on their storyboard one section at a time as the coaching cycle dialogues between the learner and coach go on. In the executing phase of the Improvement Kata the entire storyboard gets referenced, and even updated, with each coaching cycle.

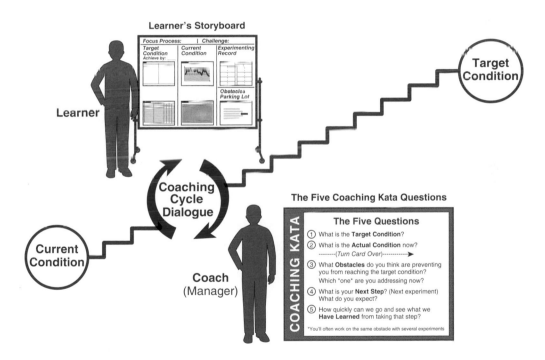

Figure 2.9. The coach's five questions and the learner's storyboard work together.

Ingredients for Good Practice

Figure 2.10 summarizes four key ingredients involved in the process of acquiring new skills, which are built into the Coaching Kata. There are other ingredients, too, of course, but anyone practicing or teaching the Improvement Kata should be aware of these four factors in how skill acquisition typically works.

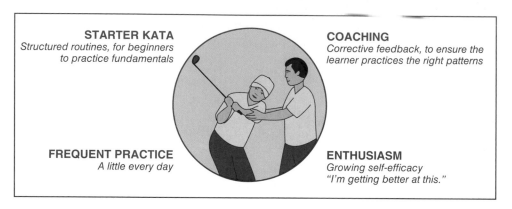

STARTER KATA
Structured routines, for beginners to practice fundamentals

COACHING
Corrective feedback, to ensure the learner practices the right patterns

FREQUENT PRACTICE
A little every day

ENTHUSIASM
Growing self-efficacy "I'm getting better at this."

Figure 2.10. Four important ingredients for learning a new skill.

Frequent ("Distributed") Practice

At the start of the learner's practice, coaching cycles are done at least once a day. This is because to develop new habits it's generally better to train for a short time frequently than in massed training sessions. Twenty minutes a day is better than two hours once a week. For example, if you practice the Improvement Kata on only one or two days a week and the rest of the time it's business as usual, then what you are actually practicing is *business as usual*. Whatever you practice every day, intentionally or not, becomes your normal routine and habit.

Improvement Kata training is based on daily practice that's coached by the learner's manager—making it part of normal daily work—not periodic training by in-house specialists or external consultants.[4]

Starter Kata

In the previous pages we briefly introduced a few of the Starter Kata used in coaching cycles, which itself is a Starter Kata. If you want to practice, then you need something *to* practice. A good way to get people to adopt a new behavior in the long term is to

---

4 Although practice is daily, there will be plateaus when it seems like you aren't making progress. At these times the learner can, of course, take a break for a few days or go back to refresh some basics.

start building their ability and self-efficacy through simple, structured routines like the Starter Kata in this book. If you start the learner out practicing a fundamental routine and they feel successful, then they're more likely to do it again because that behavior gets easier to do. You're helping the learner develop more ability and more motivation. Then you can have the learner do something harder.

Coaching

The process of learning a new skill involves targeting those aspects of the skill pattern that currently give the learner difficulty and working to correct those points. To tackle their mistakes, the learner needs periodic input from a coach who quickly detects errors and gives advice on how to correct them. Practice errors should be corrected quickly, before they start becoming bad habits.

Enthusiasm

Brain science tells us that the learner's emotions play an important role in skill acquisition. If we practice but are not enthusiastic about it, then a new pattern probably won't be learned no matter how much we practice it. In order to move beyond the plateaus that learners inevitably hit, they need to have enough motivation to tackle the mistakes and work through the rough spots. The learner should periodically be feeling *"I am getting better at this"* so she or he has the positive emotions about practice that are required for reaching higher skill levels. People learn new skills best when they are passionately interested.

This doesn't mean that every learner has to be enthusiastic right from the start, or all the time, which would be unrealistic. Rather, it's the responsibility of the coach to make sure the learner *periodically* feels a sense of progress and accomplishment, leading to a growing sense of self-efficacy. *Self-efficacy* is a belief in one's ability to succeed in specific situations or accomplish a task. The learner's experience of mastery is the biggest factor in determining the extent of their self-efficacy, meaning it develops along the way through the learner's personal experiences.

Self-Efficacy—Something to Hold Onto

Practicing the Improvement Kata helps us experience uncertainty more as an opportunity—*"I've never done that before, but I've practiced a way to figure it out and find the way."* This increase in self-efficacy happens because Improvement Kata skill gives you and your team something to hold onto when the path is uncertain. It's a kind of security blanket that provides stability in the midst of complexity and change.

All of us need something to hold onto and steady us when we step into the unknown. One option is to rely on our preconceived notions, our plan, for how things will go. But the future is not completely predictable. Instead, when people learn a scientific way of proceeding, they can shift from relying so much on their preconceived notions to also relying on a procedure, a means, for navigating the unknown, thereby becoming more open and applying their creativity (Figure 2.11). We still make a plan, of course, but we now view any plan more as just a testable hypothesis. We become more resilient, less afraid of making mistakes and being judged by others, and more comfortable in the learning zone. Practicing the Improvement Kata doesn't reduce uncertainty, it makes you more comfortable with uncertainty because you've mastered a way of dealing with it.

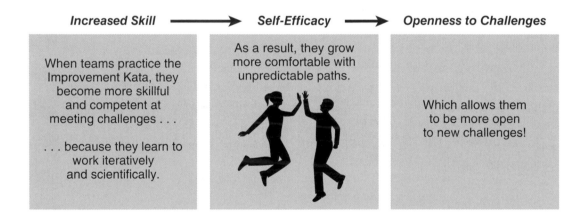

Figure 2.11. This is a chain reaction you're trying to create by practicing the Improvement Kata.

The Typical Path in Learning the Improvement Kata Pattern

Anyone who wants to learn the scientific thinking skill pattern that is modeled by the Improvement Kata will go through a route that looks something like Figure 2.12. Notice that the stages of this progression overlap:

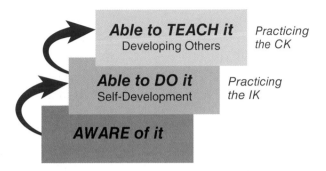

Figure 2.12. The Improvement Kata learning path.

1. **Aware of it.** At the start you may have basic knowledge about the Improvement Kata model from books, websites, videos, seminars, workshops, and so on. Though you might even be able to describe the steps, you are not able to do the new skill yet. You do, however, have a surface understanding of what it is about.

2. **Able to do it.** This is where you begin to develop your own skills and alter your mindset. At this level, you are actively practicing and applying the Improvement Kata routines yourself. A goal of this stage is to be able to string together the individual Starter Kata skill elements in behavior sequences and successfully apply the four-step Improvement Kata pattern in a real environment. Importantly, we have found no way to get around this stage before going on to the next stage of coaching others. You have to be a learner before you can teach, at least for a while.

3. **Able to teach it.** At this point your experience has given you a deeper and more instinctive understanding of the "why" behind the Improvement Kata pattern. Now you can instruct, coach, and counsel others in practicing it. You now find it fairly easy, and even automatic, to integrate scientific thinking into any problem-solving effort, and can easily recognize the lack of it. I encourage you to find a learner and begin coaching the Improvement Kata soon, which will deepen your own learning.

Summary

We're now two chapters in. The first two chapters talked about scientific thinking and deliberate practice. Bringing those two topics together is the basis for this book (Figure 2.13). *The Improvement Kata and Coaching Kata combine a practical, four-step scientific working pattern with techniques of deliberate practice, to turn scientific thinking into a lifetime skill anyone can learn.*

Scientific Thinking Pattern
+
Techniques of Deliberate Practice
= *Making scientific thinking a skill that can be learned by anyone*

Figure 2.13. The concept behind *The Toyota Kata Practice Guide*.

Combining these two topics is useful for anyone and any team that wants to develop creative, entrepreneurial skills and operationalize concepts like "Learning Organization" and "Systems Thinking." Practicing the set of Starter Kata in this book is intended to increase your competitive capabilities, because the more you develop skill and confidence in the Improvement Kata pattern:

- The more challenges you can take on

- The bigger the challenges you can take on

- The more knowledge you can build

- The faster you can move ahead

In the next chapter, we'll look at creating the environment for daily practice.

CHAPTER 3

ROLES AND STRUCTURE FOR DAILY PRACTICE

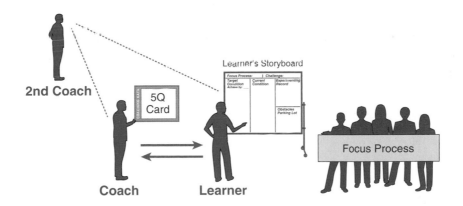

Managers as Coaches

How do you create an aligned, scientific thinking organizational culture?

Organizational culture is mindset imparted by our experiences at work, and modifying the culture involves changing the environment and deliberately practicing new behaviors. The culture shifts when enough people in the organization do the organization's work in the new ways. This suggests that practicing and coaching to modify an organization's culture should be systemic—integrated into the normal daily operation of the organization. The Improvement Kata and Coaching Kata are exactly that—a process to develop scientific skills and mindset in people through the work itself.

In any organization, the managers are by default the teachers—the *coaches* in our case—because what they say and do every day, deliberately or not, trains and shapes their people's thinking. *Manager* here refers to any person who is in charge of other people or influences what they do. Managers are probably the primary actors who spread and perpetuate an organization's culture. Ideally, what managers say and do reinforces the organization's desired way of thinking and acting every day, to help create and preserve whatever organizational culture and capability you want.

> *The center of a modern society, economy and community is not technology. It is not information. It is not productivity. It is the managed institution as the organ of society to produce results. And management is the specific tool, the specific function, the specific instrument to make institutions capable of producing results.*
>
> —Peter Drucker
> *Management Challenges for the 21st Century*
> (HarperBusiness, 2001)

Two Core Roles in Daily Kata Practice: Learner and Coach

The coach/learner relationship is at the root of the Improvement Kata approach to developing a scientific thinking mindset.[1] In an organization, the learner and coach roles usually mirror a reporting relationship, with the coach being the learner's manager, although there can be exceptions, such as peer coaching or coaching by a specialist. Most important is that the coach has some experience in applying the Improvement Kata pattern.

Many managers have been conditioned by their work to be oriented toward ad hoc action—deciding what must be done and issuing sets of directions. Some call this "firefighting." The Improvement Kata is a different way of pursuing goals, where what is learned on one day is built upon the next day. The scheduled daily coaching cycles are

---

1 This book refers to *Coach* and *Learner*. Some organizations use terminology like *Mentor* and *Mentee* or *Coach* and *Coachee*.

a cue for both the learner and the coach to pause and use the five Coaching Kata questions to reflect on the last step, review the plan for the next step, and to practice their respective skills. During the coaching cycles the learner and coach each focus on a different aspect, with the learner working on the steps to the target condition (the *what*) while the coach works on *how* the learner is approaching it. During the entire practice process the following two aspects happen simultaneously:

- **There is an improvement goal.** The learner's main goal is to effectively apply the pattern of the Improvement Kata to achieve a target condition at the learner's level in the organization. *The learner improves their focus process through application of the scientific Improvement Kata pattern, in the direction of the challenge.*

- **There is a skill-development goal.** The coach's main goal is to increase the learner's skill in applying the Improvement Kata pattern, through practice on real goals and real processes. The coach guides the thinking process, not the content, of the learner's actions, by asking questions and giving procedural guidance. *The coach's focus is on developing the learner's ability to meet challenging objectives, by guiding the learner in practicing the Improvement Kata pattern.* This grows the organization's internal capability to establish and pursue challenging, strategically relevant goals.

Although they each have a different focus, the coach and learner roles are interdependent. This is a subtle but important point. The coach is dependent on the learner to make progress toward the target condition, yet can only give the learner procedural guidance, not solutions. That's because no one knows in advance what solutions will lead to the target condition. The learner, in turn, is dependent on the manager to coach him or her effectively for skill development.[2]

Here's a way to look at it. The coach/manager can't play in the game himself and therefore needs the learner to play successfully, otherwise the organization's goals won't be met (Figure 3.1). Sometimes a learner might not reach the next target condition, or might not reach it on time. That's normal. However, if a learner consistently fails to reach target conditions, it is actually the coach who is responsible, because *if a student hasn't learned, their teacher hasn't taught.* In an elegant way, the coach is as dependent on the learner as the learner is on the coach. They're in it together.

---

2 In sports and music, a learner can often choose their teacher, but in business learners usually can't choose their manager. All the more reason to ensure that the managers in your organization are teaching what you want people to be learning.

Figure 3.1. The manager is responsible for making his or her people successful.

When we see famous athletes, we may assume that their success is due to themselves, but their coach plays a key role. The coach's job is not only difficult, it is often out of view and less heralded than that of learners who successfully reach their target conditions.

A Third Role: The Second Coach

Since coaches are practicing a skillset too, they also need a coach (Figure 3.2). The second coach coaches the first coach and is responsible for the effectiveness of the first coach's coaching. The second coach does this by periodically observing coaching cycles and giving feedback and suggestions to the coach. The second coach is either the coach's boss, one level up in the hierarchy from the coach, or a peer or a staff specialist, such as a Lean staff person. Like the coach, the second coach should have personal experience with applying the Improvement Kata. The second coach role is discussed at the end of Part III.

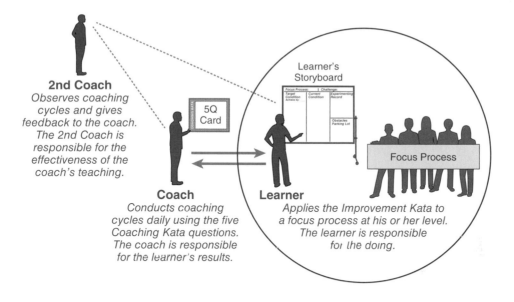

Figure 3.2. Quick descriptions of the three main roles in Improvement Kata practice.

Organization Structure Follows Purpose

Simple math. If daily coaching cycles take 20 minutes each (as described in Chapter 2) and learners are coached individually, then the number of direct reports a manager has determines how much time she would spend coaching each of her direct reports. In some organizations managers have 20, 30, or even more people reporting directly to them. If you try to deploy coaching the Improvement Kata into an organizational structure like that, it won't work.

You may have heard of Toyota's typical ratio of one group leader to about every five team leaders, who in turn have about five team members. Many organizations have tried to copy this 5:1 structure with little or no effect, because that misses the point. The reason Toyota has this structure is because it wants its managers to support their people daily in practicing and developing scientific problem-solving skills. That purpose led to the structure. Other organizations would do much better to copy the purpose and principle, and develop their own solutions appropriate for the target condition of coaching the Improvement Kata in their organization.

(continues)

The span of managerial responsibility in an organization may reflect what the organization's leaders have been focusing on. In the 20 to 30 direct reports example above, that focus has probably been cost cutting and management by exception when there is a big problem, not developing and utilizing people's skills to improve, adapt, and innovate. Cost reduction can periodically be a legitimate goal, of course, but keep in mind that we can't cut our way to greatness. What is it that your organization wants to achieve, to strive for, for its customers that would make it great? Does your organization have the skills and mindset—and coaching structure—that can make it happen?

Two Supporting Roles for Improvement Kata Practice

For the additional players mentioned below, it is helpful to think of the supporting staff truism that the learner's and coach's success is these players' success. That is, the organization delivers sustained value, achieves goals, and continuously improves primarily through the activities of its managers and their teams.

Lean or Improvement Team Staff Members, Human Resources

Since developing people is every manager's responsibility, the Lean or improvement team staff is primarily a service-and-support function to help managers be successful. The Lean staff should influence managers and try to operate through them, not try to improve work processes separately from them. They can do this, for example, by training, observing, and coaching managers as those managers in turn coach Improvement Kata application practice. If staff functions take over the role of training Improvement Kata learners, they dilute the managers' responsibility for developing their people.

However, directly moving Lean staff members to a second coach role does not work well if they do not have experience in applying the Improvement Kata. They should be encouraged to start by practicing the Improvement Kata themselves.

External Consultants

The role of an external coach is to help selected persons in your organization develop Coaching Kata proficiency as quickly and effectively as possible, so those persons can then teach and spread the Improvement Kata within the organization with decreasing reliance on outside expertise. An external coach is used more at the beginning than later. It is important that any presentations, training, and coaching related to the Improvement Kata be done by persons inside your organization as soon as possible, because the act of teaching also develops the teacher's skills. The role of the external coach is to help you get started and to support you, not to do your presenting/coaching/training for you, as that would prevent you and your organization from developing the necessary skills.

There is also a role for an external coach to come in periodically, assess the organization, and provide an external benchmark.

Conducting Coaching Cycles on a Set Schedule

For each learner, you'll be scheduling a regular coaching cycle at a set time near the start of the workday or shift. The first coaching cycle should be early in the day so the learner can take the next step that day if possible. Companies that use coaching cycles often establish a "Kata time zone," for example from 9 to 11 a.m., during which managers don't do e-mail, attend meetings, or make phone calls.

After the regular coaching cycle, the coach and learner can decide if they want or need to do any additional coaching cycles that day. With beginner learners, try to do a coaching cycle soon after each step the learner takes, so that feedback is received quickly and corrections are made right away. Once learners have become proficient they can then take multiple or more complex steps without needing a coaching input each time.

On a case-by-case basis the coach can also decide to accompany the learner, especially beginners, as the learner takes the next step, to observe the learner in action and provide additional coaching outside of the formal coaching cycle.

At this point it might seem like coaching the Improvement Kata is going to be a time-consuming add-on that eats up every day and is all that anyone is doing. Experience has shown the opposite. Practicing a scientific way of working reduces the amount of time a manager would otherwise spend on firefighting, unstructured meetings, additional dialogues, and unnecessary problem solving. As your coaching skill develops you should start to experience better results with less energy and time.

With practice, each coaching cycle takes 20 minutes or less, since each cycle is only about *reviewing* the last experiment and checking that the next experiment will advance learning. The coaching cycles are not for planning the next experiment from scratch or for doing the experimenting itself, although the proposed next experiment may be revised based on what is discussed.[3] In a coaching cycle the learner and coach identify the current threshold of knowledge and agree on the learner's next experiment to see beyond it. That's it. The learner's experiments and planning of the next step then take place between the coaching cycles.

Why Schedule Coaching Cycles Every Day?

For the Learner:

- Meeting only once every few days would mean the learner has too much time between practice sessions to actually develop new skill and mindset. Short, frequent feedback and practice are more effective for developing new habits.

- The learner is developing a habit to conduct simple, rapid, and frequent experiments toward the target condition. If coaching cycles are infrequent, then the learner's steps will tend to get too big or become multistep action plans.

For the Coach:

- A beginner coach also needs frequent practice. You are practicing to develop your coaching skill.

- The scheduled coaching cycle is a cue for both the coach and the learner to practice their IK/CK behavior patterns.

- You are seeking to be consistent in providing feedback to the learner.

If You Don't Have any Improvement Kata Coaches Yet . . . You Can Rotate Roles for Practice Purposes!

Getting to the point where managers are Improvement Kata coaches is an important element of being able to coach learners every day. However, at the start you may not have enough, or even any, Improvement Kata experienced managers. How do you coach learners in that situation?

---

3 It will probably take some practice before you can consistently do a coaching cycle in 10 to 20 minutes.

One approach to dealing with a lack of internal experienced coaches is to find an experienced external coach/consultant to coach some managers in getting started. Those managers start as learners of the Improvement Kata and then grow into the coach role.

Another temporary solution for getting started is to have people practice in rotation, whereby each person in turn takes the role of learner, coach, and second coach— at the start in name only. You literally change positions relative to the storyboard, as shown in the following examples. These rotation models are temporary, artificial structures for daily practice, to as quickly as possible develop some Improvement Kata and Coaching Kata experience and capability. They generally last for six to eight weeks of practice (for example, through three successive target conditions). All other guidelines for coaching cycles stay the same, including that they are scheduled at a set time early in the day.

Example 1: Daily Role Rotation. If you have three persons who want to practice but you don't have a coach, you can use this daily rotation model. Each member of the practice team is a learner applying the Improvement Kata to a different focus process, is coached by a designated member of the team, and you do each rotation every day. You can also add a fourth person and fourth focus process, by having two persons take the role of second coach (observer) in each rotation.

	2nd Coach	Coach	Learner	Focus Process
Rotation 1			*You*	Process 1
Rotation 2	*You*			Process 2
Rotation 3		*You*		Process 3

Example 2: Periodic Role Rotation. In this rotation model the members of one practice team all use the same focus process and periodically rotate their roles within their team, for instance rotating roles every 10 coaching cycles. Here, too, you can add a fourth person to a practice team by having two persons take the role of second coach.

	2nd Coach	Coach	Learner	Focus Process
	→ Roles rotate *within* each team ←			
Practice Team 1			*You*	Process 1
Practice Team 2				Process 2
Practice Team 3				Process 3

Summary

This chapter discussed the coach/learner roles and coach/learner interactions in daily coaching cycles, which is the essential structure at the base of Improvement Kata practice. *The Toyota Kata Practice Guide* is for a learner and a coach—the fundamental unit of deliberate practice. At this point you can get going with Improvement Kata practice, and the short next chapter prepares you for that.

In the box on the following pages we widen the perspective for a moment, to take a look at how the base coach/learner pairing can be multiplied and deployed throughout an organization, with the intent of generating scientific thinking organizational culture.

A Look at the Big Picture: Developing Scientific Thinking Organizational Culture[4]

We may think of innovation as a flash of brilliance by certain individuals, because that's how it often looks in the history books. However, a lot of improvement, adaptation, and innovation is actually the cumulative effect of multiple experimenters, all pointed in a direction. The *action of innovation* is the day-to-day enterprise of iterating toward a challenge, often undertaken across an entire organization. People throughout your organization are the creators and innovators.

A corollary to this is that a small group of managers cannot conceive of and direct all the adaptations that are necessary to meet truly challenging strategic goals. The Improvement Kata and Coaching Kata handle that dilemma by fostering a common, scientific way of working that teams apply toward shared, strategically relevant goals. The routines of the Improvement Kata and Coaching Kata are scalable, in an interconnected way, as a way of *managing* (Figure 3.3).

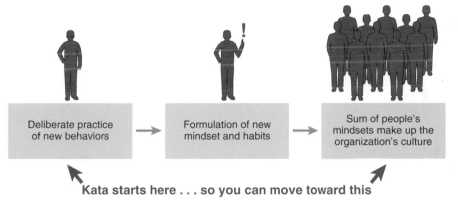

| Deliberate practice of new behaviors | → | Formulation of new mindset and habits | → | Sum of people's mindsets make up the organization's culture |

Kata starts here . . . so you can move toward this

Figure 3.3. Kata help you build capability for decentralized but well-aligned striving toward the organization's goals.

Note that this is not about developing people out of friendliness. It's about reaching tough goals that you can't achieve fast enough via a command-and-control management approach. It's about recognizing that reaching these kinds of goals requires mobilizing the brainpower of many people in the organization. In many business sectors, long-term

(continues)

---

4 This topic is the subject of the book *Toyota Kata Culture* (McGraw-Hill, 2017).

competitive strength may boil down to a combination of (1) understanding customer needs, (2) defining challenging strategies for how you want to compete on those dimensions, and (3) developing and utilizing your organization's capability to navigate the unpredictable paths toward those challenges.

What It Looks Like When IK/CK Practice Gets Expanded Up and Down an Organization

The coach-learner pairing repeats *across* each level of an organization. Each organization member has a next-level-up coach (his or her manager), and in the other direction each is coach to a group of learners (Figure 3.4). The roles are fractal,[5] interlinking all members of the organization with a common language, structure, and way of working. Every coaching cycle is a chance to course correct toward the organization's goals.

Every coach and learner can start with the same practice routines because everyone in the organization can use this same underlying pattern of thinking and working, even though the content of what's being worked on differs from area to area and level to level. Practicing and coaching the Improvement Kata pattern becomes a part of nearly every task, goal, or problem, as managers use those activities as opportunities to grow their people's problem-solving skills. The objective is not just to achieve a goal, but to simultaneously get better at *how* to achieve goals.

By practicing the IK and CK in chains of coaching like this, you are:

- Aligning the organization by creating shared purpose and connection

- Making the creation of a scientific thinking culture part of normal daily work

- Creating a shared skillset, which produces capability and power that your organization can utilize to pursue challenging strategic goals

- Developing a common working language

- Making innovation happen at every level

---

5 A *fractal* is something that has the same or similar pattern that repeats at each scale level.

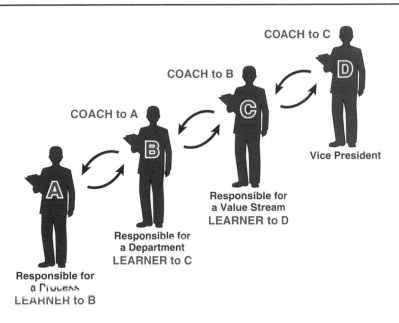

COACH to C

COACH to B

COACH to A

D

Vice President

C

Responsible for
a Value Stream
LEARNER to D

B

Responsible for
a Department
LEARNER to C

A

Responsible for
a Process
LEARNER to B

Figure 3.4. The coach/learner roles repeat across each level of the organization.
Each level coaches the next level down.

Ultimately Developing Your Own Way

In some organizations, practice of scientific thinking grows into a prevailing way of doing things. In other organizations, it might not go beyond a few interested teams, and it may or may not stand the test of time.

Chapter 1 described three stages that a learner practicing a Starter Kata goes through: Follow → Fluency → Detach. In a sense, an organization may move through similar stages as it goes from using the Starter Kata in this book to ultimately finding its own way (Figure 3.5). The organization uses the original Starter Kata until a critical mass of managers develop fluency with the overall Improvement Kata pattern and are coaching their people in it. At that point, we can begin to talk about a scientific thinking cultural shift. The intention and fundamental patterns of the Starter Kata are still evident if you look closely, but the organization is probably starting to evolve its own routines and language, and now uses scientific thinking as its normal way of reaching goals—perhaps without even calling it that.

(continues)

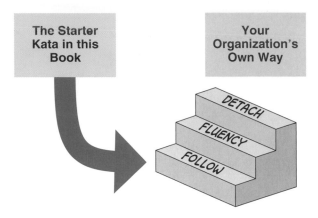

Figure 3.5. Building on practice of the Starter Kata,
your organization can develop its own routines and language.

A Note About Organization-wide Deployment

Planning a perfect deployment of new skills across an organization is impossible. Unforeseen obstacles, problems, and weaknesses will naturally arise, and it will be important to spot them, learn from them, and adjust your deployment accordingly. In fact, those obstacles, problems, and weaknesses are helpful because they show you what you need to work on next. You're conducting experiments toward a desired culture, which means you should apply the same scientific pattern of the Improvement Kata to your effort to develop Improvement Kata skills. Use the Improvement Kata to deploy the Improvement Kata.

To facilitate that learning and adapting, you should determine early on what small team of people will have the responsibility for shepherding your deployment.[6] That team should conduct regular reflections about the deployment (using the five Coaching Kata questions as the headings for those reflections) and introduce deployment course corrections as needed. Hopefully you are already thinking, *"Yes, we need to apply scientific thinking to our deployment, too!"* because intentionally modifying an organization's culture is a significant undertaking.

- This is not about just adding something on top of how you currently manage, but rather a change in how you manage.

---

6   Some organizations even call this team the "shepherding group."

- This cannot be delegated and simply monitored. Managers should be among the first to practice and learn the new skills themselves, before they can coach others. Start your practice with your strongest managers, and have them coach the next set of managers.

- To make the pattern of the Improvement Kata a habit, it should be practiced and coached as part of every day's normal work.

- Nobody will be an expert at first. Everyone should be comfortable with making mistakes, correcting, and learning.

- Ultimately you have to evolve your own system, based on your practice and experience. "Shepherding" plays a key role here.

The main constraint on the speed and range of a deployment in an organization is how much internal Coaching Kata proficiency you are able to develop. Your deployment, and the associated process of continuous improvement, can expand as you develop more capability to coach among your managers, as illustrated by the exponential growth curve in Figure 3.6. Of course, just calling managers "Coaches" will not work. Developing their Improvement Kata and Coaching Kata skills takes practice and time.

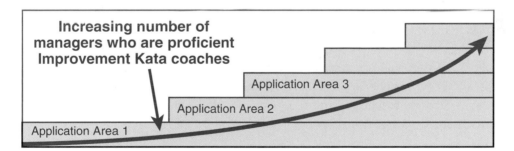

Figure 3.6. The speed of your deployment depends on how much coaching proficiency you can develop in your managers.

The good news is that the Improvement Kata and Coaching Kata patterns are fractal— following the same pattern at all levels—which helps you greatly with their deployment. Although each organization's effort to deploy Improvement Kata skills is unique and not predictable, everyone practices the same Starter Kata within the same basic learner/ coach structure.

CHAPTER 4

GET READY TO PRACTICE

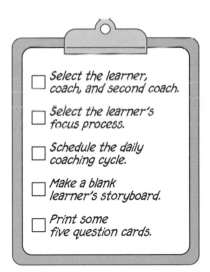

- Select the learner, coach, and second coach.
- Select the learner's focus process.
- Schedule the daily coaching cycle.
- Make a blank learner's storyboard.
- Print some five question cards.

One of the best places to start Improvement Kata practice is where you work, whether or not you have committed leaders above you. There are real work processes that you can improve there, and persons who can coach one another. Establish some competence with the pattern and practice routines of the Improvement Kata at your workplace, and then you can take your new skills wherever you want.

This short chapter recommends what you should organize in advance for your initial practice.

Select the Learner, Coach, and Second Coach

The coach is usually the learner's manager, although peer coaching works too. The coach should ideally have some experience in applying the Improvement Kata pattern, but if not you can temporarily utilize an external coach consultant or one of the rotation models described in Chapter 3.

The second coach is typically the coach's boss, a peer, or a staff specialist. The second coach should also have personal experience with applying the Improvement Kata, although at the start this may not be the case in your situation. Get started with what you have.

Select the Learner's Focus Process

For our purposes, a *process* is a series of activities that a person or a group of persons undertake as they interact with routines, materials, and equipment to produce an output or get something done. There are many kinds of processes: production, administrative, hospital, material handling, order entry, lab procedures, customer returns, and so on (Figure 4.1).[1]

Figure 4.1. There are many kinds of processes.

The main objective for a beginner learner the first time out is to get familiar with the four-step Improvement Kata pattern and the basics of its Starter Kata practice routines, not to achieve a big goal or solve a big problem. For a learner's first practice, try to use a visible, easy-to-understand work process so the learner can concentrate on practicing

---

1 Several processes linked together make up a "value stream." Here, however, we are talking about having the learner focus on one individual work process, not a value stream.

the pattern of the Improvement Kata rather than getting overwhelmed by the details of a complicated focus process.

"Routine work" is a good choice as a focus process for a beginner learner's first practice, such as manual processes that repeat their cycle every 30 seconds to five minutes (Figure 4.2). With this kind of process the learner can easily get a baseline understanding of the current condition, conduct several experiments toward a target condition, and measure the effects, all within two weeks. To find such a focus process, you may need to temporarily take the learner outside of their normal work area. Or you might select a smaller set of activities that is part of a larger process, such as a subassembly.

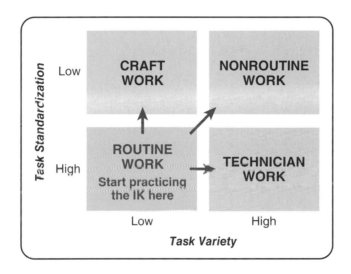

Figure 4.2. Routine work is a good choice for a learner's first focus process.
(Diagram adapted from: Liker and Meier, *Toyota Talent*, 2007. Modified from: Perrow, Charles,1967.
"A Framework for the Comparative Analysis of Organizations," *American Sociological Review* 32: 194–208.)

The coach should decide what the learner is ready for next. After the first two weeks of practice, most learners can probably start to apply the Improvement Kata to more complicated processes, which should then ideally be in their own work area. Unlike with the initial practice, the selection of the focus process should now be increasingly based on need, connected to a larger, strategic goal, such as a higher-level challenge or future-state value stream design. From this point on, the coach should ensure that the learner's practice has a meaningful, strategically connected improvement goal rather than just being random improvement. We'll talk more about this in the "Step 1: Understand the Direction or Challenge" chapter in Part II.

Schedule Your Daily Coaching Cycle

Get out your calendars. For each learner, schedule one regular daily, 20-minute coaching cycle at a consistent, set time near the beginning of the workday (Figure 4.3). Schedule it early in the day so the learner can take the next step that same day if possible.

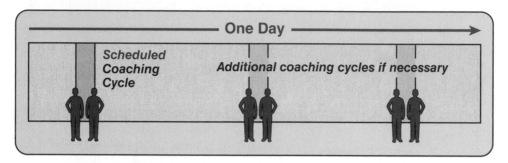

Figure 4.3. Schedule the regular daily coaching cycle early in the workday.

Make a Blank Learner's Storyboard

Start with the exact storyboard format shown in Figure 4.4 and in the Appendix. The working area of the storyboard should be at least 90 centimeters (three feet) tall. There is no need to make the storyboard permanent at this time. You can print it out on a large sheet of paper, draw it on a whiteboard, etc.

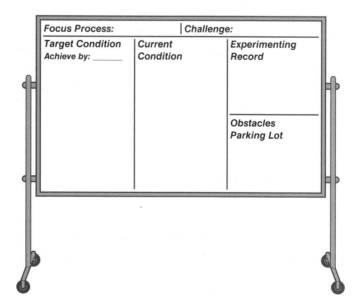

Figure 4.4. Start with this storyboard format.

The learner's storyboard will be a "living document," meaning that it contains the running story of the learner's application of the Improvement Kata to the focus process and is used to support the interaction between learner and coach during their coaching cycles. In the planning phase of the Improvement Kata, the sections of the storyboard will get built up one at a time, and in the executing phase the entire storyboard will be used.

Ideally, the learner's storyboard should be located near the focus process, so that coaching cycles happen as close as possible to where the work is being performed. **This means that the coach comes to the learner for the coaching cycles**, not the other way around.

Details that are posted on the storyboard may need to be added or corrected in response to coaching input during the coaching cycle dialogue, and if possible the learner should adjust the storyboard immediately.[2] Keep a pencil and eraser at the storyboard for this purpose.

Print Some Five Question Cards

You need at least one card each for the coach, learner, and second coach. Note that the cards are two-sided. Read through the questions on the card front and back to see their logic and flow. Note how the questions are nested, meaning that the next question is a subset of the previous question.

The five questions are the main headings of a coaching cycle, and the five question card is the coach's script for conducting coaching cycles. In every coaching cycle the coach will ask all the questions on the front and back of the card, one at a time, exactly as they are written on the card. The learner knows in advance what main questions the coach will ask. Some learners even post the five question card on their storyboard. After each question on the card the coach can also ask their own clarifying questions to probe the learner's thought process, gain more information, and help identify the current threshold of knowledge.

What's Ahead in this Book

Dear Learner and Dear Coach,

Parts II and III of *The Toyota Kata Practice Guide* are the recipe for your initial practice. For the **learner**, Part II describes how to do the Starter Kata for each step of the

---

2 Wherever possible, the coach will want to correct practice errors right away.

Improvement Kata pattern (Figure 4.4). For the **coach**, Part III contains guidelines and instructions to the Starter Kata for coaching an Improvement Kata learner.

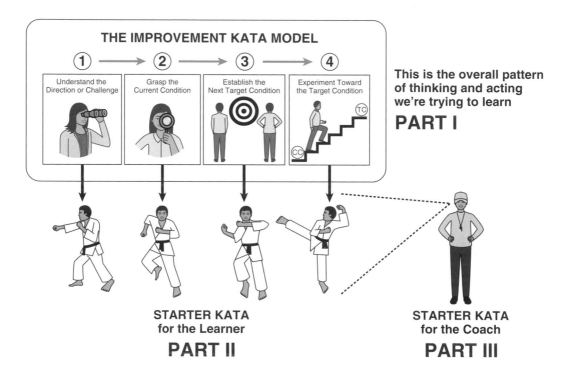

Figure 4.5. The layout of *The Toyota Kata Practice Guide.*

The Starter Kata presented here are well-tested routines to help you develop the skill of greater scientific thinking. Begin by practicing the Starter Kata formally and meticulously just as they are described, even though it may feel awkward and unnatural. The place to start is to practice each routine and learn the fundamental patterns that it imparts.

However, as you master the skill elements and they become more like second nature, the less rigid your practice needs to be. As you develop proficiency, the Starter Kata will look less like separate items to check off and more like parts of a natural flow with fuzzy lines between them.

For instance, as you work to understand a challenge, you may also immediately start recognizing certain things about your focus process's current condition in relation to that challenge. As you work to grasp a current condition, ideas about an appropriate target condition will probably also appear in your head. As you try to define the next target condition, you'll easily recognize where you still don't understand the current condition deeply enough and simply go back and get what you're missing. As you conduct experiments toward the target condition, you'll also deepen your knowledge about the current condition and gain insights that add more detail to the target condition.

You'll also start to recognize that, no matter what, *every step you take is an experiment* that could revise what you thought so far. And at that point, I think you can start calling yourself a scientist. Or, better yet, an explorer of realities that we'll never entirely know. You may even start to think of uncertainty as a joy, because it means there is no end to exploration and interesting discovery in our lives. That's what scientific thinking and continuous improvement are about.

When your practice gets to the point where scientific thinking becomes a connected flow like that, you'll be able to apply its power in almost any situation. Proficient practitioners, with skills derived from hands-on experience, apply the Improvement Kata pattern automatically. They quickly see what's important in any situation and depart from the strict Kata by stringing together ingrained fundamentals in ways that adhere to the principle but suit the situation.

And my hat will be off to you.

Suggestions for You as a Learner

One of the delights of life is to be a learner, and as we get into Parts II and III, both the learner and the coach will be learners in their respective roles. Let me offer the following suggestions:

1. **Adopt some "beginner mindset."** A first step for any learner is to acknowledge that whenever we want to acquire a new way of thinking and acting, we're going to be a beginner in that particular area. Caution! The more you are already familiar with a topic, the less you may be open-minded to learning something new about it. How positive your attitude about your practice is will significantly impact how much you are able to rewire your brain for the new skill. Ultimately, you've "gotta wanna."

2. **Assume that you'll experience failures, plateaus, and setbacks.** At first a new skill pattern is likely to feel awkward and ineffective because the fast habits you already have get in the way of the new habits you're trying to develop. That feeling is normal and actually a sign that a learning process is underway. At various points you may feel like "*I don't think this is going to*

work for me," which can prevent the new pattern from imprinting. Take a short break from practicing if you need to. Sooner or later, with your coach's help, your efforts will produce some positive results, which should build up your enthusiasm and desire to go on. Eventually you'll find yourself performing the new skill without even thinking about it.

3. **Concentrate on one Starter Kata at a time.** Don't worry too much about the entire behavior sequence of the Improvement Kata. You'll get there. Focus instead on practicing each Starter Kata so that it starts to feel natural and you're having success. Work on your errors and don't move on until you get better. In time, then, you'll tie the Starter Kata skills together into the entire scientific thought and behavior sequence that's modeled by the Improvement Kata.

4. **Think of mistakes as opportunities to improve and as helpful indicators of what you need to work on next.** Mistakes are "teachable moments" and are especially useful because you and your coach can use these experiences as indicators for what to correct and work on. Ask yourself, *"What should I adjust and do differently here?"* Then practice that right away.

5. **Listen to your coach.** Your coach is there to accelerate your learning by helping you stay focused, suggesting corrective adjustments, and ensuring that you experience successes. That's why the coach is giving you input, ideas, and feedback. It's not personal. It's not you that the coach is evaluating, but only your current level in performing a new skill element. In time, you may even find it strange to practice without a coach, because without a coach you can't tell what you are doing wrong and may be burning in a bad habit.

Your enthusiasm and persistence as a learner will make the difference as to how far you go in deepening the skills and mindset you're trying to learn, and turning them into new habits. With my best wishes for your practice, let's get going.

PRACTICE ROUTINES FOR THE LEARNER

(The Improvement Kata)

Practicing a Scientific Way of Working and Thinking

Welcome to the practice chapters for the four-step Improvement Kata pattern. The four steps of the Improvement Kata are presented in a linear fashion here, which makes them easier to practice and absorb, and is a good way to get started. As your experience grows, you'll find that in reality the steps tend to overlap.

Part II has five chapters:

Chapter 5: Understand the Direction or Challenge (Step 1)
Chapter 6: Grasp the Current Condition (Step 2)
Chapter 7: Establish the Next Target Condition (Step 3)
Chapter 8: Experiment Toward the Target Condition (Step 4)
Chapter 9: The Summary Reflection

Each of the practice chapters has two parts—a **concept overview** and **instructions for the Starter Kata**—which are indicated by the two icons below.

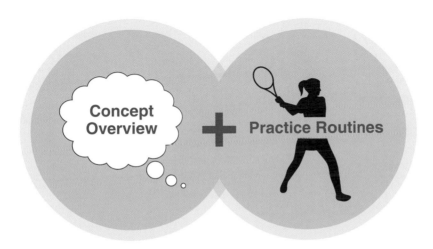

The four-step pattern of the Improvement Kata has two phases: planning and executing. The first three steps make up the planning phase, which is covered in Chapters 5 through 7. The fourth step makes up the executing phase, which is covered in Chapter 8. When the process is completed, it can be followed by a summary reflection to review and plan the next pass through the Improvement Kata. This is covered in Chapter 9.

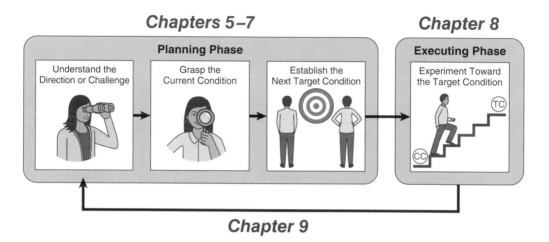

Planning Phase (Chapters 5–7)

A foundation for effective, scientific problem solving and improvement

When we are faced with a tough goal, we have a natural tendency to jump right into action. After all, the sooner we get going, the sooner we'll get there, right?

Not necessarily.

We often don't view planning as action, and thus end up getting poorer results, because in our zeal to get moving we jump to conclusions and start trying to "implement" preconceived ideas too quickly. As was described in Part I, that's a natural tendency of our brain, which quickly fills in missing information without alerting us that it is doing so, and makes us feel like we know more than we actually do.

The planning phase of the Improvement Kata pattern is a countermeasure to this brain tendency. It involves:

1. Getting some clarity about the **challenge** that's coming from above, and what it means for you and your team.

2. Analyzing your focus process, through direct observation and measurement, to understand its **current condition**, especially as it relates to the challenge.

3. Establishing the **next target condition**—a goal that's smaller and nearer than the challenge—based on the current condition and aimed at the challenge.

The planning phase sets you up to be effective in the executing phase, where each step toward the target condition is an experiment from which you may learn something.

Executing Phase (Chapter 8)
Working like a scientist to reach the next target condition

Experiment Toward the Target Condition

Defining your next target condition is important, but great execution is also important. If you have those two together, just about anything is possible.

In Chapter 8 the learner strives toward the target condition iteratively through experiments. Learning how to plan and conduct good experiments, and how to do that quickly, are skills you'll practice with the Starter Kata in this chapter.

Summary Reflection (Chapter 9)

Whenever either the target condition or the target condition achieve-by date is reached, the overall four-step pattern of the Improvement Kata starts over and gets repeated. On each pass through those four steps the learner practices all the individual Starter Kata. Notice, however, that the Starter Kata for the *executing* phase will naturally get practiced more than the other Starter Kata, since several cycles of experimentation repeat in that phase. This means that getting enough practice with the Starter Kata of the up-front *planning* phase will require the learner to pursue a few successive target conditions and thereby go through the entire Improvement Kata pattern a few times.

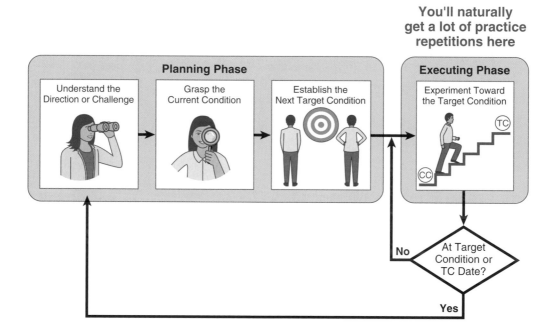

Ultimately the entire Improvement Kata pattern should become an automatic way of thinking for you. Follow the instructions for practicing each of the Starter Kata, remember the guidelines for good practice from Chapter 2, and listen to your coach!

CHAPTER **5**

UNDERSTAND THE DIRECTION OR CHALLENGE (STEP 1)

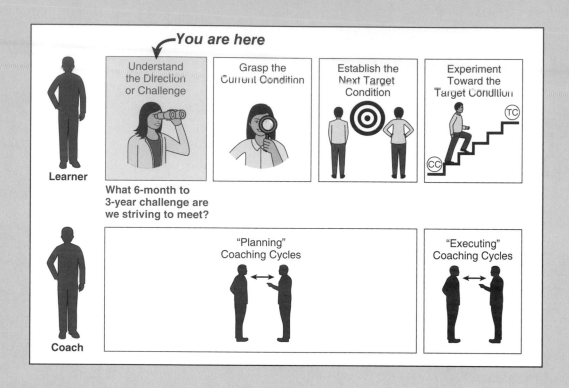

You are here

| Learner | Understand the Direction or Challenge | Grasp the Current Condition | Establish the Next Target Condition | Experiment Toward the Target Condition |

What 6-month to 3-year challenge are we striving to meet?

| Coach | "Planning" Coaching Cycles | "Executing" Coaching Cycles |

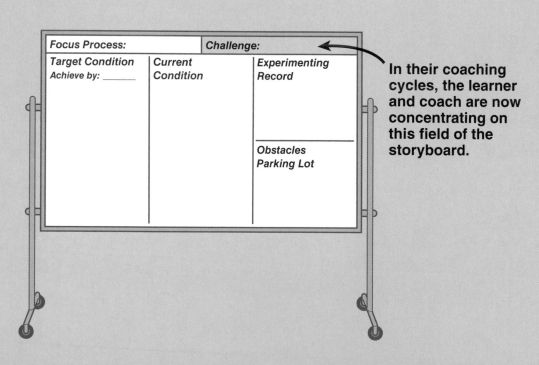

Focus Process:

Challenge:

Target Condition
Achieve by: _____

Current Condition

Experimenting Record

Obstacles Parking Lot

In their coaching cycles, the learner and coach are now concentrating on this field of the storyboard.

Strategy Before Goals

The Improvement Kata pattern begins with a sense of direction. It's about striving for a desired new condition with a compass, not a map.

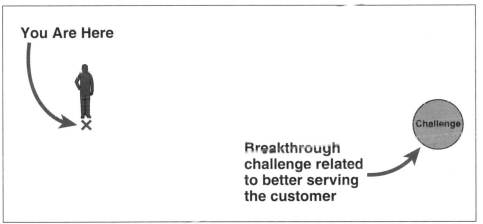

You Are Here

Challenge

Breakthrough challenge related to better serving the customer

Based on a graphic by Bill Costantino

The first step of the Improvement Kata pattern is to reference or connect to an overarching strategic challenge, which serves as the context for the rest of the Improvement Kata steps that follow. Think of the challenge as the *purpose* of your improvement efforts.

Having an overarching challenge makes people's target conditions meaningful. It's difficult to stay engaged with something that doesn't have a purpose, but surprising things can be achieved when we are pursuing an important goal. The combination of a tough challenge plus an effective way of meeting it is powerful because it can move your organization into new territory.

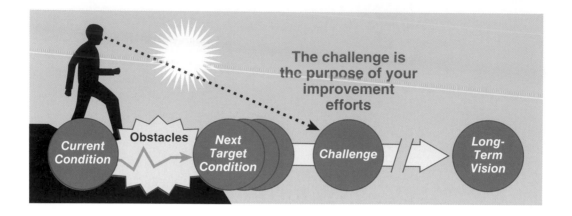

*When people see themselves as components in a system [and] work in coop-
eration to achieve a shared aim, they feel that their efforts hold meaning.
They experience interest and challenge and joy in the work.*

—W. Edwards Deming,
The New Economics (MIT Press, 1993)

Long-Term Vision: The Big Idea That's Way Out There

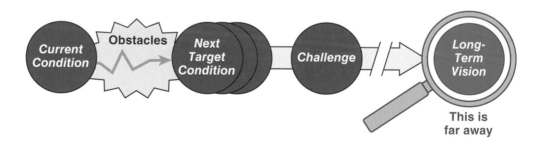

Which way is our organization heading? A vision is the loftiest goal for your organization. It's a long-range, almost utopian ideal about value you want to provide for
customers. It's your dream, sometimes referred to as "true north." For example, a long-
term vision for a maker of drills might be, *"Holes where you want them when you want
them"* (what the customer really wants is a hole in something, not necessarily to own a

drill). A vision may be impossible from the perspective of current technologies, conditions, and competencies, which is OK. It's far away, described only in general terms, and you may never actually get there. It's something you commit to pursuing for life.

A compelling vision can be an important beacon for an organization, but it's not such a good guide for daily improvement efforts because visions are by their nature vague and distant.

A Strategic Challenge: The More Practical, Day-to-Day Direction-Giver

Where is our organization going next? An overarching strategic challenge is an actual destination that's a distinctive and concrete value proposition related to better serving the customer. It's a picture of success—a description of a new level or pattern of performance that will differentiate your organization's offering from other offerings—that lies six months to three years in the future. A challenge is:

- A clearly described new customer experience that you would like to offer, which will cause you to stretch and grow. As you try to describe a challenge, think of completing the sentence *"Wouldn't it be great if we could . . ."*

- Something you can't yet achieve with your current system and processes.

- Not easy, but not impossible. It's achievable, but we don't know how yet. It cannot be reached quickly and takes a series of target conditions to reach. A challenge describes a destination, not how to get there.

- Is measurable, so you can know if you are there or not.

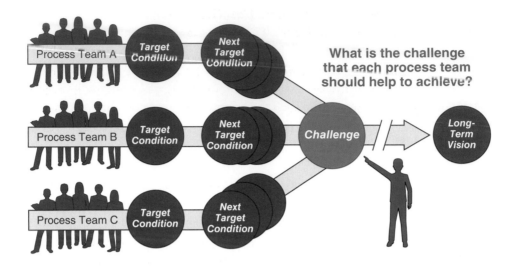

A main function of a challenge is to act as a theme that helps connect an organization's strategy with execution. The challenge helps align and connect individual improvement efforts, ensuring that what process-level teams work on has a shared focus and fits together.

For that reason a challenge is often expressed as a catchy *challenge statement*. For example, an automotive service shop might have a six-month challenge of all customers being registered within five minutes of arriving, communicating that with the challenge statement *"Give Me Five."*

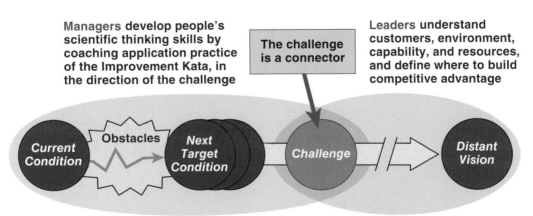

Danger: Efficiency and Cost Cutting Alone Are Not a Good Long-Term Direction

Strategy should focus on how you differentiate yourself from your competitors, not just on operational efficiency. Just pursuing low cost is unlikely to be a source of sustained competitive advantage, because it can lead you into a quality-sapping commodity trap that comes from seeking ever-lower-cost inputs. Going for efficiency alone can ultimately lead to a dangerously static and vulnerable organization.

Rather than managing the operational side of the business only to be efficient, with the Improvement Kata approach managers guide activities to support strategic themes that grow and distinguish the business. Those themes can include efficiency and cost reduction, of course, but over time shouldn't be limited to that. Defining a strategic goal is about building unique value—distinctive differences that are valuable to customers and serve as a rallying point for the organization.

To the Learner

This first step of the Improvement Kata is simple for the learner. The learner's task here is to understand their challenge, record it on the storyboard, and, ultimately, be able to show how their target condition connects to and supports the challenge. A learner's challenge typically comes from one level above. As a result there is less of a structured practice routine at this step. The hard part here is defining a good overall challenge, which is a task for leaders.

What the learner cares about at this step is what larger goal he or she should have in mind as they work to grasp the current condition, establish the next target condition, and conduct experiments at their particular focus process. The first step of the Improvement Kata pattern is about seeking alignment and making sure you are working on the right thing.

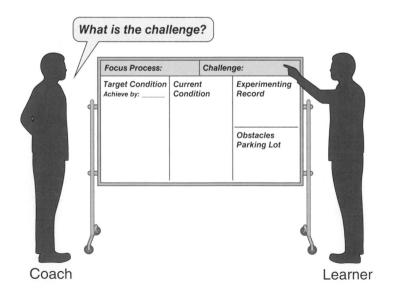

In each coaching cycle, before getting to the five Coaching Kata questions, the coach will ask the learner to name the focus process and reiterate the challenge that the learner is working toward. There are fields for this information at the top of the storyboard. This connects the learner's target condition to a larger objective and frames the rest of the coaching cycle dialogue.

Once an overarching challenge has been defined at the leadership level, it gets broken down into smaller objectives at each organizational level, through the coach/learner dialogues that repeat across the levels of the organization. Each person is a learner to the coach above him or her, and in turn a coach to learners in the level below, which is how local application of the Improvement Kata pattern gets linked to a larger objective. In many cases the target condition at the level above a learner is what becomes the challenge for the learner.[1]

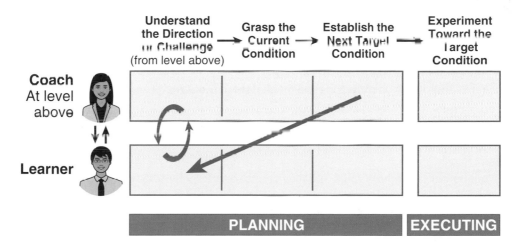

Of Course, in Reality There Is More Than One Goal in an Organization

The learner's practice of the Improvement Kata pattern won't always link formally to an overarching strategic goal. It just has to make sense within a larger picture, which is what's meant by "Understand the Direction." Every organization has multiple objectives, and people are expected to reach a variety of targets. You cannot stop working on

---

1 For a detailed and illustrated description of how this process works, see the book *Toyota Kata Culture* (McGraw-Hill, 2017).

the variety of fronts necessary to the business and put all improvement activity into one challenge and the associated target conditions. A goal is to develop many people who are proficient with the Improvement Kata pattern so it can be applied in any number of areas.

TO THE LEADERS

Establishing a Challenge at the Organization Level

A challenge typically has a time frame of six months to three years. The most basic practice for establishing an overarching challenge for the organization is to complete this sentence, with the customer in mind:

> *"Wouldn't it be great if we could . . ."*

The following questions help you to think outside the box and complete that sentence. For now, don't worry too much about technical limitations and things you can't yet do, since that could limit your thinking too much right at the start.

1. What is the distant, very long-term **vision** for our organization? What challenge will now help us move in that direction?

2. What do our **customers** value that they are not currently getting from us?

3. What special product or service **capability** do we want to develop?

4. What **changes** are happening in our environment that could make our current capabilities less special?

5. What does **success six months to three years from now** look like?

The overall challenge should describe a measurable desired state that people in the organization can relate to and rally around. However, the challenge is not just a number. It should be descriptive in a way that is relevant to the work being done in the organization. A good challenge focuses a team's attention and effort and is often published as a compact, inspiring *challenge statement*. Here's a case example.

Wouldn't it be great if we could . . . build one customer
kitchen at a time and put it right on the truck.

At a kitchen cabinet manufacturer, the normal operating pattern in the assembly department was to batch build one type of cabinet for a period of time (sink cabinets, corner cabinets, overhead cabinets, etc.) and then change over to assemble a different type. Finished cabinets were moved into storage until all of the different cabinets for a particular customer order were on hand, at which point the mix of cabinets for that customer's kitchen would be taken out of inventory and shipped.

The leadership of the company recognized that a customer just wants their particular set of cabinets, and that it would be an advantage to be able to assemble one customer's kitchen at a time, rather than batches of cabinet types. If the cabinets for one kitchen were assembled together they could even be loaded directly onto the truck and shipped. The company's leaders put forth the following challenge statement, with a time horizon of 18 months:

"Build to Truck, One Kitchen at a Time"

You can imagine people's dismissive initial reaction to this challenge. It was significantly different from the current approach, hard to see how it could technically be possible, and would require changes in many parts of the value stream, such as assembly, logistics, wood cutting, material ordering, and so on. There were many obstacles.

Eighteen months later, after a lot of focused, incremental improvement efforts throughout the organization, the people in the plant had met the challenge and were indeed assembling one kitchen at time. At the end of each assembly process a roller conveyor moved the just-assembled cabinets directly into a delivery truck, with no stopover in the storage warehouse. When you visited the various processes along the kitchen cabinet value stream, the teams there would enthusiastically show you the incremental innovations they had developed, which ultimately allowed the challenge to be reached. They would tell you stories of the experimentation it took to overcome the obstacles and get there.

There is no end to great challenges. They may start out seemingly impossible or hard to imagine, yet often become something positive and deeply satisfying . . . if you and your team have a scientific thinking way of working toward them.

(continues)

Writing a Good Challenge Statement

A good challenge statement can be an important element of any group endeavor. Suggestions for writing a challenge statement include:

- Choose the time frame for the challenge, within six months to three years.

- What new value do you want to offer the customer? Go for something great.

- Write the challenge as if you were already there, describing the new reality or condition you expect to see happening then.

- Be sure to write the challenge statement in measurable terms so you can tell if you are achieving it or not. There should be a clear goal line.

- The challenge should be difficult, but it does need to ultimately be possible.

Two common errors are that a challenge statement is too broad, which makes it ineffective as a direction giver, or too narrow and solution focused, which fails to leave room for developing new, yet unknown solutions. For example:

Too Broad	GOOD STATEMENT	Too Narrow
"Shorten the Lead Time"	*"Same Day, Next Day"*	*"Outsource subassemblies"*
You won't know when you are there.	(Build the product the day the customer orders, and ship it the next day.)	Rules out other solutions.

Dropping Down from the Organizational Challenge to a Value Stream Design

Going down a level from the organization's leaders, a future-state value stream map is often the next level of providing direction and challenge for Improvement Kata practice. A future-state value stream map is sometimes even called a *challenge map*. The future-state map illustrates how you want one value stream to be functioning and performing six months to three years in the future, and thereby provides an even more concrete sense of direction.

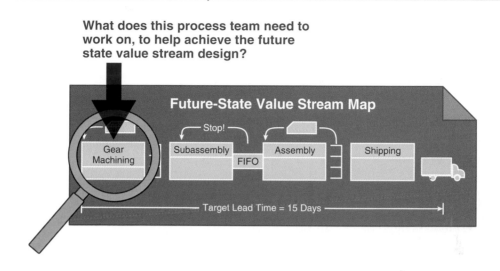

What does this process team need to work on, to help achieve the future state value stream design?

A **value stream** encompasses the course, or stream, of actions required to take a product or service from "raw material" to the hands of the customer, in one product family or business unit. **Value stream mapping** is a method for analyzing the current state and designing a future state for that series of actions. At the value stream level, current-state mapping is equivalent to grasping the current condition, and future-state mapping is equivalent to establishing the target condition. The popular book *Learning to See* gives you instructions for value stream mapping.

What If Your Organization Does Not Currently Have an Overarching Challenge?

It's easy to envision how a descriptive, compelling challenge can help galvanize the members of an organization into concerted action. However, the senior management of your site may not yet have formulated a meaningful strategic challenge. This is not uncommon.

If not, drop down one level, map your value stream (current state and future state), and see what comes out of that. Without constructive directional guidance from the leader level, future-state mapping at the product-family level can temporarily take the lead and provide the necessary sense of direction and challenge for your initial Improvement Kata

(continues)

practice. If the challenge is coming entirely from the value stream level, then the challenge statement should be written at that level too. That is, a future-state map should usually include a theme or challenge statement, whether that statement comes from senior management or from the value stream design team.

In the long run, of course, future-state mapping can't be a substitute for strategic direction provided by the organization's leadership.

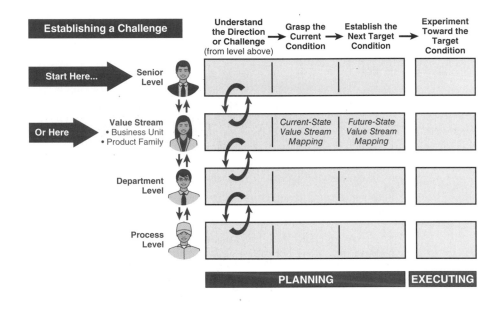

CHAPTER **6**

GRASP THE CURRENT CONDITION (STEP 2)

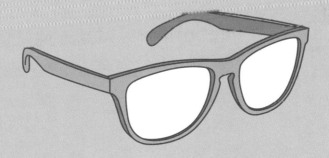

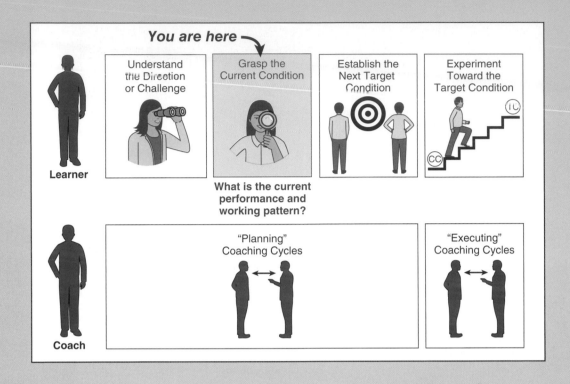

You are here

| Learner | Understand the Direction or Challenge | Grasp the Current Condition | Establish the Next Target Condition | Experiment Toward the Target Condition |

What is the current performance and working pattern?

| Coach | "Planning" Coaching Cycles | | "Executing" Coaching Cycles |

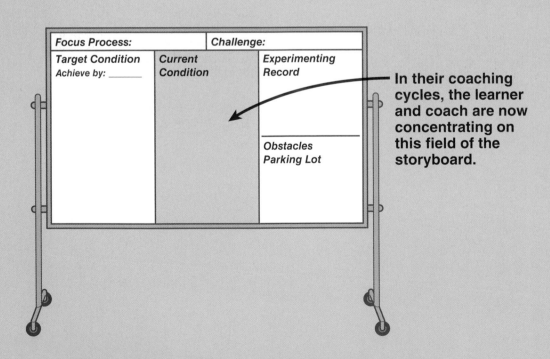

Focus Process: ___ Challenge: ___

Target Condition
Achieve by: _____

Current Condition

Experimenting Record

Obstacles Parking Lot

In their coaching cycles, the learner and coach are now concentrating on this field of the storyboard.

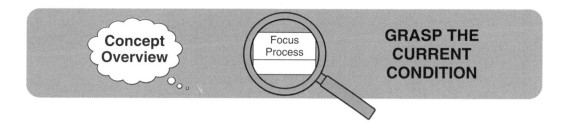

Where Are We Now?

Don't go into an improvement situation with preconceived notions or jump into action without knowing the real current condition. To establish an appropriate next target condition, you should first get a good grasp of your starting position.

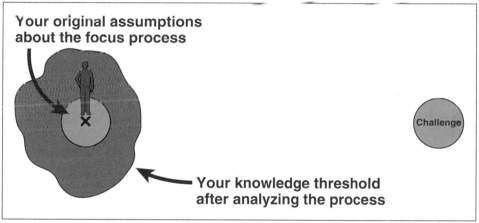

Based on a graphic by Bill Costantino

Grasping the current condition involves personally observing and studying the focus process to objectively and quantitatively analyze how it currently operates and performs. This chapter gives you a step-by-step Starter Kata for doing that with almost any work process. You may have to make some adaptations in elements of this process analysis routine to make it fit different kinds of processes, but the five basic steps usually stay about the same.

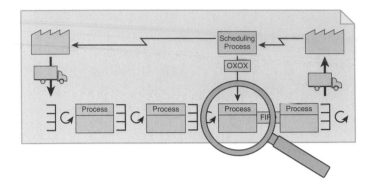

"Process analysis" is a good name for this Starter Kata, because it is designed for grasping the current condition at the level of an individual process. A "process" is the series of activities that a person or a group of persons undertake as they interact with routines, materials, and equipment to produce an output or get something done.

Note that at *high levels* in the organization, how to grasp the current condition depends on the particular strategic purpose being pursued, and at the *value stream level*, current-state value stream mapping is often used for grasping the current condition.

Reality Is Not Obvious

A common error in grasping the current condition is to make assumptions. We cannot depend on our impressions and intuition for an accurate assessment of the current condition, no matter how well we think we already know the focus process. In fact, the more familiar you are with a process, the harder it can be to see it objectively. Process analysis is time well spent because it leads you to better decisions and improvements down the line. Go and analyze what's really happening rather than listening to people's beliefs, or your own beliefs, about what is happening.

However, you can't simply tell someone to "go grasp the current condition," because each of us will see different things as being important. For the same reason, you cannot simply ask people in the process or responsible for the process about the current condition. The process analysis Starter Kata gives you a structured routine to go and see and measure for yourself. Practicing the systematic routine of this Starter Kata helps anyone assess and understand the characteristics of a process in a consistent, objective, mathematical, and efficient way.

We can't just use my impressions or ask people what they think. We need to observe and measure!

The Purpose of Process Analysis

The steps of process analysis are designed to give you a deeper understanding of the focus process than you can get from à la carte observing, interviewing, and looking at past data. It is critical to understand the operating patterns and other characteristics of the focus process before you develop the next target condition.

Note that process analysis is not *problem* analysis. It's not about identifying problems, wastes, or potential improvements. At this point you're just trying to see and understand what's there, without judgment. Practice that impartial mindset. The purpose is to get a baseline understanding of the current performance and operating patterns of the focus process—that's all—as a prerequisite for then establishing a next target condition.

Go through all five steps of the process analysis Starter Kata, because the information you obtain from any single step is not enough. It's the activity of slowing down and going through the entire process analysis that gives you a deeper grasp of the focus process.

However, you don't need to get a perfect understanding of the current condition at this step. You'll add information as you move forward and learn more. This chapter is about grasping the *initial current condition*, and your knowledge about the focus process will keep deepening when you try to establish a target condition, and then as you experiment toward that target condition. The "Current Condition" field on the learner's storyboard gets updated before each coaching cycle to reflect the learner's latest knowledge about the latest current condition.

Focus on Understanding Process Patterns, Not Just Outcomes

To deeply understand the current condition, don't just measure the focus process's outcomes, such as units/day, productivity, quality, or customer ratings. The process analysis Kata emphasizes also understanding how the focus process is operating that produces those outcomes. That's why this step of the Improvement Kata is called "current condition" rather than "current results." You should understand the means, not just the ends of what's happening. Why? We generally can't sustainably improve process outcomes—such as productivity or quality—by directly attacking them, since they are a result of how the process operates. Instead, you figure out what the **current operating pattern** is that generates those outcomes, and then you design a **target operating pattern** (in the next step of the Improvement Kata) that you predict will generate the outcomes you want.

A common problem in assessing a current condition is relying primarily on analysis of past data, with little or no direct observation of the focus process. With the process analysis Starter Kata, you directly observe and measure the operation of the focus process, live, to the extent possible. You'll be observing and timing operating cycles of the focus process's actors and equipment, which lets you spot patterns in the work that were invisible or appeared to be random events. These insights are part of what guide you to developing an appropriate next target condition. In many cases you'll come to understand the current condition so well that the next process target condition becomes almost obvious. In fact, if what the target condition should be is not clear, it often means you need to go study the current condition some more. Grasping the current condition is an important and powerful step in the Improvement Kata.

How to Get Started

You may already have an approach for analyzing a process. Put that aside for now and practice the process analysis Starter Kata as it is designed, until you absorb its basic steps and can do it easily—like practicing some musical scales.

At the beginning, follow the steps of the process analysis Starter Kata in order, as closely as you can in your situation. Changing the steps or their order at this point just makes it harder for beginners to learn. You're also creating team skills. Unless people in your organization take the time to practice and learn a common, systematic way of understanding and communicating about a process, they will too easily slip back into shooting from the hip based on each person's individual perspective and impressions.

Once you develop some proficiency with the steps of the process analysis Starter Kata, you can:

- Vary the order of the steps. Experienced practitioners naturally and smoothly move back and forth between the steps of process analysis as they encounter or seek out information.

- Build on the steps and combine them with your existing approach to best suit your organization's processes, products, and culture.

It is easiest to apply the process analysis Kata to repetitive, short-cycle processes, rather than to long-cycle processes or processes where the work content varies a great deal. That's a good place to do your first process analysis practice, even if it is not your normal focus process.

To illustrate the five steps of the process analysis Starter Kata, the "practice routines" section of this chapter uses a manufacturing process as an example, because it has a fast cycle and is easy to observe. Note, however, that the example focus process itself is not important. The five steps are generic and vary less from case to case than you might think. What does vary is how difficult it may be to apply them to a particular process. Check yourself: Are you skipping a step of the process analysis Starter Kata because it doesn't work, or because it is hard to figure out how to apply it to a particular focus process? At this point your coach might give you some suggestions and say, *"Please try again."*

Guidelines for Practicing Process Analysis

❑ For beginner learners choose a process that is easy to understand and analyze. The first goal here is to internalize the routine of process analysis, not to tackle the most important or most difficult process to improve. Once the learner has developed some familiarity with the steps of process analysis, he or she can practice applying this Starter Kata to more difficult processes.

❑ Have the learner follow the process analysis steps as closely as possible, one at a time. Don't let a beginner learner jump ahead, because you're trying to imprint a pattern. Competent-level learners can then vary the sequence of steps according to the situation.

❑ However, as the learner moves through the analysis steps in order, he or she will often have to go *back* to review or recalculate an earlier step based on what he or she is learning. That's normal. One can't get each step right the first time.

(continues)

- A key to the process analysis Starter Kata, as with any Kata, is to not overthink it, but rather to go ahead and do it a step at a time. Learn with the body. A routine like this can seem complicated when you've never done it this way before, but it will seem easy after you've done it a few times. As a beginner, follow the instructions as closely as you can.

- Don't let the learner use averages, because averages mask process variation.

- Break the practice of process analysis into "chunks":

  o Have the learner complete one process analysis step at a time.

  o Upon concluding one step of the process analysis, have a beginner learner summarize and present that step in a coaching cycle before going on to the next step.

  o In coaching cycles, the learner should present current condition information in the same order as the five steps of this Starter Kata. You're trying to imprint a pattern of thinking, and even a language.

  o Each time the learner presents their ongoing process analysis, have him or her begin the presentation back at step one of process analysis. The learner should go over the entire process analysis each time he or she presents it, to help internalize the pattern, until all the steps are completed and a full picture is obtained. This is a common technique in music practice.

- With a beginner learner, the coach should go along during the process analysis, and to a degree also analyze the process, working in parallel with the learner. This way the coach can better evaluate and give feedback on what the learner is doing.

- At the beginning, doing a process analysis may take a few days, but as you gain experience with the process analysis routine you can often do it in a few hours. For practice it can be fun to set an increasingly shorter time to do a process analysis. Pick another process and do it again. Can you get to the point of doing a complete process analysis in just a few hours?

QUICK TIPS

Process Analysis with Office and Service Processes

Find the pattern of working!

"Pattern" is a good word to use when you seek to understand any process. There is a repeating pattern in nearly all work that humans do, because that's how our brain works.

Practicing the Improvement Kata with office and service processes can be difficult at the beginning because the work content often varies, takes a long time, and may even be invisible. However, even when the work content varies, people carrying out the tasks will have certain repetitive ways of doing them. That's a key part of what you're trying to see and measure in process analysis with any process: What is the current way of doing things?

It can take longer to observe and measure the current work patterns in office and service processes. But once you start to recognize the patterns you can measure, graph, and sketch them and, based on that analysis, define the next target pattern to aim for.

Process Analysis with a Fully Automated Process

Focus on the surrounding human processes.

Fully automated processes are still dependent on things that people do, such as:

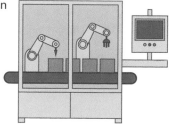

- Machine tending (monitoring, stocking, loading, adjusting, etc.)

- Changeovers

- Logistics (moving material in and out)

(continues)

- Reacting to problems

- Planned maintenance

You may be surprised at the degree to which variability in these surrounding human work processes will affect the performance of an automated machine. You can apply the steps of the Improvement Kata, including process analysis, to any of those human-centered processes rather than to the machine itself.

STEP 1: Process Outcomes. Review the process's outcome performance, which gives you a sense for what the process is creating and a frame for the rest of the process analysis.

STEPS 2–5: Pattern of Working. Now get inside the focus process to understand its characteristics and operating pattern, which are what generate the outcomes.

---

1   **GRAPH PROCESS OUTCOME PERFORMANCE**
How is the process performing over time?

2   **CALCULATE THE CUSTOMER DEMAND RATE AND PLANNED CYCLE TIME**
How frequently should the process do what it does?

3   **STUDY THE PROCESS'S OPERATING PATTERNS**
☐ Draw a block diagram of the process steps and sequence.
☐ Time exit cycles and draw run charts, to make variation visible.
☐ Record your observations about the current operating patterns.

4   **CHECK EQUIPMENT CAPACITY**
Are there any equipment constraints? What are they?
(This step is only for processes that include automated equipment.)

5   **CALCULATE THE CORE WORK CONTENT**
How many operators would be necessary
if the process had no variation?

QUICK TIPS

The Basic Equipment You'll Need:

- A stopwatch that measures in seconds

- Graph paper

- Pencil, eraser, and ruler

- Calculator

- Blank current condition / target condition form (see Appendix)

- Timing worksheet (see Appendix)

Practice Courtesy at the Focus Process!

- Approach the process via its manager or supervisor.

- Introduce yourself to the people in the process and explain what you are doing. Explain that you are watching the work, not the person.

- Do not interrupt people while they're working.

- Before you leave say *thank you*, and show any notes you've taken.

- Keep your hands out of your pockets while you are at the focus process, because everyone is working here.

Some Process Analysis Terminology:

Facts: Something you observe. Example: The actual occurrence of scrap.

Data: Something you measure. Example: The scrap rate.

Outcome metric: This is a "result" metric, measured after the fact, that summarizes how a process or system has performed in aggregate over several cycles. An outcome metric itself cannot be directly influenced because it is the product of other variables. Examples: lead time, output per hour, cost, labor cost, productivity, quality.

Process metric: This is a metric that occurs in each cycle of the focus process and can be directly observed and measured in real time to assess how a process is operating now. A process metric is often one of the variables that affects the outcome metric and is something that can be directly influenced. Example: The time each work cycle takes.

Working with the Current Condition / Target Condition Form and the Storyboard

The current condition / target condition form (see Appendix) is both a process analysis checklist and, together with the storyboard, a place to record your findings. This form plus any additional pages of data, such as your block diagram and run charts, should be posted in the "Current Condition" field of the storyboard.

As you gain experience you can modify and evolve this form to suit your particular environment and needs. However, as with any Starter Kata, first practice using it as designed.

In the planning phase of the Improvement Kata, the spaces for describing the current condition and target condition are together on one form so you can cross-reference characteristics of the current condition and target condition. At this time you will be using the *left side* of the form. Later, once the target condition is established, the form gets cut into two pieces along the line shown, and each side is placed in its corresponding field on the storyboard.

Remember, what you are working on now is determining the *initial current condition*. In the executing phase of the Improvement Kata the "Current Condition" field of the learner's storyboard will be updated before each coaching cycle to reflect the latest current condition.

CURRENT CONDITION / TARGET CONDITION		Outcome Metric	
Learner:	Coach:	Focus Process	Process Metric
		Current Condition Date	Target Condition Achieve-by Date
1 Outcome Performance	Actual output		
	Operating time		
	Is there overtime?		
2 Customer Demand & Planned Cycle	Requirement		
	Takt time		
	Planned cycle time		
3 Operating Patterns	Process steps and sequence		
	Variation		
	Observations about the current operating patterns		
4 Equipment Capacity	Automated equipment constraints?		
5 Core Work	Calculated number of operators		

Left Side

STEP 1: GRAPH PROCESS OUTCOME PERFORMANCE
How is the process performing over time?

Once the focus process has been selected, begin your process analysis by looking at data on how the process has been performing over time. Doing this should help you understand what the focus process produces, who its customers are, when it operates, and how it is performing.

Some examples of outcome metrics for the focus process include quantity, productivity, quality, cost, wait time, service ratings, and so on. You can change the outcome metric you are following or add outcome metrics at any time. You may already have this information, since it is historical data. Graph it in a simple run chart, as illustrated below, and post it on your storyboard.

An additional piece of information to collect at this step is how much overtime beyond the scheduled work time, if any, has been required for the focus process to produce the outcomes.

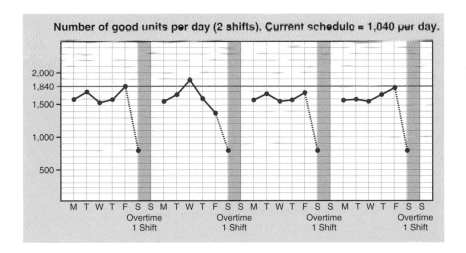

Keep in mind that it can be difficult to tell how accurate historical data is. If possible, set up a system to continually measure and collect this data, because you'll want to keep an eye on the outcome metric(s) as you conduct experiments in step four of the Improvement Kata pattern.

Post this graph in the "Current Condition" field of your storyboard.

STEP 2: CALCULATE THE CUSTOMER DEMAND RATE AND PLANNED CYCLE TIME
How frequently should the focus process do what it does?

In this step you're trying to figure out at what rate the focus process *should* be cycling. It may seem strange to be thinking about desired cycle time when you're analyzing the current condition, but it is an important lens, or benchmark, that you'll use in the next steps to compare with what is actually happening. The purpose of determining a desired cycle time is to help you understand customer demand and then let you assess where the focus process currently stands relative to that. Notice that cycle time is a process metric.

 It may be tempting to simply ask someone what the desired cycle time should be, but don't rely on that. Instead, base your determination on a calculation that *you* make, which starts with understanding the needs of the focus process's customer. With that information you can calculate a desired cycle for almost any work process. Any process has both a customer and a pattern of working. When you bring those two things together, there's usually some kind of desired cycle.

There are two numbers you are trying to get in this step: (A) the rate of customer demand, expressed in seconds/minutes/hours/days/etc., per unit, which is often called the "takt time," and (B) the desired or target rate at which the focus process should be cycling, which is often called "planned cycle time." Later, in step three, you'll measure and graph the current actual cycle time.

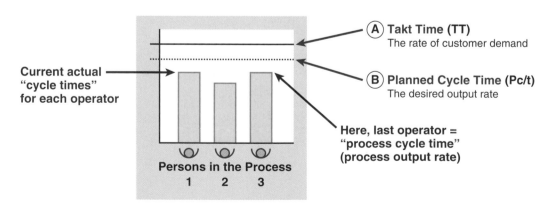

The planned cycle time will usually be faster than the customer demand rate to accommodate problems such as unplanned downtime, changeover time, and swings in demand and still be able to serve the customer in a timely fashion. However, this creates a buffer, so try not to overdo it. An 85 percent planned cycle time guideline is explained on the following pages.

Questions to ask in this step of process analysis are:

- *What is the focus process's product or unit of output?*

- *How often does the focus process's customer or customer process want this unit of output?*

- *How often do we want the focus process to make one unit of its output?*

Note 1: Don't worry if you can't get a perfect picture of demand and calculate perfect numbers at this time. Get as close as possible and come back and fine-tune the numbers as you move forward and learn more.

Note 2: Since customer demand changes over time, you'll need to recalculate takt time and planned cycle time periodically.

A. Calculating Takt Time (TT): Available Working Time Divided by Demand Quantity

The takt time calculation for the focus process is simply the available work time at that process (the numerator) divided by the number of units of process output the customer requires in that time frame (the denominator). See the example calculation on the next page.

Note that the available work time is the time per shift or day or week (etc.) minus any *planned* downtimes—when the process intentionally pauses—such as breaks. However, do not subtract out any *unplanned* downtime or changeover time at this point, so that the takt time calculation gives you a picture of the real customer demand rate.

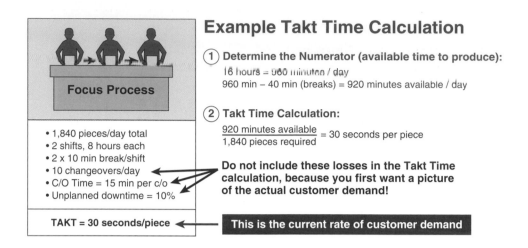

Example Takt Time Calculation

(1) **Determine the Numerator (available time to produce):**

16 hours = 960 minutes / day

960 min – 40 min (breaks) = 920 minutes available / day

(2) **Takt Time Calculation:**

$$\frac{920 \text{ minutes available}}{1,840 \text{ pieces required}} = 30 \text{ seconds per piece}$$

Do not include these losses in the Takt Time calculation, because you first want a picture of the actual customer demand!

Focus Process

• 1,840 pieces/day total
• 2 shifts, 8 hours each
• 2 x 10 min break/shift
• 10 changeovers/day
• C/O Time = 15 min per c/o
• Unplanned downtime = 10%

TAKT = 30 seconds/piece ← **This is the current rate of customer demand**

B. Calculating Planned Cycle Time (Pc/t)

This is the actual rate, or cycle, at which you want the focus process to operate. You'll be using this number in the remaining steps of process analysis. At this point you just need an initial number for the rate at which you think the focus process should cycle, which you can fine-tune if necessary as you learn more.

Once you have calculated takt time (the demand rate), now you subtract your typical losses, such as changeover time, unplanned downtime, scrap, and rework from the available work time (numerator) in order to arrive at a *planned cycle time* (Pc/t).

A word of caution: The more potential losses you subtract from the numerator of the planned cycle time calculation, the more your cost rises. You end up cycling the process too fast, which requires more operators and easily leads you to overproduce relative to the actual customer demand, resulting in potentially harmful buffers. For that reason there is a useful alternative calculation. A good place to start with planned cycle time is to simply multiply the takt time by .85 (85 percent) to arrive at an initial planned cycle time that is only 15 percent faster than the takt time. Later, as you start experimenting, you'll learn more about the process and can adjust the Pc/t number accordingly.

You can think of the planned cycle time as a target that you will be working toward. That is, rather than simply covering all process problems with a much faster cycle, strive through your experiments to be able to cycle the focus process no faster than 15 percent below the takt time. That makes you address the problems rather than burying them out of sight.

STEP 3: STUDY THE PROCESS'S OPERATING PATTERNS

This step is the heart of the process analysis Starter Kata.

Step three consists of the following three main activities. The findings from each of these activities should be posted in the "Current Condition" field of the storyboard.

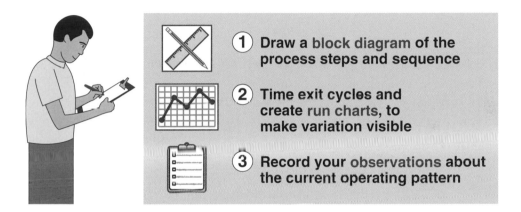

1. Draw a **block diagram** of the process steps and sequence
2. Time exit cycles and create **run charts**, to make variation visible
3. Record your **observations** about the current operating pattern

Before you do these three activities, first get a sense for the boundaries of your focus process by walking the flow of the product or service. You can refer to a current-state value stream map to see where the inputs to the process come from and where its output goes. However, be sure to go and walk these flows yourself, starting at the "customer" process that receives the focus process's output, and going upstream all the way through to the process that supplies your focus process. What do you think are the boundaries of where your focus process starts and ends?

QUICK TIPS

In step three of process analysis you can and should communicate with people about process details, but do not interview or ask people to tell you what are process problems or improvement ideas. Practice the routines of this step to study the focus process and learn to see and understand the true situation for yourself.

Draw a Block Diagram of the Process Steps and Sequence to Show the Flow of Work

A block diagram is a simple but remarkably useful tool. It is a row of squares to which you add information to visually depict the steps and sequence of how the work in the focus process is done. Note that the block diagram is a process-level diagram, not a value stream map. In office/service processes a "swim-lane diagram" can be useful for the same purpose as a block diagram. (Many online resources describe that tool.)

Begin by defining the start and end points of the process you are observing. You may decide to adjust these process boundaries as you draw and get to know the process better.

At this stage you're trying to understand the current work pattern and flow, *not* the physical layout. To do this, draw a *straight-line* sketch of the workstations in the process, with each one shown as a square of the same size, regardless of what the actual workstations and layout look like. Each square simply represents a workstation, table, fixture, or machine. Do not draw to scale or worry much about the physical layout. What you are drawing is the work flow. The block diagram can have multiple branches, of course, if that's how your focus process flows.

You can add whatever information you like to your block diagram. The example below (an assembly process) illustrates information that typically gets noted:

- Name of the workstation or processing step

- Number of operators (three in this example) and their range of work

- Batch sizes (how many units are processed by one person before passing them on)

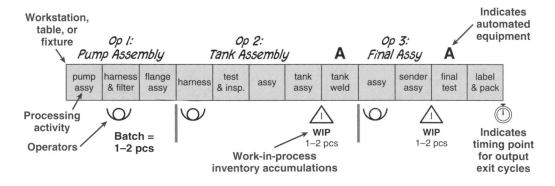

- Where work-in-process inventory tends to accumulate (WIP triangle)

- Where there are fully automated machines that can cycle unattended (useful in step four)

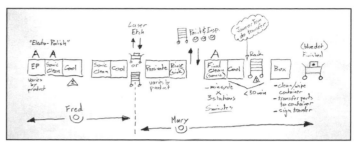

You can keep adding details to your block diagram as you go through the other steps of process analysis. Your block diagram may get messy, which is normal.

Time Exit Cycles and Draw Run Charts to Make Variation Visible

In this step you'll be making run charts of a metric called "exit cycles." These run charts are another highly useful tool for gathering, understanding, and communicating current-condition information. Exit cycle run charts illustrate process variation over time, and making them provides many clues to the current operating pattern of a process. Understanding the variation in a process is important because it can affect so many other aspects of the process. The run charts look like this:

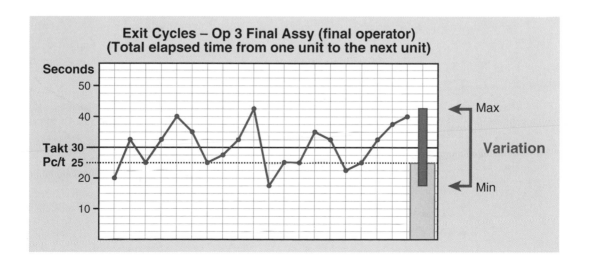

You should always try to make exit cycle run charts for your focus process, even though it can be difficult and time-consuming in the case of long-cycle or custom processes. Preparing them forces you to observe and study the process in more detail than just watching, and leads you to a deeper understanding. You will be getting lots of practice with this, because in the executing phase of the Improvement Kata, run charts often get retimed and redrawn before each coaching cycle, to document the *latest* current condition.

How to Make a Run Chart

First you need to time "exit cycles" for each operator in the process. An exit cycle is the actual time between completed units of the product or service that is coming out of that operator's portion of the process. It's not how long, but *how often*. It's not the operator's work content, but how much time elapses from unit to unit.

Exit cycles for the last operator position in a process—the one closest to the output end—often give you a metric for the output variation of the whole process. Check the box on the timing worksheet (see figure) if you are timing the operator exit cycles that represent process output. Timing operator cycles further upstream gives you a picture of variation that is occurring *inside* the focus process.

Time 20 to 30 "exit cycles" for each operator in the process. To do this, select a reference point in the operator's work pattern, and start your stopwatch when the operator gets to that point. Now let your stopwatch run until the operator returns to this reference point in the cycle, no matter what interruptions or delays might take place. You are

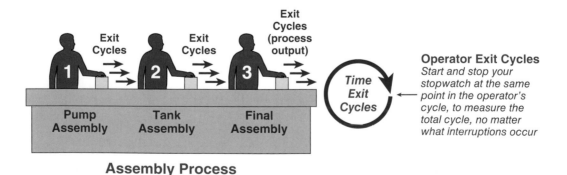

Operator Exit Cycles
Start and stop your stopwatch at the same point in the operator's cycle, to measure the total cycle, no matter what interruptions occur

timing full cycles, so just let the stopwatch run until then. Also do not skip or discard any cycles, no matter what happens, because they are all data.

As you do this, please keep in mind that you are timing and understanding process characteristics, not the operator. You're not trying to change how people work, only to begin to understand the variation that is occurring in the focus process and what may be causing it.

Record the times you measure on the timing worksheet, and be sure to write any observations you make about the current operating pattern in the area provided. Using the data from the timing worksheet and some graph paper, you can now draw your run charts by following the steps on the next page.

TIMING WORKSHEET

Process *Assembly*

Date *May 16, 2017*

Metric *Exit Time*

Operator *3-Final Assy* [X]

Check box if this is process output

Cycle	Observed Times (Data)	Observations about the current operating pattern (Facts)
1	20 seconds	
2	33	
3	25	
4	33	
5	40	Fixture got stuck
6	35	Wrong components in box
7	25	
8	27	
9	33	
10	43	Operator moves finished goods
11	18	
12	25	
13	25	
14	35	Parts stuck in supply chute
15	33	Waiting for operator 2
16	23	
17	25	
18	33	
19	38	Helped operator 2
20	40	Operator replenishes own material
21		
22		
23		
24		
25		

Drawing a Run Chart, Step by Step

Step 1: Draw in the target times

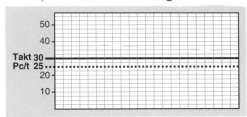

1 If you have a takt time and a planned cycle time for the process, draw horizontal lines for them on the graph.

If you don't have a TT or Pc/t, simply draw a line for the exit cycle time or rate you'd like to have. These numbers can be adjusted later if necessary.

Step 2: Add the data points

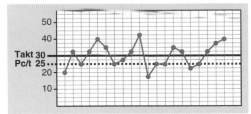

2 Plot & connect the data points.

Notes: • Do not use any averages because they obscure variation.

• Include all data points, even outliers. Try to depict the real situation.

Step 3: Find the lowest repeatable time

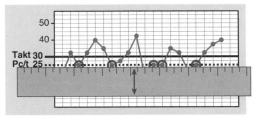

3 Find the "lowest repeatable time" by moving a ruler up from the bottom until the data points start repeating.

The lowest repeatable time in this example is approximately 25 seconds.

Steps 4 & 5: Summarize the amount of variation

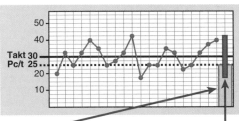

4 Draw a wide bar ("the candle") to show the lowest repeatable time.

Draw a thin bar ("the wick") to show the range of variation (highest point to lowest point). Range here = 18–43 seconds

5 Calculate the amount of positive and negative variation relative to the Pc/t

Positive Variation:
(Highest point – Pc/t) ÷ Pc/t
(43 sec – 25 sec) ÷ 25 sec
% pos variation here = 72%

Negative Variation:
(Lowest point – Pc/t) ÷ Pc/t
(18 sec – 25 sec) ÷ 25 sec
% neg variation here = 28%

Interpretation for this Example: (Op 3 Final Assembly)

The lowest repeatable cycle time is approximately 25 seconds, with 72% positive variation and 28% negative variation relative to the planned cycle time.

Note: The helpful "candle" and "wick" terminology used here comes from Brandon Brown and Bill Kraus.

You can make run charts like this for nearly any process. Maybe it's a customer issue, maybe it's your job hunt, maybe it's a global issue like carbon emissions. Here are current condition exit cycle run charts for the other two operators in our example focus process.

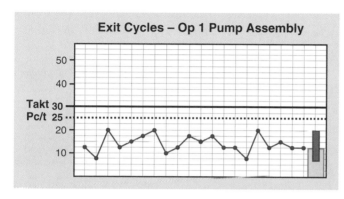

Range = 8–20 seconds

The lowest repeatable cycle time here is approximately 13 seconds, with 0% positive variation and 68% negative variation relative to the planned cycle time.

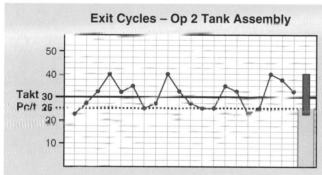

Range = 23–42 seconds

The lowest repeatable cycle time here is approximately 26 seconds, with 68% positive variation and 8% negative variation relative to the planned cycle time.

Now summarize your snapshot of the variation in the focus process by combining all the variation summary bars (the "candles" and "wicks") in a variation summary chart that looks like this.

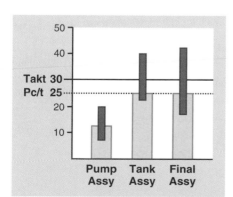

**Variation Summary Chart
Current Condition—Assembly Process**

In this example the lowest repeatable times seem OK (can meet the planned cycle time), but the variation in Ops 2 and 3 is too great for the planned cycle time to be consistently achieved.

The individual run charts and your variation summary chart belong on the "Current Condition" field of your storyboard. Regularly making run charts is one of the most useful process analysis practices. Based on them you can visually and numerically describe several key aspects of a process's current condition, and in the next step of the Improvement Kata you can establish a target condition for those aspects of your focus process.

Record Bullet-Point Observations
About the Current Operating Pattern
What else do you notice?

When you stand at a process and time 20 to 30 exit cycles, you are going to see things related to its current operating pattern. What do you notice? As you get the exit cycles data, also jot down any notes in the "observations" column of the timing worksheet. Then summarize your key observations in the space provided on the current condition / target condition form. Simply describe what you see happening in the work, without any judgment, noting your observations in bullet form as shown in the example CC/TC form at the end of this chapter. In our example, these observations include:

- Operators get their own parts.

- Work-in-process inventory (WIP) tends to accumulate before the two automated workstations.

- The last operator has to periodically move containers of finished goods out.

The tricky part here is tuning your mind to see patterns, not problems. Our mind quickly picks out issues or problems to address, and even solutions, but it's too soon for that because you don't have a target condition yet! Your bullet-point observations should mostly just describe additional characteristics of how the focus process currently functions.

It takes practice to learn to see this way. Once you acquire this skill you'll look at processes a little differently—realizing that there are patterns everywhere—and you'll move away from making quick judgments and scattershot improvements.

Digging Deeper

Drawing run charts is a core, standard step of the process analysis Starter Kata that helps you see below the surface. You should almost always practice using them. But run charts also raise new questions. Why are some cycles long and some short? Why are there certain patterns?

At this point in process analysis—after you have made the run charts—you can go "off Kata" and use any additional analysis tools that you think might be useful for further understanding how your focus process is functioning. Examples are flow charts, spaghetti diagrams, histograms, check sheets, scatter diagrams, Pareto diagrams, control charts, work balance charts ("yamazumi" charts), and daily time diaries. For example, you might collect and separate (stratify) data by products, equipment, operators, materials, shifts, day of the week, time of day, and so on.

Any additional analysis you do should be added to the "Current Condition" field of the storyboard.

Advanced Beginners: You Can Even Do Some Experiments

Another way to learn more about the focus process is to conduct an "exploratory experiment." Temporarily introduce a small change in the process to observe how the process reacts and what obstacles arise. This can tell you a lot.

STEP 4: CHECK EQUIPMENT CAPACITY
This optional step applies only to automated equipment.

The point of this step is to ensure that any automated equipment in the focus process is able to cycle fast enough to meet the planned cycle time. It is also effectively a check of the current *technical* volume capacity for a process.

This check applies only to *automated* equipment—equipment that is able to go through its cycle unattended while the operator does something else—as found in hospital labs, manufacturing processes, and so on. Many processes do not have any automated equipment. Also, do not worry about equipment that requires operator manipulation, such as hand tools, hand welding, ultrasound scanners, and so on. Their times are already captured in the operator exit cycles that you timed in step three of the process analysis.

First identify any automated equipment with the letter "A" on your block diagram. Then draw a machine capacity chart for those machines, as shown on the next page.

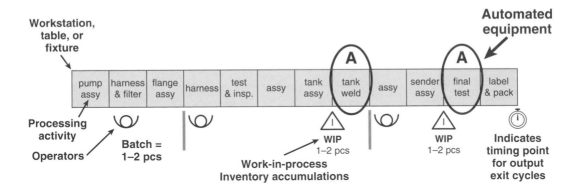

Drawing a Machine Capacity Chart, Step by Step

Step 1: Draw in the target times

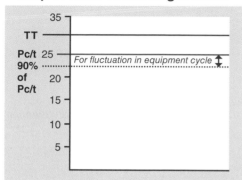

(1) Draw in lines for the takt time (if calculated), planned cycle time, and a line representing 90% of the planned cycle time.

The 90% line is a maximum cycle time for the automated equipment if you want the process to consistently meet the planned cycle time.

Step 2: List the automated machines

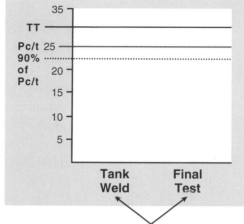

(2) List the automated machines in the process (equipment that can cycle unattended).

Step 3: Add the machine time

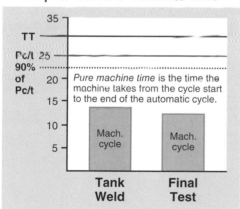

(3) Graph the pure machine time to process one unit, machine start to machine stop.

You usually only need to measure a few cycles to obtain this number, since machine cycle times are often pretty consistent.

Step 4: Add unload/load times

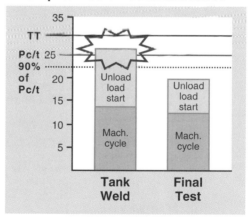

(4) Add unload and load times to the machine times. This is the time it takes to unload and load the machine *if* the machine has to wait during unloading and loading.

Pure machine time + unload/load time
- equals -
Total machine cycle time

Interpretation for this Example:
- The current tank welder cycle is too long to support a planned cycle time of 25 seconds.
- Half of the total machine cycle time is unload/load time.

Interpreting the Machine Capacity Chart

Total machine cycle time is the sum of the start-to-stop automatic machine run time plus any time for unloading and reloading, etc., during which the machine has to wait before it can start operating. However, if the machine can be unloaded and loaded while it is already cycling on the next unit, then ignore the unload/load time because it occurs in parallel.

In order to achieve a smooth, consistent work flow, a basic guideline is that any automated machine's total cycle time should be no more than 90 percent of the planned cycle time. The extra 10 percent exists to accommodate fluctuations in machine cycles. This guideline applies only to the automated equipment, not to the operators. (In completely automated processes 95 percent may be acceptable.) In other words, the fastest planned cycle time that a process with automated equipment can run is its longest total machine cycle time divided by .90. This is an estimate of the focus process's current capacity.

If a piece of automated equipment cannot cycle fast enough to meet the planned cycle time, you will need to either reduce that machine's total cycle time or lengthen the available work time in the takt time calculation, which lengthens the planned cycle time for the focus process.

In the example shown on the previous page, the current tank welder cycle time is too long to support the planned cycle time of 25 seconds. Interestingly, though, half of the total machine cycle time consists of unload/load time. Looking ahead, three options to keep in mind for dealing with this capacity bottleneck are listed below.

Options here include:

- Reduce the machine cycle time.

- Reduce the unload/load time.

- Lengthen the available work time, which raises the planned cycle time.

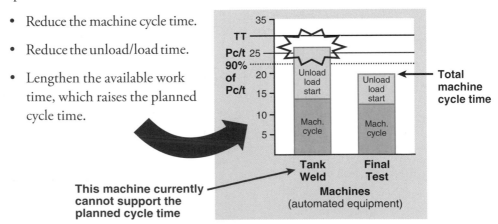

STEP 5: CALCULATE THE CORE WORK CONTENT

How many operators would the process require if it had no variation (was problem free)?

The purpose of this step is to help you understand the core work activity that has to be done to give customers what they need. When we look at a process, many things catch our eyes, which can make it difficult to see and understand the essential.

One way to help get a sense for the core work is to calculate the theoretical number of operators if the process had no variation. This is not about reducing the number of operators, because the calculated number of operators would only be sufficient if you first are able to achieve a tight range of variation in the process.

The Number-of-People Calculation in Two Steps

Step 1. You first need an estimate of the total work content necessary to complete one unit of the product or service in the current condition. Get this by adding together the lowest repeatable times from the exit cycle run charts (the "candles") for each operator in the process.

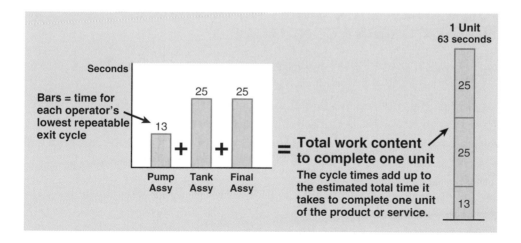

Step 2. Divide the sum of the lowest repeatable exit cycles from step one (the estimate of the total work content to complete one unit) by the planned cycle time. The resulting number is an estimate of the number of operators required if the process was problem free.

In making this calculation, subtract from the sum of lowest repeatable exit cycles any *consistent* wait time—occurring in nearly every cycle—that you observed any operators having, since this is not time required to process a unit of the product or service.

Add the resulting number of operators to the current condition / target condition form to represent the core work content in the focus process.

An **example calculation** is shown below.

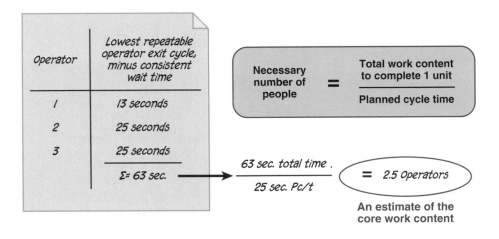

SUMMARIZE YOUR ANALYSIS OF THE INITIAL CURRENT CONDITION

You've invested some time to conduct a systematic analysis. Based on the steps of the process analysis Starter Kata, you now probably have a good understanding of the focus process. But there are usually still some open questions and knowledge gaps, too, which is normal. You are free to add more current condition information anytime, as you learn more in the next steps of the Improvement Kata pattern. You can also go back and get the missing current condition information now.

Post your current condition / target condition form (see next page) plus your block diagram, run charts, machine capacity chart, any calculations, and other current condition information in the "Current Condition" field of your storyboard.

Then get ready to turn your attention to establishing a target condition. After so carefully studying the focus process, you may already have some ideas about how it should be operating. You can move into developing a target condition by practicing the Starter Kata in the next chapter.

CURRENT CONDITION / TARGET CONDITION

			Outcome Metric	*Units per day*

Learner: *Frank Hartford*   **Coach:** *Mary Smith*   **Focus Process** *Assembly* | **Process Metric** *Exit cycles* |

		Current Condition — Date *May 16–17 2017*	Target Condition — Achieve-by Date
1 Outcome Performance	Actual output	*1,520–1,900/day (see graph)*	
	Operating time	*Two shifts*	
	Is there overtime?	*Yes, Saturdays. See graph*	
2 Customer Demand & Planned Cycle	Requirement	*1,840 pieces per day*	
	Takt time	*30 seconds*	
	Planned cycle time	*25 seconds (85% of takt)*	
3 Operating Patterns	Process steps and sequence	*See block diagram* *3 operators*	
	Variation	*· See run charts. Output variation = +72% / -28%* *· Lowest repeatable times are OK, but variation at Op2 & 3 is too large.*	
	Observations about the current operating patterns	*· Operators get own parts* *· WIP accumulates before the automated equipment* *· Last operator moves own finished goods out*	
4 Equipment Capacity	Automated equipment constraints?	*Tank weld cycle is too long at 27 sec. Should be ≤ 22.5 sec.*	
5 Core Work	Calculated number of operators	*63 seconds / 2.5 operators*	

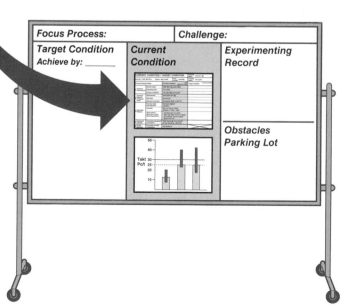

Your process analysis information goes here on the storyboard

CHAPTER **7**

ESTABLISH THE NEXT TARGET CONDITION (STEP 3)

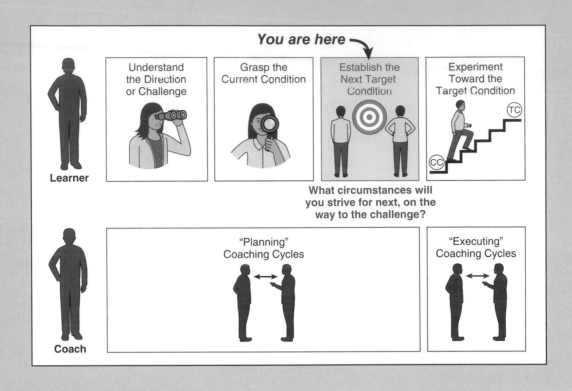

You are here

| Learner | Understand the Direction or Challenge | Grasp the Current Condition | Establish the Next Target Condition | Experiment Toward the Target Condition |

What circumstances will you strive for next, on the way to the challenge?

| Coach | "Planning" Coaching Cycles | "Executing" Coaching Cycles |

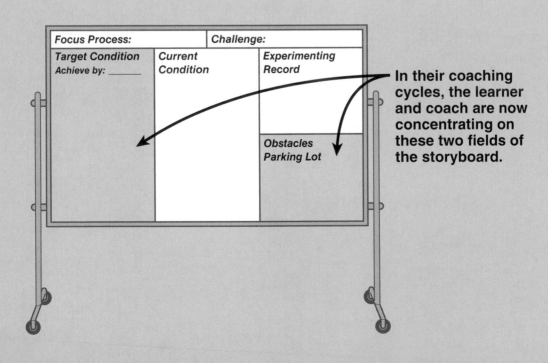

Focus Process: **Challenge:**

| Target Condition Achieve by: _____ | Current Condition | Experimenting Record |
| | | Obstacles Parking Lot |

In their coaching cycles, the learner and coach are now concentrating on these two fields of the storyboard.

Where Do We Want to Be Next?

At this point you understand the challenge direction and have analyzed the current condition of your focus process. Now you can define how you want that focus process to be operating in the near future by establishing a target condition for it in the direction of the challenge.

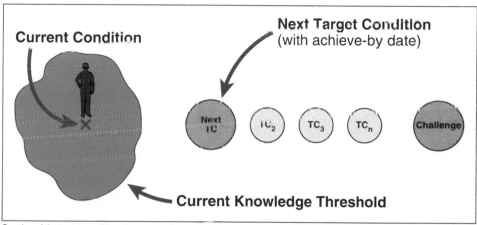

Spacing of the target conditions is not to scale   Based on a graphic by Bill Costantino

A *target condition* is a description of a goal point on the way to the more distant challenge. It describes in some detail where you want to be next, but not how to get there. That will be figured out through experimenting in the fourth step of the Improvement Kata pattern.

Taking Advantage of Unfolding Reality

It will usually take a series of target conditions to reach a challenge. What may be different for you is that **you only define one target condition at a time, rather than trying to lay them all out as a road map in advance.** You're now only specifying the *next target condition*, and when you get there you'll have a better and more realistic idea about what the target condition after that one should be.

This is a little like golf where it takes several swings to get onto the green of a distant hole. You may have a plan in mind for how you would like to get there, but the path that will actually get you there is not completely predictable. For the first swing you have a target condition of where you want the ball to land. Based on how that goes and where the ball actually lands, you then decide on the next target condition in the direction of the green. In Improvement Kata practice, when you reach one target condition's achieve-by date you reflect on what you've learned and then establish the next target condition accordingly.

Working this way gives you the ability to learn from and adjust to unfolding reality, as opposed to pretending that you know what's in the as yet unlit territory ahead of you. You can and often should make a plan, of course, but that plan is a hypothesis, a prediction, and shouldn't just be blindly followed. The Improvement Kata process progressively sheds light on your path, and on your plan, while you are underway.

Not Too Far Away

A target condition should always have a specified achieve-by date, which is usually between one week and three months out. Longer than that is often ineffective and should probably be broken down into smaller target condition increments. A beauty of a target condition is that it is within reach, not too far outside your current threshold of knowledge, but in the challenge direction. This manageable stretch helps to draw out and focus your creative capability. Once you and your team have reached the first few target conditions, the more distant challenge may not seem quite so tough, and even inspiringly doable.

Here is a quick comparison between a challenge and target conditions:

Challenge	Target Conditions
Comes from a level above the learner. 6 months to 3 years out.	Developed by the learner, in a back-and-forth dialogue with the coach Achieve-by dates are only 1 week to 3 months out. A series of target conditions is necessary to reach the challenge.

A Positive, Forward-Looking Mindset is an Important Element for Mobilizing Ingenuity, Creativity, and Teamwork

Once you've experienced the role of a target condition, you may find it difficult to work without one. A target condition is a mindset of moving toward something, rather than just reacting to problems. You're working toward a condition you want—be it large or small—not trying to get away from something you don't like.

A target condition makes the goal the focus, rather than who is most persuasive. A target condition functions as a set of constraints that help you work scientifically, just as a scientist defines their research question before they begin experimenting. Without a target condition, teams may flounder around with random improvement, troubleshooting, and acting on opinions—going in several directions and wasting time and energy.

A target condition enables more effective effort toward a mutual end by helping you discover what you *need* to work on, rather than spinning your wheels thinking about what you *can* work on. In defining a target condition and then striving to achieve it, you discover exactly what is preventing you from getting there, and those obstacles are the ones you work on. You may have heard the saying that *obstacles show you the way*. Just work on what you find in the way to your target condition, not everything you *could* work on.

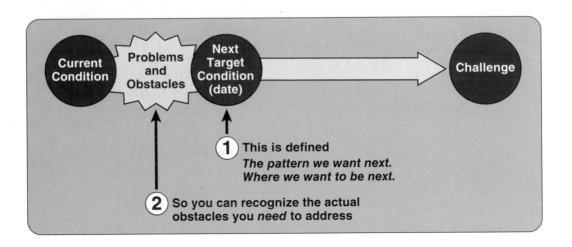

In this step of the Improvement Kata, once you have defined the next target condition you also start to identify and record on the storyboard what you perceive as obstacles to that target condition. Starting this list—called the "obstacles parking lot"—is important, because obstacles are what you will experiment against in the next step of the Improvement Kata.

WITHOUT A TARGET CONDITION

- **Disorganized discussion about *solutions*.**

- **Exchange of opinions. Debate about my idea versus your idea. *"Who's right?"***

- **Prioritization by dominant individuals.**

- **No experimentation.**

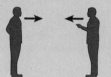

WITH A TARGET CONDITION

- **Structured discussion about next experiment toward a common picture of success.**

- ***"What do we need to work on next to reach our objective?"***

- **Moving forward scientifically.**

Scientific Thinking Is Common to Any Problem Solving

Problem solvers sometimes make a distinction between trying to operate to a standard ("maintaining") and trying to raise the standard ("improving"). Interestingly, the striving mindset of the Improvement Kata is fundamental to both of those modes, and to nearly all problem solving. In both cases there is a gap between something you want to be happening and what is actually happening. In both cases there is a desired set of circumstances—a target condition—that you don't yet know how you will reach, and you're going to learn how by experimenting to get there.

Three Elements of a Good Target Condition

A target condition should ideally contain a specified achieve-by date, a target outcome, and a description of the operating pattern that you predict will generate that outcome (described to the extent that you can at this point—don't fake it). These *when*, *what*, and *how* aspects are three ingredients of a target condition for your focus process.

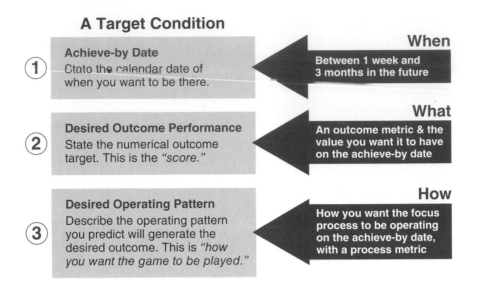

A Target Condition

(1) **Achieve-by Date**
Ctate the calendar date of when you want to be there.

When
Between 1 week and 3 months in the future

(2) **Desired Outcome Performance**
State the numerical outcome target. This is the *"score."*

What
An outcome metric & the value you want it to have on the achieve-by date

(3) **Desired Operating Pattern**
Describe the operating pattern you predict will generate the desired outcome. This is *"how you want the game to be played."*

How
How you want the focus process to be operating on the achieve-by date, with a process metric

Note that it's called *target condition*, not *target*. A target condition describes both a desired outcome and the operating attributes that you think will generate that outcome. An outcome metric alone, such as "5 percent scrap rate," is only a target, not yet a target condition. Outcomes usually can't be altered by direct attack because they are a *result* of the way the focus process operates. You should also begin to define the process operating pattern that you think will lead to a 5 percent scrap rate, such as how machines are to be maintained, how each process step should go, and so on. Those factors *are* directly changeable and thus something you can act upon. The focus process's operating pattern and characteristics are your "construction site" for achieving the desired outcome performance.

Here's an example. Suppose you weigh 180 pounds and have a challenge of weighing 160 pounds in six months. Currently you eat mostly processed food, consume about 2,800 calories per day, and rarely do physical activity. For your first 30-day target condition in the direction of the challenge, you might establish an outcome target of consuming 2,500 calories and doing some moderate exercise every day. That's great, but those outcomes will be the result of doing something. A *target condition* also describes the pattern of eating and exercise that you want to have in place, which you predict will generate those outcomes. For instance, you might aim for an operating pattern of drinking flavored sparkling water instead of sugary soft drinks, including a steamed vegetable with olive oil in each dinner, and taking a 30-minute walk every day. Now with all of these elements together you have a target condition!

Target Condition

Achieve-by Date
June 30 (30 days)

Desired Outcome Performance
• Consume 2,500 calories/day
• Moderate exercise every day

Desired Operating Pattern
☐ Sparkling water, not soft drinks
☐ Steamed vegetable at dinner
☐ Walk 30 minutes/day

What's in this box is predicted to produce the desired outcome.

To reach the desired outcome, work on what's in this box. It's the "construction site."

There will, of course, be obstacles to the desired operating pattern, because it represents a change. Those obstacles are what you will be experimenting against in the next chapter.

When it comes to defining a target operating pattern, try to go deep, not wide. Get as detailed as you can at this point about how you expect the focus process to operate. For instance, in a service organization the operating pattern might describe a customer experience

> **Desired Operating Pattern**
> Describe the operating pattern you predict will generate the desired outcome. This is *"how you want the game to be played."*

your team designs. In a bakery, it might specify how the customer is greeted, how products are displayed, and what steps the service provider should go through in serving a customer. In a manufacturing process, it might describe a desired sequence and timing of work steps, the location and size of work-in-process buffers, how a quality check is to be done, and so on. A basketball player might have an outcome goal of 80 percent of free throws made, and a desired operating pattern that describes the position of the player's body, hands, and eyes during the free throw routine. A golfer working on hitting the ball a certain way might have a desired pattern for her stance, the clubface angle, and the path of the clubhead. A teacher may have an outcome goal of all students passing a standardized test, and a desired operating pattern, such as 25 percent of class time devoted to in-class group practice. **In all of these examples you combine an outcome goal with an operating pattern that's predicted to achieve that outcome.**

Pretend You Are Already There

A target condition describes a condition as if it's already a completed thing, not as actions. One useful trick for doing this is to *describe the target condition as if you were already there*; as if that condition were already in place. Pretend you have traveled forward in time to the achieve-by date and are looking at the focus process. The target condition is a description of what you see.

To help you with this, a rule of thumb is that **there should be no verbs—such as *minimize, reduce, improve, increase*—in a target condition.** This forces you to simply describe the conditions you want in place when you get there. For example, "Maximum cycle time of 38 seconds" is target-condition (destination) thinking, whereas "reduce cycle time variation" is not. Try to describe what you want to be happening, versus what's wrong or what you don't want to be happening.

Don't Fake It—You Can't Change a Target Condition, But You Can Add to It

Defining the desired operating pattern portion of a target condition at this point is a bit of a balancing act, because you are describing it without knowing exactly how you will get there. This gets easier and even normal with practice. However, don't fake it by trying to specify in detail something you don't yet understand. Don't cross over your threshold of knowledge. If you find yourself *guessing* about what operating pattern details you want, stop. You have two choices here:

- Go back and study the focus process some more to get the details you need (more advanced learners can even try some experiments).

- Leave some operating pattern details in the target condition blank for now, and add them later as you learn more from your experiments in the next step of the Improvement Kata.

In other words, it's OK if the "desired operating pattern" portion of your target condition is still incomplete when you move into the next step of the Improvement Kata. This happens all the time. It's better to flesh it out later, as you experiment in the executing phase of the Improvement Kata and your knowledge of reality increases, than to guess.

This brings up a key point about target conditions: **Once a target condition has been agreed upon by the learner and coach, you can still add more detail to it as you learn more along the way, but you cannot *change* the target condition or its achieve-by date.** This constraint is applied so that we (a) take time to understand the current condition; (b) think carefully in setting the next target condition; and (c) are persistent and creative in working on the obstacles, rather than easing up on the target condition if the going gets tough.

From time to time you won't reach a target condition by its achieve-by date, which is normal. You'll still learn something that's useful for the next target condition. It means a prediction you made was not confirmed, and you would lose those learnings if you instead had changed the target condition or its date along the way.

A corollary to this is that the first target condition for a focus process will probably not be your best target condition, because you're still learning more about the current condition. This is one reason why the first target condition's achieve-by date should often be just one or two weeks out. The sooner you can adjust based on what you have learned, the better.

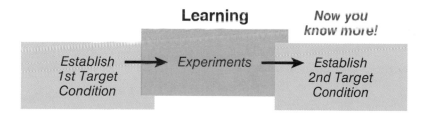

Just as Important: What's Not in a Target Condition

A common error in establishing a target condition is to include solutions, or to think of solutions as the target condition. It's *target condition*, not *target solution*. **A target condition does not include actions you plan to take.**

Beginner learners will often already have some strong ideas about solutions at this stage, but these are actually potential countermeasures that come later.[1] It's too early to limit yourself to solutions, and doing so limits your thinking. *A target condition only describes*

---

1 Learning not to do this comes with practice.

focus-process attributes you want to have in place by a future date, not planned actions. First describe how you would like the focus process to be operating on the achieve-by date. You develop and discover countermeasures later, as needed, through experiments.

Incorrectly Focused on Solutions

Desired Outcome Performance
A visual board in every patient's room

Here the learner already has an answer, so there is no process of experimentation, discovery, and learning. The stated goal is already inside the learner's threshold of knowledge.

Focused on a Target *Condition*

Desired Outcome Performance
Information in every patient's room is complete and accurate

Here the learner does not yet know exactly how s/he will reach this goal. It lies outside the current threshold of knowledge and will necessarily involve a process of experimentation and discovery.

If a learner is prematurely focusing on solutions, ask what *effect* the learner envisions those solutions having. That will be closer to a true target condition, which leaves room for solutions you haven't thought of yet.

Here is a visual depiction of the difference between target conditions and solutions.

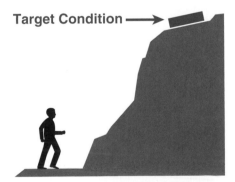

A place you want to be on a future date. Defining this is what this step of the Improvement Kata is about.

These are steps, techniques, and countermeasures that you then find are necessary for getting there.

In establishing a target condition, you are confronting a threshold of knowledge and setting a goal beyond it. A goal that you already know how to reach—one that involves little experimentation and learning—is not really a target condition, but more of a reshuffling of existing abilities and knowledge. In that case you are probably standing still rather than improving.

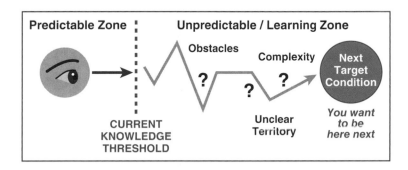

A Target Condition Is More About "And" Than "Or"

Establishing a target condition is not about choosing between known existing options, but about creating a new option. For instance, saying, *"Would you rather have 100 percent inspection and three operators in the process, or sampling inspection and only two operators in the process?"* is not target condition thinking. Target condition thinking would be, *"We want 100 percent inspection and only two operators in the process."* Notice how target condition thinking is more associated with the word "and" than the word "or," and how it pulls you beyond your knowledge threshold.

Of course, as soon as you say, *"We want 100 percent inspection **and** only two operators in the process,"* someone may cross their arms and understandably exclaim, *"Well, why don't you tell me how that is going to be possible!"* There is only one answer. Respond by saying:

> *"I don't know. And if we already knew the answer, then anyone could do it. What we do know is how to work (the Improvement Kata pattern) in order to get there."*

You could go ahead and list reasons why people think it won't work, but those are only obstacles.

Since many businesspeople are trained to use return-on-investment calculations for making decisions, we should be clear that a target condition is not about the highest payoff or lowest risk option. Don't use an ROI or cost-benefit calculation to determine a target condition. *First* establish where you want or need to be next on the way to your challenge. This is a *strategic* question. The target condition should then, of course, be achieved within your budget and other constraints, but it will probably take some trial and error, ingenuity, and resourcefulness to get there. When you do get there your focus process, and your organization, will have reached a new level of performance. Viewing the world as if there are only already-known, binary options—called a "false dilemma" or "black-and-white thinking"—is a kind of static thinking because it fails to allow for options that are still unknown to us, that may take work to develop.

Remember, a target condition is not something you are trying to reach right away, and you don't need to know in advance how you will reach it. It is the result of a series of experiments, and you don't yet have the answers for how you will achieve it within your constraints.

To the coach: You should appreciate how difficult it can be for a beginner learner to envision and describe a new, out-of-the-ordinary future condition. *"How am I supposed to describe it if I don't know how we will get there?"* Thinking about a target condition pulls the learner out of a zone of apparent certainty and runs counter to the more common business approach of defining only outcome metrics and advocating adaptations of existing practice for getting there. Don't expect the learner to get it right the first time, and be ready to kick it back-and-forth with the learner as described in the following pages.

 Practice Routines **ESTABLISH THE NEXT TARGET CONDITION**

Steps to Establishing a Target Condition

1. Review your challenge
2. Agree on the achieve-by date
3. Define the desired outcome performance
4. Define the desired operating pattern
5. Start the "Obstacles Parking Lot"

STEP 1: REVIEW YOUR CHALLENGE

Before you establish a target condition for your focus process, be sure you understand your particular challenge, from the first step of the Improvement Kata pattern. Ideally that challenge is the frame within which your target condition will be defined, although there are exceptions. There are probably other goals that you need to achieve too.

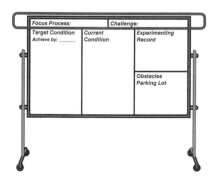

The challenge should already be noted at the top of your storyboard. Remember that in many cases the target condition at the level above you will become a challenge for your level. Another possible challenge is the future-state design for the value stream and, specifically, how your focus process needs to function in order to help make that design possible.

STEP 2: AGREE ON THE ACHIEVE-BY DATE (WHEN)

Achieve-by Date
State the calendar date of
when you want to be there.

Between 1 week and
3 months in the future

This step is usually led by the coach. The coach considers the learner's current Improvement Kata skill level and steers how much of a stretch the next target condition will be for the learner by: (a) proposing how far out the achieve-by date lies, and (b) giving feedback on the details of the target condition the learner is developing and proposing. A good target condition will take the learner just over the edge of his or her current skill level and lead you into a learning mode.

A common error in establishing a target condition is setting it too far into the future, which makes it too large in scope. For beginners, shorter achieve-by dates are better for learning because the learner can make a course adjustment sooner and get more repetitions with all four steps of the Improvement Kata. Two weeks is enough time to understand and significantly improve several aspects of a focus process, but a short enough time to keep the learner from feeling like he or she has to solve a complex issue all at once. The following table is a guideline, and there are exceptions. Be sure to set an actual calendar date for the achieve-by date, not just "in two weeks."

Learner Skill Level	Achieve-by Date
Novice or Beginner	≤ 2 weeks out
Competent and above	≤ 1 month out[2]

To increase the learner's self-efficacy it is important that the target condition challenges the learner, but also that the learner periodically experiences a sense of accomplishment. As mentioned in Part I, if a target condition is *too easy*, meaning the learner already knows they can do it, then there is no real increase in self-efficacy when the learner gets there. If a target condition is *too hard*, then the learner might get to the

2 Many experienced Improvement Kata practitioners do not set target conditions further than one month out.

achieve-by date thinking, *"I knew I couldn't do this,"* and the person's self-efficacy may actually decrease.

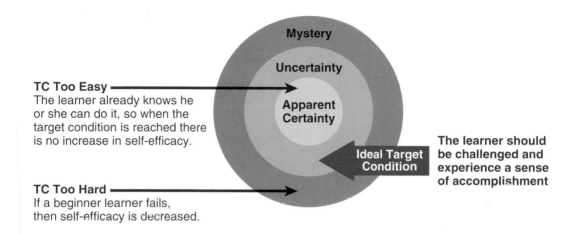

A good target condition is difficult and could even make the learner a little fearful, but then the coach provides frequent support via corrective feedback that helps the learner achieve it. A good statement to periodically hear from a learner is, *"Wow, I didn't think I could do that!"*

Work with the Current Condition / Target Condition Form Again, but Now on the Right Side

Use the current condition / target condition form you started in the *Grasping the Current Condition* step, which should be on your storyboard. The columns for the current condition and target condition are still connected on the same form at this time, so you can cross-reference characteristics of the current condition with those of the target condition you are establishing.

CURRENT CONDITION / TARGET CONDITION				Outcome Metric	Units per day
Learner: *Frank Hartford* Coach: *Mary Smith*			Focus Process *Assembly*	Process Metric	*Exit cycles*
		Current Condition	Date *May 16-17 2017*	Target Condition	Achieve-by Date *June 7 (2 weeks)*
1 Outcome Performance	Actual output	*1,520-1,900/day (see graph)*			
	Operating time	*Two shifts*			
	Is there overtime?	*Yes, Saturdays. See graph*			
2 Customer Demand & Planned Cycle	Requirement	*1,840 pieces per day*			
	Takt time	*30 seconds*			
	Planned cycle time	*25 seconds (85% of takt)*			
3 Operating Patterns	Process steps and sequence	*See block diagram 3 operators*			
	Variation	*· See run charts. Output variation = +72% / -28% · Lowest repeatable times are OK, but variation at Op2 & 3 is too large.*			
	Observations about the current operating patterns	*· Operators get own parts · WIP accumulates before the automated equipment · Last operator moves own finished goods out*			
4 Equipment Capacity	Automated equipment constraints?	*Tank weld cycle is too long at 27 sec. Should be ≤ 22.5 sec.*			
5 Core Work	Calculated number of operators	*63 seconds / 2.5 operators*			

Right Side

As you work to define the next target condition, note that *not everything has to change*. Depending on how far out your achieve-by date is, sometimes only one or two aspects will be changed on the right-hand, target condition side of the form.

However, a common approach is to first fill in the "target condition" side of the form with how you want the focus process to be operating overall—often changing quite a few characteristics—and then backing off that to better suit the achieve-by date. In that case the overall target condition is like a challenge, which is then approached in smaller target-condition steps. We'll illustrate this iterative process in the next pages.

Once you and the coach agree on the next target condition, cut the form along the vertical line shown and place each side in its corresponding field on the storyboard.

STEP 3: DEFINE THE DESIRED OUTCOME PERFORMANCE (WHAT)

Desired Outcome Performance
State the numerical outcome target. This is the *"score."*

An outcome metric & the value you want it to have on the achieve-by date

Either the learner or the coach can propose the outcome performance to be reached by the achieve-by date. This is the measurable outcome target. Ideally you should be able to mathematically connect this numerical target to your challenge or a future-state value stream design.

Continuing with the example from the previous chapter, the outcome metric during the process analysis was "units per day." So the learner might begin by simply writing the current daily requirement of 1,840 pieces—in two shifts with no overtime—onto the CC/TC form as shown here.

CURRENT CONDITION / TARGET CONDITION			Outcome Metric	*Units per day*	
Learner: *Frank Hartford* Coach: *Mary Smith*		Focus Process *Assembly*	Process Metric	*Exit cycles*	
		Current Condition	Date *May 16–17 2017*	Target Condition	Achieve-by Date *June 7 (2 weeks)*
1 Outcome Performance	Actual output	*1,520–1,900/day (see graph)*		*1,840 /day*	
	Operating time	*Two shifts*		*Two shifts*	
	Is there overtime?	*Yes, Saturdays. See graph*		*No overtime*	
Customer Demand	Requirement	*1,840 pieces per day*			

As you can probably already see, this outcome target is, of course, too ambitious for the two-week achieve-by date and will certainly need to be adjusted before this target condition is finished. It's an ideal, and just a starting point in the iterative process of establishing the next target condition.

STEP 4: DEFINE THE DESIRED OPERATING PATTERN (HOW)

Desired Operating Pattern
Describe the operating pattern you predict will generate the desired outcome. This is *"how you want the game to be played."*

How you want the focus process to be operating on the achieve-by date, including a process metric

The learner should now develop and describe the desired process operating pattern and operating characteristics, to the degree that he or she can. This is done in that back-and-forth dialogue with the coach. That is, the learner lays out a target condition and proposes it to the coach, receives feedback, and goes back to fine-tune the design accordingly. This repeats until the coach and learner come to a consensus about the next target condition.

The learner may adjust or rewrite the target condition several times—going back again to rethink or gather more information—before consensus is reached. This is normal, and it is a worthwhile effort because the target condition is the frame for the experimenting in the next step of the Improvement Kata.

The coach might ask:

> *"What would the focus process need to look like in order to get the outcome you desire?"*

> *"What do you want to change, and what will you keep the same?"*

One way to begin this process is for the learner to cross-reference each line in the current condition / target condition form, looking at the current condition characteristic on the left and jotting down on the right what that characteristic should be like in the future, with the desired outcome performance that was recorded above in mind.

This will generate a set of focus-process characteristics that is usually too ambitious for the achieve-by date, but it does provide an overall picture of what may need to be done. As always, there may be parameters that the learner cannot change, such as safety, quality, or budget.

Using the example from the last chapter, the learner's first picture of the desired operating pattern might look something like the target **variation summary chart** and filled-in **CC/TC form** in the following figures. The factors on the target condition side of the form that are changed from the current condition are marked with blue arrows. The other factors stay the same.

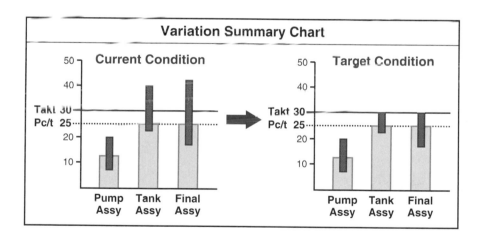

Items with an arrow are changed
from the current condition

CURRENT CONDITION / TARGET CONDITION			Outcome Metric	Units per day	
Learner: *Frank Hartford* Coach: *Mary Smith*		Focus Process *Assembly*	Process Metric	Exit cycles	
		Current Condition Date *May 16-17 2017*	Target Condition	Achieve-by Date *June 7 (2 weeks)*	
1 Outcome Performance	Actual output	*1,520-1,900/day (see graph)*	*1,840 /day*		←
	Operating time	*Two shifts*	*Two shifts*		
	Is there overtime?	*Yes, Saturdays. See graph*	*No overtime*		←
2 Customer Demand & Planned Cycle	Requirement	*1,840 pieces per day*	*1,840*		
	Takt time	*30 seconds*	*30*		
	Planned cycle time	*25 seconds (85% of takt)*	*25*		
3 Operating Patterns	Process steps and sequence	*See block diagram 3 operators*	*See block diagram 3 operators*		
	Variation	*• See run charts. Output variation = +72% / -28%* *• Lowest repeatable times are OK, but variation at Op2 & 3 is too large.*	*No more than +15%*		←
	Observations about the current operating patterns	*• Operators get own parts* *• WIP accumulates before the automated equipment* *• Last operator moves own finished goods out*	*Parts are delivered* *Batch = 1 pc (1x1 flow)* *Not done by operators*		← ← ←
4 Equipment Capacity	Automated equipment constraints?	*Tank weld cycle is too long at 27 sec. Should be ≤ 22.5 sec.*	*Cycles at 22 sec or less*		←
5 Core Work	Calculated number of operators	*63 seconds / 2.5 operators*			

The outcome target is to produce the required quantity of 1,840 pieces with the same personnel and equipment, but without overtime. To achieve this the learner predicts that at least the following operating characteristics will be necessary:

- As shown in the "target condition" variation summary chart on the previous page, all positive variation should fall within the 15 percent difference between takt time and planned cycle time. The amount of positive variation shown in run charts should not exceed +15 percent.

- Getting the variation to be no more than +15 percent means that periodically moving supplied parts in and batches of finished goods out (called "out-of-cycle work") should be done by someone other than the operators, such as a material handler on a scheduled route.

- The tank-welder cycle should be at least 15 percent faster than the planned cycle time, or no longer than 22 seconds.

The learner presents this array of characteristics to the coach. If the coach agrees that this is a useful prediction, the coach might say:

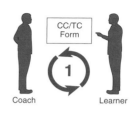

Coach   Learner

"OK, now please propose where you want the focus process to be on the two-week achieve-by date."

The learner goes back to consider the situation more closely.

Continuing with the example, it is clear to the learner that the current tank-welder cycle time of 27 seconds means the focus process currently does not have the machine capacity to support a planned cycle time of 25 seconds. It makes sense to address this capacity bottleneck issue first, before working on other aspects of the desired operating pattern.

In the machine capacity chart from the process analysis, the learner sees that half of the welder's 27-second cycle time is manual unload and load time. This is an opportunity because it should be easier to reduce this by five seconds than to take five seconds out of the welding time itself. The learner predicts that lowering the tank welder cycle to 22 seconds or less will eliminate the tank-welder bottleneck and result in no less than 1,700 units produced per day and no more than +25 percent variation at tank welding. The learner records this on the right side of the CC/TC form, as shown by the blue arrows below.

Items with an arrow are changed from the current condition

CURRENT CONDITION / TARGET CONDITION			Outcome Metric *Units per day*
Learner: *Frank Hartford* Coach: *Mary Smith*		Focus Process *Assembly*	Process Metric *Exit cycles*
		Current Condition Date *May 16–17 2017*	Target Condition Achieve-by Date *June 7 (2 weeks)*
1 Outcome Performance	Actual output	*1,520–1,900/day (see graph)*	*No less than 1,700 /day*
	Operating time	*Two shifts*	*Two shifts*
	Is there overtime?	*Yes, Saturdays. See graph*	*Yes, Saturdays*
2 Customer Demand & Planned Cycle	Requirement	*1,840 pieces per day*	*1,840*
	Takt time	*30 seconds*	*30*
	Planned cycle time	*25 seconds (85% of takt)*	*25*
3 Operating Patterns	Process steps and sequence	*See block diagram 3 operators*	*See block diagram 3 operators*
	Variation	*• See run charts. Output variation = +72% / -28% • Lowest repeatable times are OK, but variation at Op2 & 3 is too large.*	*< +25% at Tank Weld*
	Observations about the current operating patterns	*• Operators get own parts • WIP accumulates before the automated equipment • Last operator moves own finished goods out*	*No changes at this time*
4 Equipment Capacity	Automated equipment constraints?	*Tank weld cycle is too long at 27 sec. Should be ≤ 22.5 sec.*	*Cycles at 22 sec or less*
5 Core Work	Calculated number of operators	*63 seconds / 2.5 operators*	

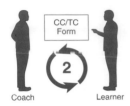

The learner proposes this as the next target condition, with an achieve-by date that is two weeks away. The coach might ask:

"How do you want the unload/load process at the welder to go, so that it takes five seconds less than it currently does?"

The learner may have ideas about this based on what the learner saw while gathering data for the machine capacity chart during step two of the Improvement Kata. More likely, however, is that the learner is now at a threshold of knowledge. There are two options:

1. Stay in step three of the Improvement Kata and go back to the tank welder to observe and analyze the manual unload/load process, and then add corresponding detail to the target condition.

2. Move into step four of the Improvement Kata and add detail to the target condition as the learner goes forward and learns more.

Coach and learner agree on option 2, since the basics of the next target condition are now established. The learner cuts the current condition / target condition form in half and posts each half in its corresponding section on the storyboard.

Note that the contents of the next target condition after this one are not yet known, and will depend partly on what the learner learns in pursuing this target condition. This target condition is not the last!

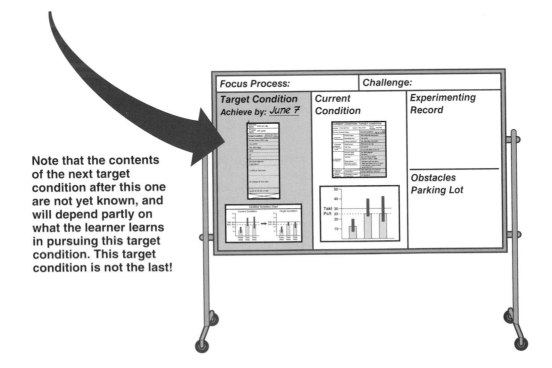

STEP 5: START THE OBSTACLES PARKING LOT

Having established the next target condition doesn't quite complete this step of the Improvement Kata pattern. You should also begin recording initial obstacles on a simple list kept in its own field on the storyboard. At this point the coach will ask you:

> *"What obstacles do you think will prevent us from getting closer to the target condition?"*

Going back to the weight-loss example, that target condition included this operating pattern:

Desired Operating Pattern
- ☐ Sparkling water, not soft drinks
- ☐ Steamed vegetable at dinner
- ☐ Walk 60 minutes/day

In that example, some obstacles might be:

- No place to walk after work

- I have never cooked steamed vegetables before

In the assembly process example we've been using here, the next target condition centers around getting the unload/load process for the tank welder to take 5 seconds less than it currently does. When the coach asks the learner what he or she sees as obstacles at this point, the learner might answer, *"The main obstacle I see right now is that I do not know much about the unload/load process at the tank welder."* The coach responds, *"That's a great start to your obstacles parking lot. It's fine to leave it at that for now, until we learn more."*

Note how the learner did not cross over his or her knowledge threshold and instead stated the lack of knowledge as an obstacle.

Obstacle Parking Lot

- *Don't know enough about unload/load process*
- _____
- _____
- _____
- _____
- _____
- _____
- _____
- _____
- _____
- _____

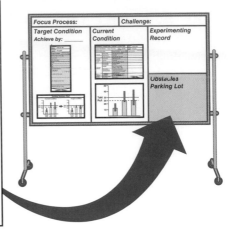

A word of caution: Don't turn the obstacles parking lot into an action-item list, which is a frequent error made by beginner learners and coaches. The obstacle parking lot (OPL) is simply a place to record perceived and discovered obstacles, each of which may or may not get addressed. The purpose of the OPL is:

1. To act as a holding place that acknowledges potential obstacles and helps prevent you from working on several obstacles simultaneously, which is usually an unscientific approach.

2. To help you recognize how flawed our perceptions and predictions can be. Obstacles that are overcome get crossed off, of course, but you will often also add previously unseen obstacles and cross off presumed obstacles that turned out not to be problems after all.

QUICK TIPS

A common error with the obstacles parking lot is to name the lack of a solution as an obstacle. Lack of a countermeasure that you might have in mind is just a preconceived solution stated in reverse, and not an obstacle. Here are some examples:

This is a countermeasure or solution, not an obstacle	This is an obstacle
"Lack of a standard." "No parts dryer."	"Variability in how the work is done." "High moisture content in the parts."

Another common error is to state obstacles too vaguely. If you can't be specific about any obstacles, it may mean that you don't understand the situation at the focus process well enough yet. Go back and look again rather than making up obstacles. It may also mean you are not accustomed to being specific. Try to develop a habit of being as specific and measurable as possible as you complete the following sentence:

"We currently can't move closer to the target condition because . . ."

You're now ready to start working toward the target condition by practicing the Starter Kata in the next chapter. Defining what you want to achieve—the target condition—is important, but what happens once you start working in that direction is equally important. Finding ways to overcome the obstacles is where a lot of satisfaction, self-efficacy, and even a useful humbleness come from.

CHAPTER 8

EXPERIMENT TOWARD THE TARGET CONDITION (STEP 4)

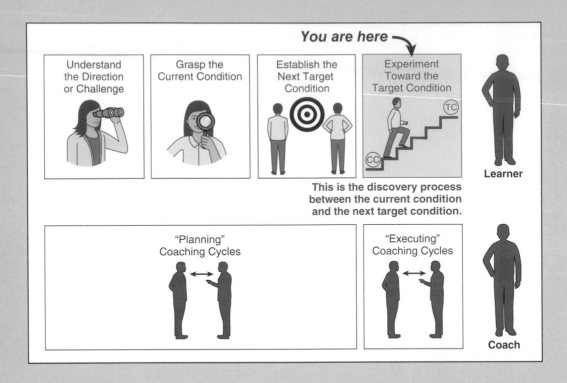

This is the discovery process between the current condition and the next target condition.

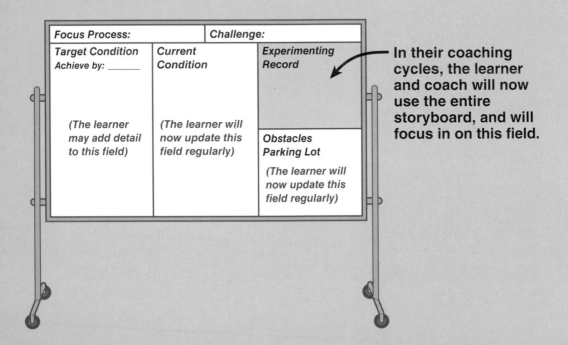

In their coaching cycles, the learner and coach will now use the entire storyboard, and will focus in on this field.

Building Your Path to the Target Condition

Now that you have a target condition, how do you get there? Most importantly: assume that the path is unclear, and be open to steps other than those you thought would get you there. The path to your target condition cannot be completely determined in advance through logic, calculation, or debate.

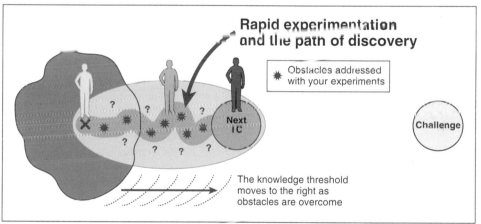

Based on a graphic by Bill Costantino

We often have plans or preconceived solutions and intend to implement them, but most reality is neither linear nor predictable enough for that alone to be an effective way to achieve target conditions. You won't have all the answers up front, because we can't see all the variables that influence a situation, nor the many ways in which those variables are interrelated. In fact, the unique variables in each workplace are probably one reason why benchmarking solutions from one organization and bringing them to another has often not been effective for generating improvement. Rather, it's a good idea to work like a scientist, *who learns his or her way forward by experimenting*.

The Improvement Kata doesn't give you solutions for how to reach a particular target condition, because the scientific process can't tell us what's ahead. It only confirms or refutes the results of experiments, which helps you discover and build a route based on a growing understanding of reality. This chapter gives you a structured starter routine for how to conduct experiments. An *experiment* is taking a step with the intent of learning something. I use the words *step* and *experiment* interchangeably in this book.

The magic of this approach is that you don't have to know all the steps in advance. Donald Schön called experiments a *conversation with the situation*.[1] You test your idea via an experiment and the focus process talks back to you, which will often surface something you didn't know before. Consider for a moment that any step you take, in all of life, is actually an experiment.

Of course you don't reach the target condition through a single experiment, and many experiments will have outcomes other than what you expected. You take one step, encounter new information, evaluate it, maybe revise your understanding based on what you learned, and then plan the next step toward the target condition accordingly. By repeating this—as rapidly as possible—you are simultaneously investigating and moving forward, because your experiments help you see what you need to do to get closer to your target condition. Experiments allow you to be action-oriented, but without too quickly jumping to solutions. It's a little like when you walk at night with a flashlight and can only see as far as its light shines into the dark. To see farther you have to take a step. Then the light shines on things that you couldn't see before.

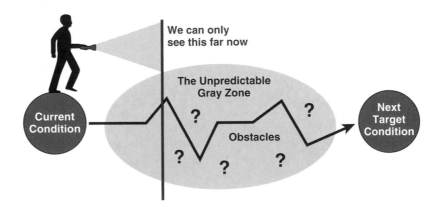

1 Donald Schön, *The Reflective Practitioner* (Basic Books, 1983).

Experimenting at Your Threshold of Knowledge

The threshold of knowledge is the point at which you have no facts and data and start guessing or extrapolating. If you hear yourself saying things like the following, then you are probably at or past your knowledge threshold:

- Words such as *I think*, *probably*, *maybe*, *could*, *most likely*, *well . . .* , *on average*, *90 percent of the time*

- "Let's reduce/increase it by 50 percent." (A 50 percent "guesstimate" is common when we lack a specific, calculated number.)

- Referring to old data

- Making arguments about what must be true

- Referring to anecdotes without hard data

Recognizing your current threshold of knowledge is important, because it shows you where to conduct your next experiment. It's your *learning edge*, and here's what you should do there:

1. **Acknowledge the knowledge threshold.** This can be difficult to do until you get some practice, because our brain tends to jump right over knowledge thresholds to possible solutions. The more you practice the Starter Kata in this chapter, the more you will begin to see how many knowledge thresholds we unknowingly and carelessly cross over in our thinking and discussions every day. You may be surprised.

2. **See farther by conducting an experiment.** When the path ahead is uncertain, do what the pros do: experiment! Don't deliberate about who has the best idea about what might lie beyond the knowledge threshold. Deliberate about what would be a good experiment to run in order to learn more. And once that's decided there is no need to continue the conversation. Go run that experiment as quickly as you can, so your flashlight will shine farther.

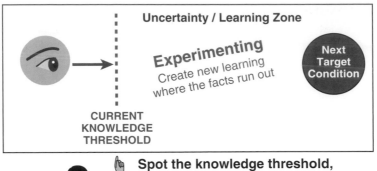

Spot the knowledge threshold, acknowledge it, and conduct your next experiment here as quickly as possible.

Consider the image of a country road below. We could sit in a conference room and discuss what each of us thinks is on the other side of the hill, but without new data doing that practices and reinforces an unscientific mindset. It's OK to stay in the conference room a little longer to discuss ideas for how you want to test and learn more about what's on the other side of the hill, but you'll actually see farther by trying something, not by discussing. Base your decisions on evidence that presents itself from the next experiment along the way, not on the strength of someone's arguments and opinions.

In a coaching cycle your coach might ask:

What is your threshold of knowledge now, and what do you need to learn next?

The ability to be aware of knowledge thresholds and to design good, cheap, quick, experiments there are important skills and mindset for developing your adaptiveness, agility, and resilience.

It's the Scientific Learning Cycle

Scientific thinking is always provisional, à la *"This is what we think we know, and our plan is a hypothesis."* To obtain and maintain a sufficient grasp of reality, scientists undertake a *prediction → test → data → evaluate* cycle of interaction with a situation, which builds up layers of learning. You can use this cycle as a practical way of working through the uncertain gray zone to your target condition. This learning cycle is the soul of improvement, adaptiveness, and innovation. In fact, a popular phrase that's used in the Kata community to help us keep thinking scientifically is: *"There may be an even better idea behind this one."*

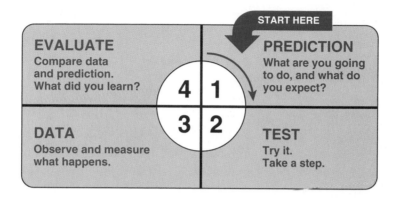

In the Lean community the learning cycle is usually called Plan-Do-Check-Act or Plan-Do-Study-Adjust. However, this kind of jargon can be unfortunate, because it creates an unnecessary and even counterproductive distinction between it and the rest of life. We would probably do well to use normal, widely understandable words such as *prediction* → *test* → *data* → *evaluate*.

Before we get into the Starter Kata for step four of the Improvement Kata pattern, let's look at **three key points about experimenting**.

1. Experimenting Is Not About Implementing Solutions

You may already have ideas about possible solutions for reaching your target condition, but most of the steps you take won't come from a predetermined implementation plan, Pareto analysis, or brainstorming. They come out of the "chain" of experiments, where what you learn from taking one step often leads you to shift your stance and sets the stage for the next experiment. Scientific thinkers let the results of their experiments show them what to work on next, not their preconceived ideas and assumptions. You are building a path to the target condition, link-by-link.

Point 1

One corollary to this is that the path to the target condition will not be a straight line. The experimenting procedure is specified, but the path is not. Things will occur along the way that cause you to revise your ideas. The target condition remains the same, but the path can shift as you learn.

Another corollary is that not every step will bring a measurable benefit. Some steps do and some don't, but that's not the point. **It is achieving the target condition that brings the benefit, not the individual steps.**

Experimenting is not free, of course. Picture yourself as working within an **"experimenting zone"** that's defined by these boundaries: (1) There is a measurable, not-optional target condition with a firm achieve-by date, (2) you have budget constraints that you cannot exceed, and (3) you cannot compromise safety or quality. It's *within* these boundaries—within this "experimenting zone"—that you conduct your experiments.

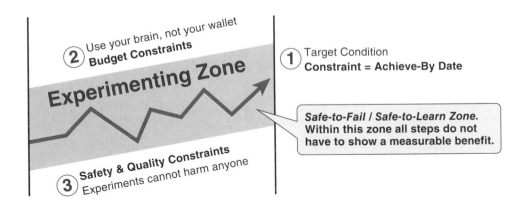

2. Prediction Error, or Surprise, Is a Big Part of How Experimenting Helps You Learn and Improve

If the result confirms the hypothesis, then you've made a measurement. If the result is contrary to the hypothesis, then you've made a discovery.

—Enrico Fermi

The core dynamic of scientific thinking involves comparing what we think will happen with what actually happens, and adjusting based on what we learn from the difference. Note the word, *difference*.

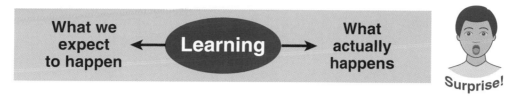

Unexpected outcomes go hand-in-hand with the improvement process, and you may learn to love them (if you can keep your experiments cheap and cheerful). How does this work? "Learning" by definition means something you don't yet know. When a result is as predicted, it confirms something you already thought and strengthens your existing neural pathways. Not much new learning there. But when a result is *different* than you predicted, then you are about to learn something new to you. Prediction error leads you out of your assumptions and provides new information that you can use to advance your design.

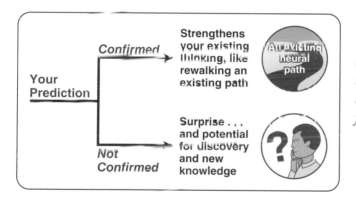

The most exciting phrase to hear in science, the one that heralds new discoveries, is not "Eureka" but "That's funny . . ."

—Isaac Asimov

Implementation is all about positive results, but in an *experiment* a negative result can be even more useful than a positive one. In an experiment you're looking for facts and data that poke holes in your idea, not so much for confirmation of your idea. This may seem counterintuitive, but once you practice it, it will make sense and can be of great use to you for finding the path to your target condition.

You will always get results, just not always the ones you expected or predicted. So be ready to revise and take another step in order to reach your goal. Of course, since we rely on prediction error as one of the main ways to learn, then your experiments should be designed so that prediction error will not harm anything. There's more on that in the practice section of this chapter.

Finally, to facilitate learning from an experiment you should **write down** in advance what you expect to happen. Afterward you should write down the data about what actually happened. Only then you can objectively compare these two things. The Starter Kata for this step of the Improvement Kata will have you do it exactly this way.

3. Quick and Frequent Experiments = More Learning

If you have to eat crow, eat it while it's young and tender.
                                                    —Thomas Jefferson

The faster you are able to learn, the more successful you'll be in reaching the target condition on time. As illustrated with the flashlight analogy, you often can't see further until you test your idea, so the sooner you test your prediction, the sooner you can see further.

Small steps are not slow steps! Quick and frequent experiments advance your knowledge rapidly, at low cost. Emphasizing small steps, one at a time, reduces the fear of failure and the stress of trying to do too much all at once. Of course, for small steps to get you to the target condition, you should take a lot of those steps.

Try to prototype and test your idea before the next coaching cycle. Think *hold* before *tape* before *weld* (try quick test methods before more permanent ones). In fact, whenever possible conduct your experiment right away, on the spot. Get good at doing that.

Frequent and rapid experiments keep learning and progress toward the target condition coming at a fast pace, which keeps both the learner and the coach motivated. When experiments are delayed and learning occurs at a slow pace, daily coaching cycles may lose their allure and value. If that starts to happen, don't reduce the frequency of your coaching cycles—instead work to increase the frequency of your experimenting.

Your coach might ask:

> *"How can we test that today? Can we do an on-the-spot experiment right now?"*

> *"What can you try right away, to see if the idea is worth pursuing further?"*

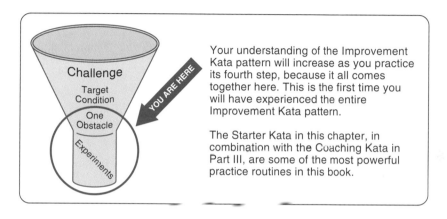

Your understanding of the Improvement Kata pattern will increase as you practice its fourth step, because it all comes together here. This is the first time you will have experienced the entire Improvement Kata pattern.

The Starter Kata in this chapter, in combination with the Coaching Kata in Part III, are some of the most powerful practice routines in this book.

How to Conduct Experiments—Powerful Routines for Achieving Any Target Condition

In this step of the Improvement Kata, the coach's five Coaching Kata questions and the learner's experimenting record are used together in the daily coaching cycles that are conducted at the learner's storyboard. In combination, these two Starter Kata help teach effective, systematic experimentation. The following pages explain how to use the learner's experimenting record. The five Coaching Kata questions are covered in Part III.

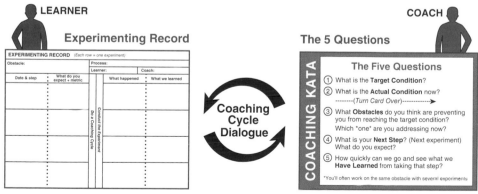

The coach asks the five Coaching Kata questions *before* each experiment that the beginner learner conducts.

First, Select One Obstacle and Write It on an Experimenting Record

Experimenting against a specific obstacle helps you avoid unscientific modes of working such as:

* Stabbing around for solutions that you think might achieve the target condition itself.

* Implementing something and immediately moving on rather than reflecting and learning from it.

Put an arrow on the obstacles parking lot to indicate the first obstacle you will be experimenting against, and write this obstacle into the space provided on the experimenting record, indicating this is the problem you're experimenting against. You are free to choose whatever first obstacle you want. Just pick one and get started. It doesn't matter which one, because your experimenting will reveal the important obstacles soon enough. They will wait for you. In fact, for beginner learners it's usually better not to start with the biggest or most difficult obstacle, so that you can first develop some basic skill with the experimenting routine.

It usually takes a series or "chain" of several experiments to successfully and sustainably overcome an obstacle. The idea is to "camp" on an obstacle, so that with each experiment you learn a little more about what you need to do to eliminate that obstacle and advance toward the target condition. For this reason, each experimenting record form pertains to only one obstacle. Whenever you move on to a different obstacle, start a new experimenting record.

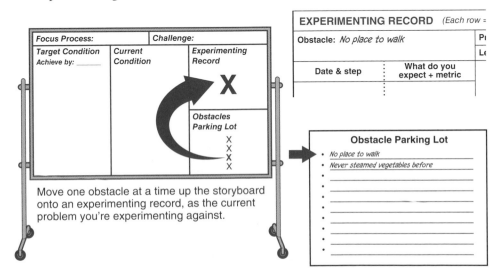

Experiments may also reveal previously unnoticed obstacles. You can add or cross off obstacles in the parking lot at any time. However, you should still try to only move one obstacle at a time up the storyboard onto an experimenting record.

Using the Experimenting Record

The experimenting record is owned by the learner and is the learner's tool for communicating his or her (a) reflection on the last experiment and (b) plan for the next experiment. The four columns in the experimenting record correspond, in order, with several of the Coaching Kata questions. **As the coach asks those questions, the learner points to and reads the responses written on the experimenting record.**

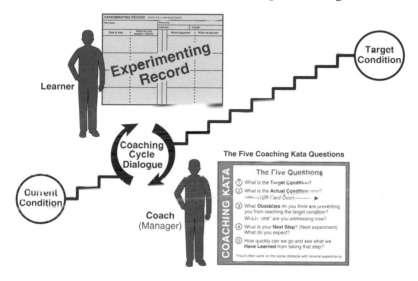

The experimenting record makes it easy to practice and teach the pattern of the scientific learning cycle because, as shown here, it embodies that pattern.

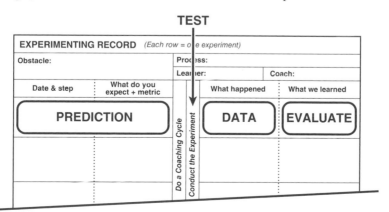

Entries on the experimenting record are made by the learner *before* the coaching cycle so the coach can see how the learner is thinking and provide appropriate feedback. The coach will either agree with the learner's plan for the next experiment or give feedback on:

- The learner's interpretation of the last step/experiment (reflection).
- The learner's proposed next step (the design of the next experiment).

During the coaching cycle your coach may suggest adjusting what's written on your experimenting record, so have a pencil and eraser on hand. Information on the experimenting record can be erased, revised, or rewritten during a coaching cycle.

As with any Starter Kata, you should first practice using the experimenting record exactly as it is designed. Once you internalize its pattern you can modify the form to suit your environment. There are many different adaptations of the experimenting record in use around the world, yet they embody the same essential scientific thinking pattern.

The Layout of the Experimenting Record

The experimenting record Starter Kata is used as follows:

- The experimenting record is read one row at a time, from left to right.
- Each row corresponds to one experiment (one step) against the current obstacle.
- The left side of the form is the "prediction side," which is written before the experiment. The right side is the "evidence side," which is written after the experiment.
- Each time you come to the bar in the middle of the form that says, "Do a Coaching Cycle," do not pass this point without checking with your coach.

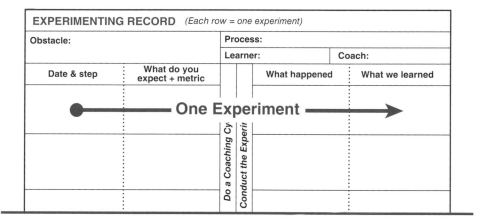

Prediction Side
Written before the experiment

Evidence Side
Written after the experiment

Making a prediction about what will happen is a fundamental element, perhaps even *the* fundamental element, of a scientific approach. For learning to take place you should predict and write down the expected results of a step before that step is taken. That creates two learning opportunities:

1. About the specifics of the step you're testing (Is "*If we do x, then we will get y*" true?).

2. About your underlying assumptions regarding the focus process and situation.

How to Use the Experimenting Record, Step-by-Step

The very first experiment you set up is based on your understanding of the initial current condition from the process analysis. After that, experiments are based on understanding the latest current condition and the reflection from the last experiment.

1. **Plan the experiment** *("I intend to...")*, indicating the proposed step and the date for that step. What is your current threshold of knowledge, and what do you need to learn next?

2. Write down the effect you predict the step will have, or what you expect to learn, and how you will measure it.

3. **Go through a coaching cycle.** The coach gives feedback on the design of the next experiment as necessary. Make adjustments based on the coach's input.

4. Once you and the coach agree, **conduct the experiment.**

5. Record the facts (observations) and measured data about what happened. No interpretation yet!

6. Now reflect on the outcome of the experiment by comparing the predicted result (2) with what actually happened (5) and summarize what you learned.

7. Move down a row. Based on what was learned from the last experiment, propose the next step and date. What is now your threshold of knowledge, and what do you need to learn next?

8. Write down your next prediction and how you will measure it.

Now it's time for the next coaching cycle.

QUICK TIPS

PREDICTION SIDE:

Before the coaching cycle the learner proposes the first **step**, what the learner **expects**, and how this will be measured. This is done in the first two columns of the form.

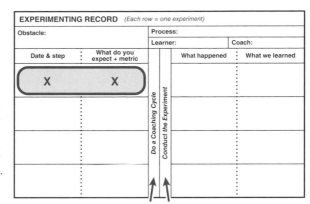

Now the learner and coach do a coaching cycle.

Then the learner conducts the experiment.

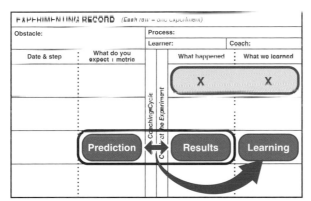

B

EVIDENCE SIDE:

Once the step (experiment) is done, the learner fills in **data** on what happened, reflects by comparing that with the expectation, and notes what was **learned**.

PREDICTION SIDE, NEXT ROW DOWN:

Based on what was learned from the last experiment, the learner proposes the next step, what he or she expects, and how this will be measured.

QUICK TIPS

Here's a column-by-column look at what's happening with the experimenting record.

Column 1	Column 2	Column 3	Column 4
Thinking About Theories		**Thinking About Evidence**	
Date & step	What do you expect + metric	What happened	What we learned
This column is about creating a good plan for the experiment. What is your current threshold of knowledge? Describe what you are going to test and how you are going to test it. Think of saying, *"I intend to..."*	This column is about what you think will happen, or what you expect to learn, as a result of the step described in column 1. Don't just restate what is in column 1. You should ensure that you have both a metric and a data collection method for measuring the results of the experiment. You must write down what you expect *before* the experiment. Otherwise your brain's confirmation bias may rob you of important learnings. *"A drop of ink is worth a pound of memory."* —Confucius	This column should contain only facts and data. It's a "situation report." If you are always getting the results you expected, then you are probably not running effective experiments at your frontier of discovery. There is not enough learning.	This can be the most difficult column. This is where you consider what happened and try to understand what it tells you about your thinking. You should also identify your new current knowledge threshold, which leads you to the next experiment. • What new insight did you gain about the focus process and the current obstacle? • What did you learn in regard to your theories, your thinking, and the governing variables of the focus process? Some of your experiments may also give you a better understanding of the current condition. A typical comment is, *"Wow, I hadn't really understood what was happening."*

Compare columns 2 and 3 for learning.

Getting Ready for a Coaching Cycle by Updating Your Storyboard

As soon as you have written your proposal for the next experiment on the experimenting record, you can do the next coaching cycle. Prepare for this by having all information updated and posted on your storyboard:

- Place the updated experimenting record in its corresponding field.

- Update the information in the "Current Condition" field to reflect the current condition now. This may involve making some new run charts. Note that the current condition may be different after each experiment, because anytime you make a change in a process, it's a new process.

- Update the "Obstacles Parking Lot" if new obstacles were discovered, obstacles were eliminated, or obstacles became no longer relevant.

- You can also add further detail to the "Target Condition" field.

As the coach asks you the five Coaching Kata questions, point to the corresponding information on your storyboard.

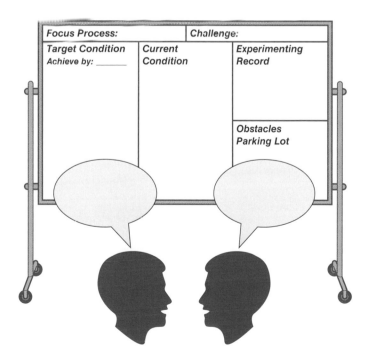

EXAMPLES (Read these example experimenting records from left to right, one row at a time.)

This is the assembly process example from the last chapter, where the obstacle was that the learner doesn't know details about unloading and loading the tank welding process. The learner's first experiment is a go-and-see step—done to learn more about that process.

First Obstacle →

EXPERIMENTING RECORD *(Each row = one experiment)*

Obstacle: *Don't know enough about the unload/ load process at the tank welder*		Process: *Assembly*	
Date & step	What do you expect + metric	Learner: *Frank Hartford*	Coach: *Mary Smith*
		What happened	What we learned
May 22. Observe the unload/load process at tank weld.	*To understand the work steps and learn if any steps can be shortened.*	*Listed the steps. (see storyboard)*	*Unclamping causes double handling of the part, which takes extra time.*

(Do a Coaching Cycle / Conduct the Experiment)

In observing the steps of the tank unloading/loading process the learner finds a new obstacle, adds it to the "Obstacle Parking Lot," and starts the new experimenting record shown below for conducting experiments against that obstacle.

New Obstacle →

EXPERIMENTING RECORD *(Each row = one experiment)*

Obstacle: *Unclamping causes double handling*		Process: *Assembly*	
Date & step	What do you expect + metric	Learner: *Frank Hartford*	Coach: *Mary Smith*
		What happened	What we learned
May 23. Attach a foot pedal for unclamping to eliminate need for double handling.	*Reduce unload/load time by 3 seconds.*	*The pedal system doesn't work with one tank type.*	*One tank type uses an extra clamp.*
May 24. Eliminate the extra clamp by adding a flange to the fixture.	*Works with all tank types. Reduce unload/load time by 3 seconds.*	*Flange scratches the tank and makes tank hard to remove with one hand.*	*Not sure how many clamps are actually needed to hold the tank.*
May 25. Eliminate the extra clamp by relocating two other clamps	*Works with all tank types. Reduce unload/load time by 3 seconds.*	*Tank is secure during welding. Unload/load time was reduced by 4 seconds.*	*New clamp configuration seems to work with all tank types!*
May 25. Monitor weld process for two shifts to check.	*If it works consistently we'll need to establish a new standard.*		

(Do a Coaching Cycle / Conduct the Experiment)

And so on...

This is the weight loss example from the last chapter, where one of the obstacles is that the learner doesn't have a place to take a walk after work.

EXPERIMENTING RECORD   *(Each row = one experiment)*

Obstacle: *No place to walk after work*		Process: *Weight Loss*		
		Learner:		Coach:
Date & step	What do you expect + metric		What happened	What we learned
Aug. 22. Take a walk in Elm Park after work.	*Good conditions to walk for 30 minutes. Path at least 1 mile long.*		*• Path is too short (only 5 minutes). • Parking costs $1.-*	*Need to try a different walking location.*
Aug. 23. Ask coworkers for suggestions.	*Able to test another location today. Path at least 1 mile long. Free parking.*		*Riverfront Trail. Works well, can return on other side of river. Feet hurt.*	*Walking in work shoes is not good.*
Aug 24. Keep walking shoes and socks in car.	*Walk 30 minutes without feet hurting.*			

(vertical labels: Do a Coaching Cycle / Conduct the Experiment)

And so on...

Reaching a Challenging Target Condition Involves Taking Many Small Steps

If you read through these example experimenting records, it may seem like they involve little steps that are hardly significant in the larger picture. That's a mistake we make because we like to highlight our milestone inventions and outcomes, our apparent leaps forward, but tend to overlook the day-to-day enterprise that actually gets us there. Important changes, improvements, and achievements are often the product of many small improvements and incremental innovations. Think of what you see on these experimenting records as the *action of innovation*.

When you realize that a lot of progress actually comes from an accumulation of steps by everyday scientists, it starts to make great sense to develop the scientific thinking capability of everyone in an organization!

What to Do During a Coaching Cycle—Responses from the Learner

Coaching Cycle

Coming

The Coaching Kata (Part III) provides the framework of questions that the coach will ask you, always in the same order, during each coaching cycle. The questions help the coach to understand your current thinking and the status of your effort to reach the target condition so the coach can give you feedback.

This table summarizes the basic information that the coach is looking for from you in response to the questions when you are in step four of the Improvement Kata pattern. In giving your initial answers, you should simply *read the information directly from your storyboard*, which you should have updated before each coaching cycle. It's a good idea to *point to each item on the storyboard as you read them*.

	COACH'S QUESTION	LEARNER'S RESPONSE
	What is the challenge?	Explain what you understand the challenge to be, which often comes from the level above you.
1	What is the target condition?	Read through the description of the target condition that's on your storyboard, pointing to the items as you read.
2	What is the actual condition now?	Read through the facts, data, and diagrams on the storyboard that describe the current condition as it is now (not the initial current condition). Point as you read.
REFLECTION	What was your last step?	Read the previous entry in column 1 of the experimenting record.
REFLECTION	What did you expect?	Read the previous entry in column 2 of the experimenting record.
REFLECTION	What actually happened?	Read the latest entry in column 3 of the experimenting record.
REFLECTION	What did you learn?	Read the latest entry in column 4 of the experimenting record.
3	What obstacles do you think are preventing you from reaching the target condition? Which *one* are you addressing now?	Read through the items on the Obstacles Parking Lot. Point out any obstacles that have been added or crossed out. Have an arrow at the obstacle you are currently working on, and point to this obstacle.
4	What is your next step? (The next experiment) What do you expect?	Propose the next step, reading the latest entry in columns 1 and 2 of the experimenting record. Use the "Checklist for Planning an Experiment" to help you plan and explain your next experiment.
5	How quickly can we go and see what we have learned from taking that step?	Propose the date and time for the next coaching cycle. The coach will encourage doing the experiment as soon as possible. Agree on the facts and data to have at the next coaching cycle.

Congratulations! You're working scientifically!

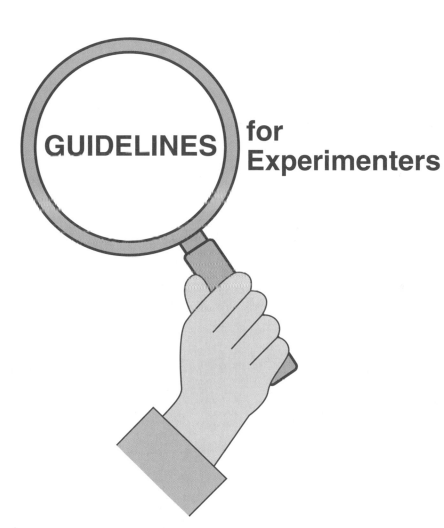

THREE TYPES OF EXPERIMENTS

The following list of experiment types goes from less scientific to more scientific. All can be considered experiments—as long as you use the experimenting record with them—since any step you take has consequences that are testable. (Remember, our definition of an experiment is *taking a step with the intent of learning something*.) Many learners like to indicate on the experimenting record what type of experiment they are doing next.

1. Go and See (Insight Through Passive Observation)

This is direct observation and data collection without changing anything, to learn more about a process or situation. "Further analysis" or "go and see" can be an experiment, as long as a prediction of what the learner expects, or expects to learn, is made on the experimenting record.

Whenever your next step is unclear to you, a good answer is often, *"Let's go and see."* Of course, to understand a situation you have to personally go to observe and measure for some length of time. It is almost always worth taking the time.

2. Exploratory Experiment (Insight Through Probing)

This is introducing a change in a process and observing how the process reacts, to help you better understand the process. If you poke the process, so to speak, it will respond. This is done to get a feel for what is there but hidden.

One of the first experiments toward a new target condition is often an exploratory experiment. An elegant tactic for a first step is to try to simply run the process as specified in the target condition. Of course, you already know it isn't going to work yet, but this quickly gets some true obstacles to reveal themselves, and then you will know what to work on.

3. Testing a Hypothesis (Insight Through a Validate-or-Refute Test)

This is introducing a specific change or countermeasure, together with a prediction of what you expect to happen, in order to test that particular idea.

If possible, try to change only one factor at a time (OFAT) and then check the result against the expected result. Such single-factor or "controlled comparison" experiments allow you to better see and understand cause and effect, which helps you develop a deeper understanding of the focus process. However, single-factor experiments are not always possible, and many times there will be more than one factor involved in your hypothesis-testing experiments. That's not unusual.

TEST AS QUICKLY AS POSSIBLE, AS SIMPLY AS POSSIBLE, AND ON A SMALL SCALE

There are two good reasons for this:
- It leads to faster learning and progress toward the target condition.
- It helps prevent unanticipated effects from causing widespread harm.

Keep in mind that the target condition achieve-by date is firm. To get there in time you should conduct your experiments as fast and frequently as possible. How can you test your prediction simply and soon? How about right now, with whatever you have? A provisional step or mockup is often OK for learning. It allows you to validate and adjust your ideas before going large-scale with them. You may be convinced of your idea—or have plenty of experience with the focus process—but it is likely to need adjusting.

In short, taking the next step quickly helps you see further quickly.

Similarly, doing small-scale experiments helps you ensure that unexpected results don't cause harm; they *limit the blast radius*, so to speak. In any experiment you might discover flaws and experience unintended consequences that could affect others and other areas. If necessary, build up a safety buffer before conducting your experiment to protect the customer of the focus process, or conduct the experiment offline in a simulation. Blindly going full-scale can end in regret.

THE NEED TO TEST

There is no need to reinvent the wheel. You should, of course, use available existing knowledge and information, such as specifications from manuals, findings from other research, experience in other areas of your organization, and so on.

However, keep in mind that even if you reference existing information, how it will work in your specific case is still a gray area where you need to conduct tests. The information you use, regardless of its source, still needs to be tested and verified in the context of your particular situation and target condition.

CALIBRATE YOUR TEAM BEFORE CONDUCTING AN EXPERIMENT

As you go to conduct an experiment, stop, turn to face your team, and ask, *"Why are we doing this experiment?"* You may get some responses along the lines of, *"To see if (idea) will work."*

Look at your team and say, *"Actually, we already know that this (idea) probably won't work."* Pause for a moment to let that sink in. Then say, *"Hardly anything works right the first time. What we need to do is look carefully at what happens and then think about what we need to do to make it work."*

Get your team to look at what's not working and to think about how to make it work. Use your team's brainpower! When you calibrate your team from a mindset of, "I don't think this will work," to one of, "Let's see what we need to do to make it work," you are switching on and engaging their brainpower. We humans have remarkable creative ability, but it often needs to be activated and aimed by a leader.

EACH STEP YOU TAKE IS AN EXPERIMENT

Taking steps toward the target condition is a way of both making progress and exploring. With every step you take you are probing the terrain, adjusting accordingly, and updating your mental representation of the situation. This is a good way to navigate uncertain, unfamiliar, and complex situations as you pursue your goal.

You don't actually know what the result of the next step will be, so don't think too far ahead. If you do, you may not be open for the unexpected results that might take you in a different but more fruitful direction than you originally thought. Get used to being in the learning zone and being right only 50 percent of the time (or less!). Concentrate on the next step, and keep an open mind. You only get to see the full path to your target condition in hindsight.

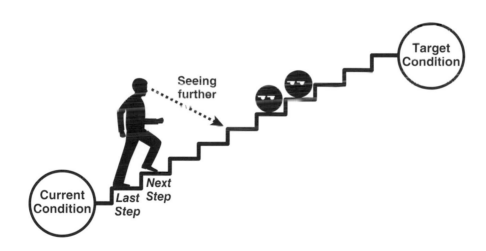

Every step taken alters the horizon, changes the field of vision, causing us to see what had been thus far circumscribed as something quite different.
—James P. Carse

WHAT ABOUT EXPERIMENTING WITH LONG-CYCLE PROCESSES?

Focus processes with long cycle times or that operate only infrequently, such as some administrative and chemical processes, can make it difficult to experiment and gain knowledge in a rapid, low-cost way. The longer the process cycle, the longer it may take to experiment, especially since you ideally need to collect several data points.

To accelerate testing in these cases, experiments often involve some type of "laboratory" simulation. The challenge becomes, "How can we artificially test this step or idea more quickly?" This approach involves conducting low-cost simulation experiments (one per day, for instance) in between less-frequent experiments on the actual focus process. You gain several learnings in the interval between actual process cycles, which culminate in one "big" experiment at the actual process under real conditions to get information that can only come from the real process.

WHAT IF AN EXPERIMENT TAKES A LONG TIME TO PREPARE?

Daily experiments may be an ideal, but just because you have coaching cycles every day does not mean that you will always be able to do experiments every day. For example . . .

Ideally you should only conduct one experiment at a time on a focus process, in order to keep cause and effect clear. However, this would mean losing valuable experimenting time if you have to wait long for a particular experiment to be prepared. In this case you can run other experiments against a different and unrelated obstacle while you wait for the other experiment to be ready, as shown in the diagram below (X = a step/experiment).

	Only one process change is done at this time	
Long step: ·········· *Preparation* ··········· **X**		
Other steps: **X** **X** **X**		

Checklist for Planning an Experiment

❑ Conduct experiments against a specific obstacle to the target condition, not randomly.

❑ What do you need to learn now? Identify your current threshold of knowledge relative to your current obstacle and conduct the next experiment there.

❑ What is your current threshold of knowledge (TOK)?

❑ How will you test your idea? Can you do a single-factor experiment, where only one thing is changed? (Not always possible.)

❑ How can you test your prediction as soon and quickly as possible? Simple and soon is better. How about now? (Think: *hold* before *tape* before *weld*.)

❑ Make sure that unexpected results won't harm anyone or anything. If necessary build up a buffer before conducting the experiment, or conduct the experiment offline in a simulation.

❑ Before the experiment, write down what you expect to happen (your prediction) on the prediction side of the experimenting record.

❑ How will you measure it? The experiment must be measurable in some way so you can determine if the prediction was confirmed or refuted.

❑ If possible the experiment should build on what was learned in your previous experiment.

❑ In order to learn from your experiment, you must be open to and willing to see that the result may not conform to your expectation. Own it!

Checklist for **Evaluating the Results of an Experiment**

❏ To check the results of an experiment, you should observe and measure several cycles. One data point is rarely enough.

❏ Make a run chart with the data from your experiment. It can also help to stratify your data by time, person, item, machine, etc. Avoid using averages.

❏ Evaluation has two phases. Be sure to maintain a clear distinction between *recording* the facts or data and *interpreting* the results:

   1. Compiling the facts and data from the experiment. (This is column 3 in the experimenting record.)

   2. Forming conclusions based on interpreting the facts and data. (This is column 4 in the experimenting record.)

❏ There are several possible outcomes, for instance:

   o The results support your prediction, and you can standardize the step.

   o The results do not support your prediction. (Interesting!)

   o The results came close, and you can see what you have to try next.

   o You can't tell and need more information.

❏ It is not at all unusual for more than 50 percent of your experiments to have results other than what you expected. The benefit you get is learning what you *need* to focus on and do to overcome the obstacle on the way to your target condition.

❏ When an experiment is successful, you'll need to think about how to institutionalize and maintain the change you made. This will likely require more experiments, since simply changing a document or telling people is rarely sufficient.

❏ It's a good idea to reflect on what you could have done differently to improve your experimental procedure, so you can become an even better experimenter.

CHAPTER 9

THE SUMMARY REFLECTION

Reflect Back and Look Ahead

When the target condition or the achieve-by date is reached, it's a good idea for the learner and coach to do a **summary reflection** together, to review plusses and minuses from the four-step Improvement Kata process that was just completed. This can be a review of the learner's Improvement Kata practice as well as the coach's Coaching Kata practice. Both the learner and the coach can come away from a summary reflection with things they would like to emphasize, try, or do differently in their next pass through the four steps of the Improvement Kata. What skills do you want to work on next?

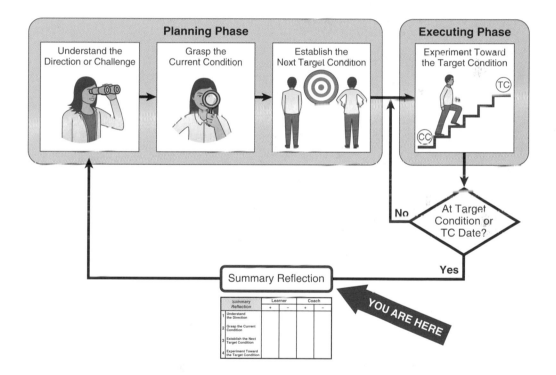

If the target condition is reached earlier than planned, conduct the summary reflection at that time rather than waiting until the planned achieve-by date. Likewise, if the achieve-by date comes up and the target condition hasn't been reached yet, stop and conduct the summary reflection at that time. Both of these situations are a learning opportunity because they are an unexpected outcome.

If you are not yet at the target condition but time is up, it is tempting to say, "Just a few more days." However, if an achieve-by date is changed, then it no longer means much and could be changed again. Don't adjust the achieve-by date. Remember, to reach the challenge you almost always have to move through several successive target conditions anyway. Learn from the unexpected outcome and then look forward anew.

Summary Reflection		Learner		Coach	
		+	−	+	−
1	Understand the Direction				
2	Grasp the Current Condition				
3	Establish the Next Target Condition				
4	Experiment Toward the Target Condition				

After the summary reflection you normally clear off and reset the learner's storyboard, and go back to step one of the Improvement Kata pattern. If you are again working on the same challenge at the same focus process, then "Grasp the Current Condition" and "Establish the Next Target Condition" may go more quickly this time, since you now know more based on the experiments you've already done.

Let me conclude Part II with a reminder that the Improvement Kata routines presented here are Starter Kata—practice routines for the purpose of helping you develop scientific thinking skills and mindset. As you internalize the patterns embedded in the Starter Kata you can adapt those patterns into your way of doing things, in a manner that suits your organization and situation.

Next up—in Part III—are the Starter Kata for the coach, which match and work together with the Starter Kata in Part II.

PART III

PRACTICE ROUTINES FOR THE COACH

(The Coaching Kata)

Learning How to Coach the Improvement Kata

If you want to learn the Improvement Kata (IK) more deeply, teach it. You should start coaching the Improvement Kata as soon as possible after gaining some basic IK proficiency. This will accelerate your learning of scientific thinking.

Coaching an Improvement Kata learner is a skill like any other, which means your practice as a coach also begins with some Starter Kata. The foundational Starter Kata for the coach is the five Coaching Kata questions, which provide the format for conducting daily coaching cycles with a learner who is practicing the Improvement Kata.

Part III has three chapters:

> **Chapter 10: Introduction to the Coaching Kata**
>
> **Chapter 11: Coaching Cycles—Concept Overview**
>
> **Chapter 12: How to Do a Coaching Cycle—Practice Routines**

The Coaching Kata is specific to teaching the scientific Improvement Kata pattern, not a general mentoring or "life coaching" routine. In any skill development effort, the coach should have some experience with the skill the learner is practicing, so the coach can assess the learner's practice and give useful feedback. To help with this, while you, the coach in training, use the Starter Kata instructions in Part III, you can also refer back to the chapters in Part II that correspond to the step of the Improvement Kata that your learner is in, to remind yourself about how the learner should be operating at that step. (See the diagram on the next page.)

Improvement Kata Chapters for the Coach's Reference

CONTENTS

Refer back to Part II as needed for details on how the learner should be practicing the steps of the Improvement Kata.

CHAPTER 10

INTRODUCTION TO THE COACHING KATA

The Five Questions

1. What is the **Target Condition**?
2. What is the **Actual Condition** now?

   --------(*Turn Card Over*)------------->

3. What **Obstacles** do you think are preventing you from reaching the target condition?

   Which *one* are you addressing now?

4. What is your **Next Step**? (Next experiment) What do you expect?

5. How quickly can we go and see what we **Have Learned** from taking that step?

*You'll often work on the same obstacle with several experiments

Reflect on the Last Step Taken

Because you don't actually know
what the result of a step will be!

1. What did you plan as your **Last Step?**
2. What did you **Expect?**
3. What **Actually Happened?**
4. What did you **Learn?**

----------------------------->
Return to question 3

The Coach/Learner Relationship

The learner needs a coach while practicing the Improvement Kata because alone they may not see and correct their own practice errors and can end up practicing poor habits. The effectiveness and speed of the learner's learning depend to a significant degree on the coaching they get. With this in mind, a job description for an Improvement Kata coach, especially with beginner learners, might be:

> *To accompany the learner and give procedural guidance as needed to ensure that although the learner struggles, he or she is ultimately successful in learning to use the Improvement Kata pattern to achieve challenging, real target conditions.*

It has been suggested that all learning is actually "self-learning," meaning that we learn from our own experiences. This is what you are supporting and enabling as a coach, and is slightly different from a "push" approach to teaching we might normally envision. The coach's responsibility is to *manage the learner's practice*, and it takes some practice to learn how to do that effectively.

We know that simply having a learner repeat a series of steps is not enough for developing new skills and mindset. The learner needs to keep ratcheting up their practice; work on their mistakes; and deal with the plateaus, setbacks, and discomfort that come with learning any new skill. That is, the learner's emotions will play a vital role. Periodically experiencing success and joy in overcoming obstacles to their target condition and in seeing their Improvement Kata skills grow is something that you influence as a coach. The coach provides support by encouraging the learner, helping the learner see when they might be working in ways counter to their skill-building goals, and finding ways to ensure that the learner makes progress. The Coaching Kata means someone's learning is in your hands and you are responsible for their success.

There is an interesting overlap of responsibility between the coach and the learner. While the learner is responsible for the doing, the coach is responsible for the results. This is like in sports or a musical performance, where the coach cannot personally go onto the field to play, but is responsible for the team's success. The coach can only develop the players. This creates an interdependence, with the coach as dependent on the learners for the coach's success as the learners are on the coach for their success.

Establishing a Dialogue Conducive to Learning	
IK Learner	**IK Coach**
Accept temporarily being a beginner in this particular skill domain (Improvement Kata) and be ready to start with some structured practice routines.	Accept temporarily being a beginner in this particular skill domain (Coaching Kata) and be ready to start with some structured practice routines.
Avoid being defensive.	Take a vested interest in developing the learner, along with obtaining improvement.
Be willing to listen to the coach and do what the coach suggests. (Of course the learner can ask about the coach's rationale.)	Discern where the learner is having difficulty, based on observing the learner's efforts.
Take responsibility for educating yourself. You "gotta wanna."	Tailor feedback and practice tactics to suit the current capability and difficulties of each learner.
	Give feedback on essential skill elements, not on every detail.
	Adjust your coaching as the capability of the learner grows.
	Avoid making the learner defensive.

What Is the Coaching Kata About?

The Coaching Kata is a practice protocol for a beginner coach to follow as they coach a learner, who is practicing the Improvement Kata. The five Coaching Kata questions are the main headings for practicing "coaching cycles," which are structured daily dialogues between the coach and a learner that take 20 minutes or less. They are the primary point of interaction between the coach and the learner. The purpose of a coaching cycle is to review the learner's current application of the Improvement Kata, engage the learner and coach in thinking about *how* the learner is working, and give feedback regarding the next practice goals for improving the learner's procedure.

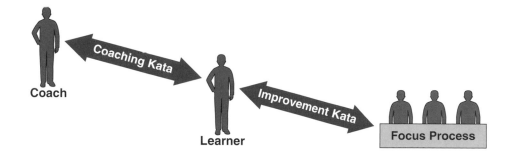

As a coach you have two main goals in a coaching cycle:

1. To develop the learner's Improvement Kata skills by supporting the learner's practice as he or she applies the Improvement Kata to a real focus process. The learner is striving to reach a real target condition *and* get better at using the Improvement Kata pattern.

2. To develop yourself as an effective coach, through your own practice of the Coaching Kata routines as you coach the learner.

As you can see, both the learner and the coach are practicing and learning. As mentioned in Part I, there is also a role called the "second coach," who periodically observes and gives feedback to you, the coach, on your practice. More on that later.

The coaching-cycle interactions are one-on-one—one coach and one learner—since every learner has different practice needs. A coaching cycle only takes 20 minutes or less, so a coach can meet with multiple learners every day. The basic structure is the same for every coaching cycle, which makes it easier for the coach to shift from meeting with one learner to the next.

Part of a coaching cycle is structured—such as the five main questions, the learner's storyboard, etc.—and part is situational. For example, the five main-heading questions are scripted, but your feedback:

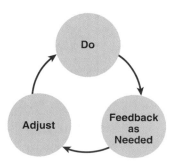

1. Depends on what you discern about each learner's thinking and where you want to bring the learner next.

2. Builds on your own library of experience from your practice of the Improvement Kata.

Once the coach has listened to the learner respond and gotten a sense for the learner's current thinking, you may give a corrective input tailored to the needs of that particular learner at that point in time. Note that you don't have to give corrective feedback in every coaching cycle. It's your decision. The coaching cycle dialogue is not about audit and compliance. It's part of a reciprocal, collaborative relationship that creates a learning experience for both of you:

- The learner and coach are engaged in a joint process of discovery around striving to reach the next target condition.

- The learner and coach are each practicing Starter Kata for their role. Every effort to give feedback to the learner is practice for the coach, and every effort to act on the coach's feedback is practice for the learner.

Two Practice Dilemmas and How the Coach Solves Them

One dilemma is that the learner is expected to learn by doing, but at the outset doesn't know what to do. The learner is supposed to practice the Improvement Kata pattern before they understand what the Improvement Kata is.

The coach bridges this dilemma by adjusting their coaching as the learner progresses. At the start you have the learner adhere to each Starter Kata quite closely, and meticulously guide the learner through them. But as soon as the learner shows some understanding of the intent behind a Starter Kata the coach can give the learner more leeway, which affords you even more opportunity to see where you need to focus your feedback.

This approach of tailoring coaching support to the evolving needs of a learner is sometimes called "instructional scaffolding," since the coach's guidance is adjusted or removed as the learner progresses.

The **second dilemma** is that to acquire new skills and mindset, the learner should be stretched beyond their current capability, yet they also need to experience some success and accomplishment, especially at the onset. Successfully overcoming the obstacles to a target condition strengthens a beginner learner's sense of self-efficacy with the Improvement Kata pattern, but failing too often can weaken it.

Here's an example. If a target condition is too easy, then the learner may arrive there and think, *"I already knew I could do that,"* and there will be little resulting growth in self-efficacy. On the other hand, if target conditions are appropriately challenging but the learner repeatedly fails to reach them, it may confirm a fear that, *"I knew I couldn't do this."* The learner doesn't need to succeed all the time, but on balance more often than not.

The coach handles this dilemma by stretching the learner out of their comfort zone *and* then providing regular feedback on the learner's procedure (not content) that helps the learner be successful in applying the Improvement Kata. You accompany the beginner learner with guidance that has the learner develop and achieve target conditions through their own activity. The learner should see that they are actually doing it themselves.

The Magnitude of the Target Condition Is Not as Important as You Might Think

I've been at countless pizza parties to celebrate a team achieving a goal, and for a long time I felt that reaching the overall goal is probably the main factor in building self-efficacy and creating joy. Working with the Improvement Kata over the last decade has given me a different perspective.

First of all, the size of the overall goal doesn't seem to matter. It only matters that the goal is challenging *to the learner*—that the learner does not know in advance how they will reach it. A team striving to save 10 seconds in their work process will experience similar emotions along the way as a team that is developing an entirely new product. This leveling effect opens the door for everyone in an organization to work in similar ways and get similar satisfaction from their work. But there's more.

The longer I watched learners practice, the more I noticed that reaching the overall goal does not actually seem to be the big factor in creating self-efficacy. Instead, it's the experience of overcoming the obstacles along the way, one at a time, that seems to build a growing sense of, *"I can do it."* The final pizza party to celebrate overall success is nice, but struggling with and overcoming the obstacles along the way seems to generate some of the most meaningful emotions.

(continues)

More than a few times I've witnessed a team member coming into a meeting saying something like, *"I was thinking about our current obstacle in the shower this morning. What if we tried this . . ."* Not only did the person come up with some terrific ideas, but sometimes this would even be the team member who was initially the most resistant to practicing the Improvement Kata. It's evident to me that our astonishing brainpower is there for us to use, if we activate and channel it by managing ourselves a little differently.

Qualifications for Improvement Kata Coaches

Since an Improvement Kata coach regularly needs to judge whether or not the learner is carrying out the Improvement Kata routines correctly and give procedural guidance, the coach should have personal experience in applying the Improvement Kata pattern.[1] The coach doesn't need to be an expert, but should have some experience with the pattern, routines, and principles. This is why in business organizations the managers, who are the natural coaches there, typically go first in practicing the Improvement Kata pattern and routines. However, having Improvement Kata experience doesn't automatically make you a good coach. There's a difference between applying the IK pattern yourself and helping someone else learn it.[2]

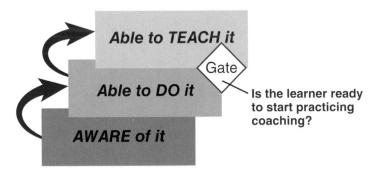

---

1 At the start you may not have any experienced coaches. See the coaching "rotation models" in Chapter 3 for a way to deal with this.

2 Note that you don't stop practicing the Improvement Kata once you start coaching. You never really stop applying the pattern of the Improvement Kata, because it is a way of thinking and working. Your skill level just reaches the point where you can begin to also coach others.

There is no universal rule for how much practice it takes to attain basic coaching competency. One useful guideline I've seen is that the coach should have conducted a minimum of 60 coaching cycles, with at least 20 of those having been observed by a second coach. Overall, criteria for being an Improvement Kata coach include:

- Experienced in both the pattern and principles of the Improvement Kata

- Willing to practice and learn a different approach to managing, which involves guiding and teaching rather than directing the content of people's actions

- Willing to become knowledgeable about the focus process the learner is improving so you can give appropriate feedback. (The coach can do this while they coach the learner.)

- Keen observer of people, with both technical and interpersonal skills

- Listens more than talks

- Truly cares about the learner's progress

- Sees coaching as a process of mutual development and trust

- Sees each coaching cycle as an experiment aimed at testing and improving their coaching techniques

Coaching as a Way of Managing

The mindset and behavior of the people in an organization—its culture—is a reflection of management. A main responsibility of managers in adaptive, agile organizations is ensuring development of their people, and thereby creating an organizational capability to work together to meet challenges. Only an organization's managers and supervisors are in a position to interact with everyone in a coaching fashion every day.

In fact, skill coaching may become a significant part of what twenty-first-century managers do, instead of just telling people what to do.[3] When managers practice the Improvement Kata and then the Coaching Kata, they will often be astounded by what their people can achieve. Once you experience this it can be difficult to go back to the old way.

---

3 It will be interesting to see if coaching capability, specifically, becomes a factor in advancement in business organizations, and a subject at business schools.

Moreover, chains of coaches and learners that cut across the levels of an organization can function as a *management system* that delivers alignment, improvement, and engagement. For more on this topic see the book *Toyota Kata Culture* (2017, McGraw-Hill).

Be aware that becoming an effective Improvement Kata coach—an effective twenty-first-century manager—also takes the right attitude. Take note of how you feel when you conduct coaching cycles with your learners. Do you feel like you're in a special position of honor and influence—over others in importance or ability—or do you feel like you're part of a larger team, working together to meet challenges and develop capabilities? Ideally you'll coach with the realization that you too are on a learning path, just like everyone else.

By practicing the Coaching Kata you are creating more Improvement Kata coaches, who can then coach other learners. You're powering the future of your organization.

CHAPTER 11

COACHING CYCLES: CONCEPT OVERVIEW

Coach Learner

Learner's Storyboard

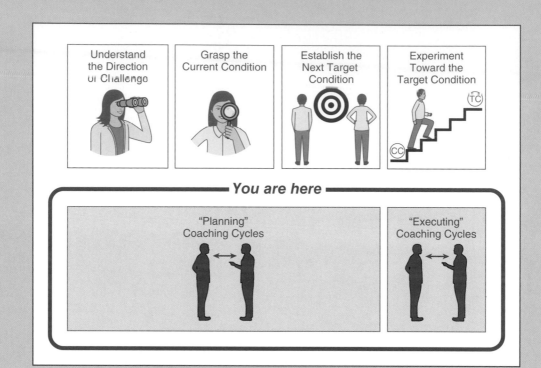

A Dialogue Routine

Coaching cycles are your primary routine for helping the beginner learner acquire the scientific thinking pattern of the Improvement Kata, and for practicing your coaching skills.[1] The next three paragraphs are a quick review.

A coaching cycle involves the coach going through the five Coaching Kata question categories with one learner, who refers to information on their storyboard while responding. This is done once per day at a scheduled time, plus as the need arises, taking 20 minutes or less each time—which is the "20 minutes" in this book's subtitle. Coaching cycles usually start and end at the learner's storyboard.[2]

Think of coaching cycles as a pause to reflect on the learner's last step, review the learner's plan for the next step, and give feedback, as necessary, on the learner's procedure. In doing this you are working to nudge the learner's practice into the corridor prescribed by the scientific pattern of the Improvement Kata, so that, over time, the learner develops a reflex of thinking that way. Coaching cycles help uncover biases in our thinking and introduce changes in how we think, by correcting practice errors quickly, before they become habits. The purpose is not for the learner to "learn the Starter Kata," but to internalize the scientific thinking pattern behind them.

A coaching cycle is not a free-form conversation, not a rigid fill-in-the-blanks process, and not about policing the learner. The structured and repetitive nature of coaching cycles—especially at the start—is where a dialogue pattern between you and the learner

---

1   The Coaching Kata and coaching cycles were introduced in Part I, Chapters 2 and 3, which you might want to reread before proceeding here.

2   Some coaching cycles are also observed by a "second coach," who is coaching the coach, as explained in the next chapter.

gets established, to help teach the scientific Improvement Kata pattern while using that pattern to meet goals. To repeat from Chapter 2, the purposes of a coaching cycle are:

- Assessing the current status of the learner's thinking, which helps the coach formulate appropriate feedback

- Identifying the current knowledge threshold relative to the obstacle the learner is working on, and making sure the learner is designing a good next experiment to see further

- Giving procedural feedback to the learner, to help the learner internalize the scientific thinking Improvement Kata pattern as they apply it to a real work process

- Understanding the current status of the focus process

- A cue for both the coach and learner to practice their respective behavior patterns and keep improving their respective skills

Coaching cycles are not all there is to coaching, of course. For instance, the coach can also decide to accompany the learner as the learner takes the next step, in order to observe the learner and/or the focus process more deeply and provide some real-time guidance or support. In the course of a workday, a manager may have many interactions with their learners, and all those interactions can reflect the scientific thinking patterns that are being stressed in the coaching cycles. Over time a manager's every encounter and interaction should begin to radiate the scientific Improvement Kata pattern, because the everyday behavior of managers functions as a role model and is one of the main forces for creating a deliberate, scientific thinking culture. Coaching cycles are the formal, structured part where it begins.

Try to Schedule Coaching Cycles for Every Day

For each of your learners, schedule a regular coaching cycle at a set time early in the workday, so the learner can carry out their next step that day if possible. It can be a challenge to arrange things so you can do at least one coaching cycle with each learner every day, but it is important to get as close to that frequency as possible. You might think once or twice per week could be sufficient, but that doesn't work well for developing new skills. Without frequent reflection and feedback, a beginner learner will automatically tend to favor existing habits over still-awkward new patterns. Practicing 20 minutes a day is considerably more effective than two hours only once a week.

As soon as you start getting better at it, daily coaching shouldn't be a burden. On the contrary, coaching cycles can be an efficient and effective way of managing, and you should be able to conduct most coaching cycles in 20 minutes or less. Remember, a coaching cycle is only for reviewing the learner's process of experimenting, not for doing the experimenting itself. The learner sees beyond the current threshold of knowledge by taking the next step (experimenting) *between* coaching cycles, not through theoretical deliberation and discussion in the coaching cycles.

If your coaching cycles consistently take longer than 20 minutes, it may indicate a flaw in your coaching. For instance, novice coaches sometimes mistakenly let coaching cycles get into lengthy discussions or cover many different factors, by treating them more like a meeting. All you need to get to in a coaching cycle is identifying and agreeing on the learner's next step; that's it. As soon as a single next step, not a list of steps, is clear to the learner and the coach, then that coaching cycle is done. At that point the learner can go take the next step, which you can review in the next coaching cycle and see further. It is perfectly acceptable for the learner's next step to be a single and small one, as long as your coaching cycles are frequent. You can make astonishing progress toward goals this way, and unnecessary time spent speculating and opining are eliminated.

Another important benefit of conducting frequent coaching cycles and taking small steps is that it gives coaches the leeway to let their learners make some mistakes and learn from them, because small steps facilitate fast course correction. A key aspect of deliberate practice is that we learn through our struggles and errors, because they show where we need to improve and they engage our emotions. These "teachable moments" are an opportunity for constructive feedback and advancing the learner's practice. With infrequent coaching cycles a beginner learner will tend to plan and take steps that are too big for swift course correction.

The Five Coaching Kata Questions

The five Coaching Kata questions are a Starter Kata that provide the framework for your coaching cycles. Going through all five of them, in order, constitutes one coaching cycle. The five questions are nested, meaning that each question is a subset of the previous question. Think of them like a funnel, starting with the **target condition**. The **current condition** is then described, relative to that target condition. The **current obstacle** being worked on springs from understanding the current condition, and then the questioning can focus down to the learner's **next step** (the next experiment) relative to that obstacle.

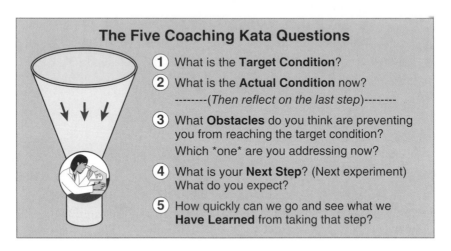

The Five Coaching Kata Questions

① What is the **Target Condition**?

② What is the **Actual Condition** now?
--------(*Then reflect on the last step*)--------

③ What **Obstacles** do you think are preventing you from reaching the target condition?
Which *one* are you addressing now?

④ What is your **Next Step**? (Next experiment)
What do you expect?

⑤ How quickly can we go and see what we **Have Learned** from taking that step?

The five questions are the main headings in a coaching cycle. They are like five *question categories*, and you can ask additional clarifying questions between them. Regardless of what you say between the five questions, at the beginning you should ask the five questions exactly as they are written on your coaching card, letting the overarching pattern sink in and become a habit for you and the learner. For instance, the target condition gets reviewed at the beginning of every coaching cycle as a "frame," even though this may start to seem repetitive and redundant when you're doing daily coaching cycles. A pattern you're trying to ingrain is to always talk first about where you are going (the target condition), and then about aspects of the current condition, and so on, relative to that.

A common mistake beginner coaches make is to deviate from the five Coaching Kata questions. If a learner sees you departing from the five-question pattern, they will tend to do the same, and soon you are both just reinforcing your current thinking rather than developing new routines of scientific thinking. When you get started it's completely normal to feel awkward following the five-question script. That's not a reason to deviate from it, but a positive sign that you're starting to learn something new. Instead, start adding your own "clarifying questions" between the five questions, based on your experiences. There's more on that in the following pages.

The five questions have great power when you know how to use them and how to respond to the answers you hear. Be careful, though. Simply asking these questions and some elaborating questions does not make you an expert coach. Their structure is easy to learn, but it takes practice and time to master the thinking behind them. As your coaching skill grows, you'll start to think even more scientifically, add the right questions and, most important, be able to listen to the learner and have approaches for providing effective feedback.

There are Two Main Purposes for the Five Coaching Kata Questions

As a coach it is important to understand the two main reasons why you are using the five Coaching Kata questions in a coaching cycle. The questions (1) reinforce the scientific pattern of the Improvement Kata and (2) are prompts for the learner to show you how they are currently thinking, so you can formulate appropriate feedback.

1. **The five questions reinforce the pattern of the Improvement Kata.** You repeat the same overall pattern of inquiry in every coaching cycle, to help convey a systematic, scientific way of thinking.

2. **The five questions are prompts that help reveal how the learner is thinking.** You're listening for the thinking pattern of the learner as the learner responds, so you can give specific, situational corrective feedback.

It's like a sports coach asking an athlete to take a few swings or a music teacher asking a student musician to play a few bars, so they can observe what the student is doing. However, since the Improvement Kata pattern is an invisible mental process, the coach relies on questions to observe how the learner is currently thinking. Having the learner update and prepare their storyboard before each coaching cycle is part of this too. It's not that you don't trust the learner, it's that you have to have a way of understanding the learner's thinking before you can give feedback.

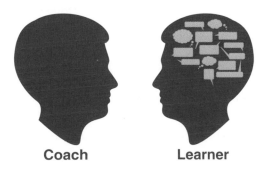

Coach   **Learner**

To facilitate this, be sure to take the time to stop talking—to pause—and listen to what your learner says. A common error here occurs when the coach prematurely draws conclusions, rather than waiting to see what conclusions the learner draws. The minds of beginner coaches are often understandably so focused on getting through the five questions that they end up not paying enough attention to what the learner is saying, and whether or not that conforms to the intent of the Improvement Kata pattern. This issue should go away with practice, once asking the five questions becomes habitual and you are able to direct more of your attention to the learner. Try to get frequent practice with the five questions by also using them at other times—for instance in meetings—not just during coaching cycles.

The coach is using a pattern of coaching that looks like this:

1. **Ask a question.**

2. **Listen.** Stop and be quiet.

3. **Compare.** Compare the learner's responses to the desired pattern of thinking—the "corridor" specified by the Improvement Kata.

4. **Instruct.** Introduce an adjustment to the learner's practice if necessary.

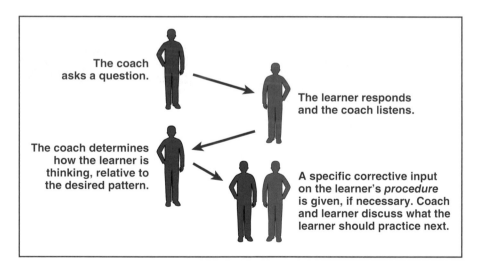

Here's a related story from Coaching Kata practitioner Michael Lombard:

> As a novice coach, I would go through and ask those questions verbatim, but I was initially so focused on the questions that I wasn't really listening to the answers. That's where my second coach would say, *"In*

reviewing how the learner answered your questions, take a look at the answers. What more do you want to know about any details they shared that would help explore the situation of what is truly happening here?" My second coach would guide me to slow down. My processing was still deliberate and slow at that point, so I needed to slow down my questioning to leave myself time to think about the answers in the context of the situation. As I got more experienced, those main headings remained as my Kata, but I could more freely expand on the questions where it was needed.

Universal Questions

The five Coaching Kata question format can actually be used during all four steps of the Improvement Kata. The questions will seem quite logical in step four—the executing phase of the Improvement Kata—but using them in the earlier planning phase can be a little more awkward. Think of it this way: as the learner goes through the four steps of the Improvement Kata, the nature of the target condition changes, as shown in the diagram below, but your coaching pattern at each step stays basically the same: reviewing the learner's last step, identifying their current threshold of knowledge, and making sure that the next step the learner has planned will lead to learning.

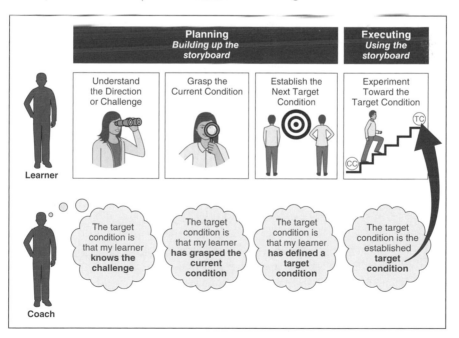

Asking Clarifying Questions

By now you should see that the Coaching Kata is more than just asking the five questions. It's about getting an understanding of how the learner is thinking. After each of the five questions you can also ask clarifying questions to trigger or probe the learner's thought process, gain more detailed information, and help identify the current threshold of knowledge. Between the five questions is where the coach's experience with the Improvement Kata comes into play, so the coach can see what the learner is doing right and wrong.

Your clarifying questions should relate back to the one of the five questions you most recently asked, seeking more detail relative to that question category. There are several examples of clarifying questions in the next chapter.

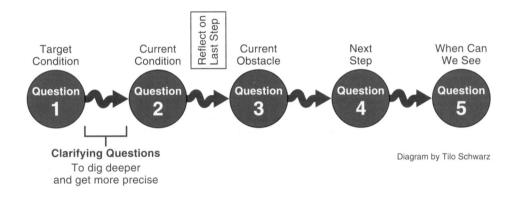

Diagram by Tilo Schwarz

The duration and complexity of your coaching cycles will ebb and flow. In some coaching cycles there may be several questions and adjustments to get the learner's practice back on pattern, and sometimes a coaching cycle will be just a quick check. With an experienced learner and coach, a five-question coaching cycle can often go quite quickly. However, whenever there is a weak point—where the learner can't answer one of the five main questions precisely with data—the coach should add some **open-ended** clarifying questions to get into a deeper and more detailed consideration and response. This is where the learner's current threshold of knowledge and next step typically become apparent, especially if the learner is reaching conclusions without evidence.

Closed-ended questions are those that can be answered by a simple yes or no—such as "*are you sure?*"—and don't give you much information about the learner's thinking. Open-ended questions require more thought and more than a one-word answer, and begin with words such as *how, what, describe, tell me more about, what do you think about? What exactly is happening? How do you know?*" You can also use the universal clarifying statement, "*Please show me.*"

An example closed-ended question is, *"Did you measure several exit cycles at the focus process?"* while an open-ended question would be, *"Can you show me your latest data about the focus process?"* Also, be careful asking your learner the question, *"Why?"* because using this word can easily feel confrontational rather than constructive, especially if you ask it repeatedly. It's usually better to use clarifying questions that begin with, *"Tell me more about . . ."* or, *"Can you show me?"*

The Coach's Five Question Card

The pocket card illustrated below is the standard starter card for the coach, containing the basic script for conducting coaching cycles. Keep the card with you as a reference, to be ready for a coaching cycle at any time. The systematic, scientific pattern of the five questions has utility all day long.[3]

Card is turned over to reflect on the learner's last step

COACHING KATA

The Five Questions

① What is the **Target Condition**?

② What is the **Actual Condition** now?
--------*(Turn Card Over)*------------→

③ What **Obstacles** do you think are preventing you from reaching the target condition? Which *one* are you addressing now?

④ What is your **Next Step**? (Next experiment) What do you expect?

⑤ How quickly can we go and see what we **Have Learned** from taking that step?

*You'll often work on the same obstacle with several experiments

Reflect on the Last Step Taken

Because you don't actually know what the result of a step will be!

① What did you plan as your **Last Step**?

② What did you **Expect**?

③ What **Actually Happened**?

④ What did you **Learn**?

----------------------------→
Return to question 3

During each coaching cycle, hold the card in your hand and ask all of the questions on the front and back of the card, one at a time and in order. The learner should also have a five question card, since the questions are not a surprise but rather a pattern the learner is practicing. Many learners post the five questions on their storyboard, as a reminder of what to expect in a coaching cycle.

---

3 A full-size template of the five question card is in the Appendix.

Begin by using the exact five question card that's shown here. As soon as you get used to what's on the card, you can start adding clarifying questions based on your experiences and suggestions from your second coach. One way to do this is to make yourself a folding question card like the one shown below. The folded card still fits in your pocket but has space on the unfolded right-hand side to add notes and your own questions that you are testing. The notes and clarifying questions on the example folding card shown here are some thought starters.

The Five Coaching Kata Questions	Your Own Notes & Clarifying Questions
COACHING KATA	
① What is the Target Condition?	• Is the target condition connected to the challenge? • What do you want to be happening? • No verbs! • Measurable? • Not "lack of something" • Achieve-by date?
② What is the Actual Condition now?	• Numbers, not opinions. • Can you show me? • How do you know? • How did you get the data? • Is there a run chart?
REFLECTION What did you plan as your Last Step?	• What was being tested? • Is the PDCA Record filled in?
What did you Expect?	• Was this written down? • Just read it!
What Actually Happened?	• Only facts & numbers. • Are the numbers written down? • Is there a run chart? • What is different than expected?
What did you Learn?	• Did the learner really reflect on this?
③ What Obstacles do you think are preventing you from reaching the target condition? Which *one* are you addressing now?	• What exactly is the problem? • True obstacles (variation), not action items or lack of a perceived solution. • Where does this problem occur? • Can you show me? • When does this problem occur?
④ What is your Next Step? (Next experiment) What do you expect?	• What is the current knowledge threshold? • Did what was learned in the last experiment frame this one? • Is expectation written down? • Please read it. • What numerical outcome do you expect? • How will you measure it? • How many cycles do you plan to measure?
⑤ How quickly can we go and see what we Have Learned from taking that step?	• Strive for cheap and fast experiments • Can we run this experiment today? Right now? • When is the next coaching cycle? • Accompany the learner if necessary.

Card folds here ⮏

Why is it called "The Five Questions" when there are more than five questions on the coach's card?

Early in our IK/CK experimenting, the following set of five questions, asked in this order, crystalized as a useful framework to help practice more scientific thinking and acting:

1. What are we trying to achieve?

2. Where are we now?

3. What's currently in our way?

4. What's our next experiment, and what do we expect from it?

5. When can we see what we've learned from taking that step?

As we continued to develop, test, and refine this Starter Kata, some secondary questions and the reflection questions on the back of the card were added. By then, however, the name "The Five Questions" had become an ingrained part of IK/CK terminology.

The Learner's Storyboard

The storyboard is the place where the learner records and maintains the ongoing details about their application of the Improvement Kata pattern to their focus process. It tells an unfolding "story," from left to right, following the pattern of the five Coaching Kata questions, and is used in each coaching cycle to support the coach/learner dialogue. The storyboard also reinforces the scientific pattern of the Improvement Kata and helps reveal the learner's current thinking to the coach.

Each focus process should have its own storyboard. If a learner is working on multiple focus processes, they will have multiple storyboards. If possible, each storyboard should be located near its focus process, so that you have the option of going and seeing the focus process during a coaching cycle.

Since the storyboard is a Starter Kata, your learner should begin with the exact layout of the storyboard that's shown here and in the Appendix. This common format also makes it easier for you to communicate with multiple learners. Over time your organization's storyboard format may evolve to suit your environment, but if you maintain a more or less standard storyboard format—whatever it is—across your organization, then coaching and communication will be easier.

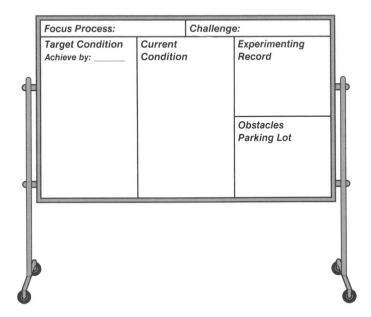

QUICK TIPS

Key Points for Using the Learner's Storyboard

- The learner owns the storyboard and should update it, not the coach.

- The learner knows the five main questions the coach will ask and prepares the latest information on the storyboard accordingly, in writing, prior to the coaching cycle. This helps the coach see how the learner is thinking without biasing the process, and avoids the risk of developing a "tell me what to do" dependency on the coach. The learner has to independently think about how to prepare the information on their storyboard before each coaching cycle.

- For the coaching cycles, the coach travels to where the learner's storyboard is located. The learner and coach refer to the storyboard throughout each coaching cycle.

- In the "Planning" phase of the Improvement Kata the learner builds up and populates their storyboard one section at a time. In the "Executing" phase the learner refers to the entire storyboard.

- In response to each Coaching Kata question, the learner should:

  o **Point to what is on the board.** This connects the question with a clear, concrete, and ideally data-based answer from the learner.

  o **First, simply read what is written on the storyboard and then wait for the coach.** This prevents the learner from drifting into verbally making up ad hoc answers, helps the coach determine how the learner is thinking, and teaches the learner to prepare information in writing *before* the coaching cycle.

    The learner may struggle with the idea of essentially reading what they have written on the storyboard, and instead may want to get right into discussing the whole story. Reading may seem too mechanical. As you get used to it, though, you'll find that this preempts overwhelming, long-winded explanations and pushes the coaching cycle to the heart of the matter, keeping it short and focused on facts and data, and revealing anything that is missing. Specifically, this practice helps to highlight the all-important current threshold of knowledge rather than obscuring it. If something is not on the storyboard, it can too easily be covered verbally via opinion and conjecture, so if it's important it should be on the board.

- Have the learner keep their storyboard neat, capturing data and details in a well-thought-out, comprehensible way. Maintaining the storyboard is part of cultivating the learner's sense of ownership of their Improvement Kata practice.

- Details on the storyboard may sometimes need to be adjusted in response to feedback from the coach. You can often have the learner do this right away during the coaching cycle. However, do not let the learner

(continues)

change something based on assumptions. In that case the learner should try to obtain the needed facts and data after the coaching cycle, and update the storyboard before the next coaching cycle. Perhaps this becomes the learner's next step.

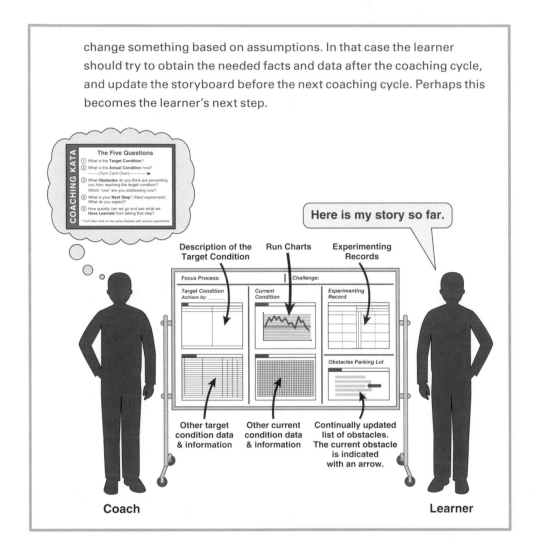

Important: Watch for the Threshold of Knowledge in Every Coaching Cycle

"Knowledge threshold" is an important aspect of scientific thinking, and it comes up in all three parts of this book. A knowledge threshold is the point at which we have insufficient facts and data, and start assuming. There's a current knowledge threshold for the learner in almost every coaching cycle, related to the obstacle that the learner is trying to overcome.

Finding the knowledge threshold is a key part of a coaching cycle, because that helps you and the learner see what the learner's next step should be. A good coaching question to have in mind in this regard is, *"What do we need to learn next?"*

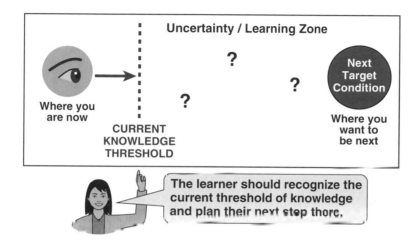

Recognizing the current knowledge threshold can be tricky because a beginner learner naturally wants to answer your questions, rather than saying, *"I don't know."* Ideally you'd like the learner to say, *"We're at a knowledge threshold here. At the moment I don't know the answer, and I don't want to jump to conclusions. Here is the next step (experiment) I intend to take to help me get the facts and data we need to learn more."*

You can encourage this kind of thinking by saying things like, *"It's not a problem if you don't know, just tell me how you plan to figure it out,"* or, *"How can we find that out?"* Scientific thinking depends on being able to acknowledge what we don't know, so that we know what to test next.

Since the learner may be hesitant to say, *"I don't know,"* a knowledge threshold will often be spotted by the coach noticing that the learner is responding imprecisely, with generalizations, assumptions, opinions, or speculation. As a coach you should develop an ear for it. When the learner does any of the following, it may indicate that a knowledge threshold has been reached. These indicators are a cue to focus in at that point, ask some clarifying questions, and encourage the learner to go and see, measure, dig deeper, or conduct a test:

- The learner uses words such as *I think, probably, maybe, could, most likely, well . . .* , on average, *90 percent of the time.*

- The learner says, "Let's reduce/increase it by 50 percent." (A 50 percent "guesstimate" is a typical response when we lack a specific, calculated number.)

- The learner refers to data that is too old.

- The learner seems overconfident, for instance acting like something must be true without being able to explain why.

- The learner refers to anecdotes without hard data.

At any time in your five-question coaching cycle dialogue, you may become aware of the learner's knowledge threshold, and at that point the learner's next step usually involves obtaining more facts and data relative to that point of weakness. Rather than continuing the coaching cycle with assumptions and opinions, you may go right to question 4 and agree on the next step. Don't let the coaching cycle structure override learning. Stop, have the learner take that step as soon as possible, and use what is learned to see further in the next coaching cycle. Note that this can send the learner back to investigate something they already thought they knew, which is not uncommon.

The key is that you (the coach) are trying to teach your learners that we see further by experimenting, rather than through conjecture. You can encourage this by handling knowledge thresholds with a positive spirit that has the learner:

- Acknowledge that knowledge threshold! A key realization is that there's *always* a threshold of knowledge.

- Capitalize on that knowledge threshold! Congratulations, you found it. Now stop and see further by conducting an experiment. Don't deliberate over answers in the coaching cycle. Deliberate instead over the design of the next experiment.

With practice you will not only start to see knowledge thresholds around you all the time, you may even begin to enjoy them as a fascinating part of life and something that helps you reach your goals.

Keep These Points in Mind

☐ There is always a knowledge threshold.

☐ It can be difficult to acknowledge knowledge thresholds until you get into the habit, because our brain tends to jump over knowledge thresholds and we don't like to admit not knowing.[4]

☐ A knowledge threshold is useful. It's exactly what you're looking for as the learner strives for the next target condition, because it reveals what needs to be investigated and worked on next.

☐ Since the five questions are nested—each question is a subset of the previous one—if one question is not answered well, then the subsequent questions won't be answered well. Once you find the learner's threshold of knowledge, don't be afraid to break the five-question sequence and help the learner plan their next step there.

☐ You see beyond a knowledge threshold by taking a step, not by talking about it.

Example: Spotting the Knowledge Threshold in a Coaching Cycle

Case example by Tilo Schwarz

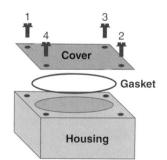

Coach Tina and learner Dan are in the middle of a coaching cycle. Dan is working on the obstacle of gaskets that get damaged during an assembly process. After beginning the coaching cycle and asking about the target condition and current condition, **Tina flips over her five question card to the back side** to reflect on Dan's last step. In the following dialogue excerpt, notice how coach Tina uses some clarifying questions to reveal the threshold of knowledge, and then gives an input to learner Dan's procedure.

(continues)

---

4 There may be an organizational culture bias to look like you have the answer, because people don't want to appear ignorant in front of the boss. Bosses can change this by practicing the Improvement Kata themselves.

Tina is asking the reflection questions on the back of her card.

"What did you plan as your last step?"

I wanted to analyze the units that need to be reworked because of damaged gaskets.

"What did you expect?"

I expected to learn what causes the damaged gaskets.

"What actually happened?"

I noticed that the gasket damage is always at screw hole number three.

"What did you learn?"

I think the damage occurs when the third screw is installed.

Tina notices Dan's unsure language and thinks, "Aha, that response suggests a knowledge threshold. We don't actually know the root cause yet." She flips her card back over to the front side, and after asking Dan to reiterate the current obstacle, she asks, *"What is your next step?"*

To advise the operators to be careful when they install the screw in hole three.

Tina then probes with some clarifying questions: *"What is actually happening when the gasket gets damaged? How exactly is the third screw causing the problem?"*

I'm not sure.

"So what do you think your next step should be?"

Hmm, I should probably go observe the process of installing the screws.

"What do you expect?"

To identify the root cause of the damage to the gaskets.

Epilogue: Later Dan discovered that the gasket damage at screw hole number three occurs because sometimes when screw number one is inserted it bumps the gasket out of the correct position. The root cause may be related to what happens with screw number one, not screw number three.

Don't Take Over the Problem Solving, Help the Learner Practice the Problem-Solving Process

In a coaching cycle, the coach is not asking questions in order to direct the learner to a particular solution (though it can feel that way to a beginner learner), but to guide the learner on procedure. The coach shouldn't be directive about *what* the learner is working on. That springs from the learner's process of experimentation, and neither coach nor learner knows in advance exactly what steps will lead to the target condition. However, once you have listened to the learner's responses, you can be directive about the learner's procedure for the next step.

Beginner coaches, especially if they are the learner's boss, may struggle with the boundary between "coaching" and "telling the learner what to do." It can be hard to keep from jumping in with your own thinking about solutions, or asking questions to lead the learner toward your preconceived ideas. Always keep in mind that the Coaching Kata is focused on getting the learner to practice thinking scientifically for themselves. Help the learner be more aware of where their problem solving is not a sound scientific process, but don't take over their problem solving. Ask open-ended questions that seek to learn how the learner is thinking, and then offer feedback *on the learner's procedure* that helps bring the learner into the corridor of Improvement Kata thinking and practice. If you are asking questions to lead the learner to your ideas for a solution, stop. But you can and should discuss the content and procedure of the learner's next experiment, which is not a solution but rather the process of developing solutions.

The Role of Encouragement

Since the learner's Improvement Kata practice occurs in the real world, rather than in a classroom, it is naturally going to involve setbacks and plateaus. We like to say "continuous improvement" or draw a staircase leading up to the next target condition, but that's not how it really works. You and your learner should practice every day, but you're probably not going to get better every day. Also, when we practice a new set of skills we are *supposed* to feel a sense of discomfort, because we're engaged in weaving new neural pathways. Practicing in our learning zone is sometimes going to involve feeling awkward, slow, unnatural, stiff, uncomfortable, and difficult.

All this makes encouragement, done right, an important element of coaching. For a beginner learner it's especially important to derive motivation from periodically feeling that he or she is successfully moving closer to the target condition and getting better at the Improvement Kata. If your learner is not getting this feeling periodically, then something in your coaching should be adjusted.

One key is to give specific praise that emphasizes new learning and growth, not just effort. You might say, *"You're not there yet, but you're on the right track,"* or, *"Look how your work has changed since two months ago. It's clear you're starting to get the hang of this."* (Be careful, you could inadvertently give the impression that you know the solution but are keeping it a secret.) With every win in overcoming obstacles to the target condition, the learner's sense that they can accomplish something grows. The learner becomes more motivated to pursue difficult goals and more confident that they will be able to achieve them.

Learn to Adjust Your Coaching Approach[5]

One of your main responsibilities as an Improvement Kata coach is to sense what the learner is ready for next, and to tailor your feedback accordingly. Don't assume every learner will pick this up in the same way or at the same pace.

The learner should internalize the patterns built into the Starter Kata, but the structured aspect of Kata practice can be confusing for the coach to handle. How do you and the learner stick to the practice script without getting too robotic? It's a balancing act. A coach should learn to sense when the learner needs strict structure, and when a more free-flowing dialogue is appropriate. As your skill increases, the nature of your coaching feedback can range from close *instructing* to looser *counseling* on a case-by-case basis.

While it is important to get the Starter Kata patterns down, adjustments often have to be made in how you deliver them based on what a learner is saying. Try to let what the learner is saying pull the response from you, rather than you deciding ahead of time what the best way to act would be. You still have to teach the patterns of the Starter Kata, but your delivery can be adjusted.

For instance, you can hold a mental checklist of the five Coaching Kata questions in mind and make sure you get answers to all of them in one way or another during a

---

5 The suggestions in this section are from Mark Rosenthal.

coaching cycle. You should stay tough-minded on the pattern you are teaching, but you can be softer and more adaptive with the learner. Of course, you should distinguish between a learner who is truly having a hard time adapting to the structured approach of practicing Kata, versus just normal discomfort that comes with practicing any new skill pattern. At the start or when in doubt, stick with the Kata.

The Coach's Notebook

Many coaches use a coaching cycle notebook to keep track of key issues from their coaching cycles, as reminders for the next coaching cycle with a learner, and to help them improve their own coaching practice. A notebook of some sort is probably a necessity when you are coaching multiple learners. Here are some ideas for what to record on the pages of your coaching notebook:

- Name of learner

- Coaching cycle date

- Start and end time

- Focus process

- Learner's next step

- Impressions of the learner's practice

- Feedback given to the learner

- Notes to yourself: What aspect of my own practice do I need to work on next?

The Role and Activity of the Second Coach

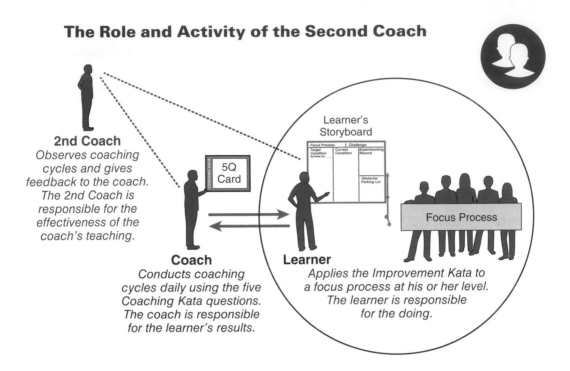

2nd Coach
Observes coaching cycles and gives feedback to the coach. The 2nd Coach is responsible for the effectiveness of the coach's teaching.

Coach
Conducts coaching cycles daily using the five Coaching Kata questions. The coach is responsible for the learner's results.

Learner
Applies the Improvement Kata to a focus process at his or her level. The learner is responsible for the doing.

If the learner isn't learning the Improvement Kata or is consistently not achieving their target conditions, then the problem usually lies in the coaching. The apparent simplicity of the five Coaching Kata questions makes coaching seem easier than it is, but it takes practice, with feedback, to master the pattern and intent of the Coaching Kata. It's the second coach who provides that feedback to you.

As already mentioned, coaching cycles are not just a forum for teaching a learner the Improvement Kata pattern and thinking, but also a forum for you to practice and experiment with your coaching skills. Of course, to make that practice effective, you should have someone to observe you and provide feedback—to "coach the coach." The second coach does this by observing you doing coaching cycles—to get a grasp of your current practice—and providing feedback to you after the coaching cycle. Having a second coach periodically watch your coaching cycles is essential for you to develop effective coaching skills.

Second Coach: Observing a Coaching Cycle

Good feedback requires good observation, and the second coach should take notes while observing a coaching cycle. The second coach can make an observation form for this purpose, such as the example below. Keep it simple, though, since note taking during a coaching cycle has to be fast. A blank sheet of paper is probably fine at the start.

COACHING CYCLE OBSERVATIONS		Process:	
		Date:	
Coach:	Learner:	Start/End:	
Question	**COACH**	**LEARNER**	
Review Challenge			
Q1: *Target condition?*			
Q2: *Actual condition now?*			
Reflect: *Experim. Record*			
Q3: *Obstacles? Which one?*			
Q4: *Next step? Experim. Record*			
Q5: *When see what learned?*			
What is the knowledge threshold?		Impressions:	
Key point(s) for this coach to practice next:		Next coaching cycle:	

Some key points for the second coach to look for during observation are:

- Is the coaching cycle dialogue following the five Coaching Kata question headings?

- Where is the learner's knowledge threshold? What is the point of weakness? Did the coach see this?

- Where is the learner's procedure not following the Improvement Kata? Did the coach see this?

- Where does the dialogue get unstructured?

- What did the coach notice and not notice?

TYPICAL COACHING ERRORS TO WATCH FOR		
Coach Asking Error	**What Is It**	**Countermeasure**
① Closed Question	Can be answered simply *yes* or *no*.	Start the question with *"what,"* *"how,"* or *"Tell me more about..."*
② Solution-Oriented Question	Advice disguised as a question.	Broaden the question.
③ Rhetorical Question	Statement of coach's opinion posed in question form.	Do not get into a judging attitude. Ask a clarifying question instead.
④ Leading Question	Pointing the learner to a solution the coach already has in mind.	Guide the learner on procedure, not solutions.
⑤ Failure to Interrupt	Being too timid to interrupt and refocus the dialogue.	Interject with a question that brings the coaching cycle back to focus.
⑥ Interrupting Too Much	Commenting while the learner is talking.	Count off 2 seconds after the learner stops speaking before replying.
⑦ Confrontational *"Why"* Question	Seeming to challenge the learner's motive and actions.	Rephrase with *"what"* or *"tell me more about..."*

Adapted from *Coaching Questions: A Coach's Guide to Powerful Asking Skills,* by Tony Stoltzfus, Pegasus Creative Arts, 2008

Sometimes it can help illuminate what is going on if the second coach times each step of the coaching cycle. For instance, once a coach and learner have had some practice, their exchange about the target condition and actual condition (Coaching Kata questions 1 and 2) should be short, while the dialogue about obstacles (question 3) and the next step (question 4) usually takes longer.

Like the coach, the second coach should probably also keep a notebook of the coaching cycles observed, to maintain a reference record of observations and feedback given to the coach. One simple way to do this is to keep completed coaching cycle observation forms, plus any other notes, in a binder.

Second Coach: Giving Feedback to the Coach After the Coaching Cycle

Some coaches prefer to get their feedback from the second coach privately, while others like to have their learners there too.[6] Be aware that since the learner, coach, and second

---

6 Some practitioners prefer for the second coach to give immediate feedback to the coach in front of the learner so that all can get over the discomfort of being a beginner.

coach may be in reporting relationships, sending the learner away can give the impression that the coach and second coach are going to talk about the learner. Explain to the learner what you are doing after the learner leaves. Note, also, that it is not the responsibility of the second coach to give feedback to the learner.

Some second coaches structure their feedback in three parts as follows:

1. **First ask the coach for *their* impressions about the coaching cycle that just took place.**

   o How did the dialogue go from your point of view?

   o Where was the knowledge threshold of the learner?

   o What were you paying attention to in this coaching cycle?

   o Where did the learner not follow the Improvement Kata pattern?

   o Where did you find the dialogue to be difficult?

   o What do you want to pay particular attention to in the next coaching cycle with this learner?

   o How do you hope this will influence the learner?

   o If you had a do over on one thing in this coaching cycle, what would you change?

2. **Then give your feedback, for instance in the following format.** Don't overload the coach; pick one or two key points for the coach to consider and practice next.

   o *"I observed that . . ."* (concrete observations you made)

   o *"I think this results in . . ."*

   o *"From my point of view you might . . ."* (specific suggestion that the coach can practice in the next coaching cycle)

3. **Agree on the date and time for the coach's next coaching cycle to be observed.** A beginner Improvement Kata coach should practice coaching cycles daily, with a second coach observing them each time and giving corrective feedback.

Looking Ahead

This chapter provides a lot of conceptual information about coaching the Improvement Kata. Don't worry, the pieces fall into place with practice, which we'll illustrate in the next chapter. In that chapter we'll go through an example coaching cycle, and then take a closer look at each step of a coaching cycle with the five Coaching Kata questions.

To conclude this Coaching Kata concept overview chapter, there is a set of coaching cycle tips on the next two pages.

QUICK TIPS

Coaching Cycle Dos and Don'ts

👍	👎
Schedule daily coaching cycles	Conduct coaching cycles only infrequently, irregularly, or "when we have time"
Conduct the learner's first coaching cycle early in the day, so the learner can do their next step (the next experiment) that day	Do the first coaching cycle near the end of the day
Proceed systematically by following the five questions	Permit unstructured, meandering, disorganized discussions
Determine whether or not the learner is operating within the corridor (the pattern) of the Improvement Kata	Ask questions to audit if the learner is doing what they said they would do
	Ask questions to get the learner to implement your preconceived solutions
Identify the current threshold of knowledge	Proceed based on assumptions
Ask the five questions while standing at the learner's storyboard	Conduct coaching cycles in your office
Have the learner point to items on the storyboard while they are talking	Just talk
Have the learner retime and graph the process metric before the coaching cycle	Use old current condition data

(continues)

Remember, question 5 is about finding out what you are learning

End the coaching cycle when the next step (next experiment) and the expectation are written on the learner's experimenting record

Ask question 5 as meaning *"When will you have it done?"*

Keep discussing possibilities and adding "action items" after the learner's next experiment has been defined. (This is a common error for beginner coaches. Each coaching cycle may result in only a small next step, which is normal. It's the rapid accumulation of these steps that brings you and the learner to the target condition.)

CHAPTER 12

HOW TO DO A COACHING CYCLE: PRACTICE ROUTINES

Practice Routines

HOW TO DO A COACHING CYCLE

This chapter shows you what to do. It (1) walks you through an example coaching cycle, and then (2) reviews each step of a coaching cycle, with the five Coaching Kata questions as the headings of those steps. (The examples in this chapter are in the "executing" phase of the Improvement Kata.) This chapter includes the following information.

INSTRUCTIONS

KEY POINTS

EXAMPLE CLARIFYING QUESTIONS

POTENTIAL WEAK POINTS

After each coaching cycle you should review how it went and decide what aspect of your coaching you want to work on in the next coaching cycle. Feedback from your second coach is invaluable in this. However, the extra edge in practicing any skill comes from working on something that you personally want to get better at. In the case of coaching, that extra edge may come from your truly wanting to help learners be successful in developing and applying their own scientific thinking. Create power in your people!

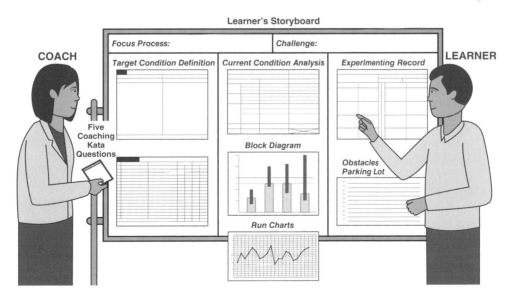

Your Overall Goal as a Coach: Giving Useful Feedback to the Learner

Let's start with the end in mind. The purpose of a coaching cycle is to review the learner's practice of the Improvement Kata and give useful feedback, as necessary, on the learner's *procedure*. There can be some content character to your feedback, too, of course, without getting into solutions. For example, you might show the learner how to make a run chart or how to arrange information on their storyboard.

Feedback is usually communicated between you and the learner, and anyone else whom you and the learner want to have present. In some coaching cycles your second coach will also be there, but this person is observing your coaching practice. The second coach does not give feedback to the learner.

The flow and elements of a coaching cycle are structured, but feedback to the learner is situation dependent, different from coaching cycle to coaching cycle and learner to learner. As you improve your coaching mastery, your feedback will get better. Imagine your task as a coach as determining whether or not this learner is practicing within the corridor of scientific thinking and acting procedure that's specified by the Improvement Kata, and to introduce course corrections as necessary to get the learner back to practicing "on pattern." Your feedback should be based on observation, should be specific, and should pertain to what the learner is doing or not doing, not to the learner's traits or characteristics as a person (this has nothing to do with the learner as a person). Your feedback can be reinforcing or corrective:

- Reinforcing feedback praises practice done well and encourages the learner to continue to strengthen that behavior. Be specific about what is good and why.

- Corrective feedback points out an area of the learner's practice that should be modified to avoid building a bad habit, and gives specific advice for how the learner should modify their practice.

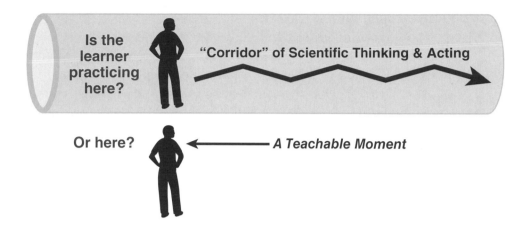

You'll find that there are two categories of feedback in a coaching cycle: Small, quick feedback that involves little tweaks to the coaching cycle dialogue itself, and forward-looking feedback that pertains to the learner's next step. Both of these kinds of feedback can be given in one coaching cycle—and often are, especially with beginner learners.

1. **Small, immediate corrective input on the learner's way of presenting information in response to the five Coaching Kata questions.**

    This is quick "pause and fix" feedback that's done at any time in the coaching cycle to immediately correct unscientific aspects in what the learner is saying or doing right now—in the coaching cycle. Just like in music instruction, it's important not to play through mistakes and develop bad habits. When you spot unscientific thinking or behavior, or thinking and behavior that doesn't follow the Improvement Kata pattern, briefly pause the coaching cycle to introduce an adjustment in how the learner is responding.

    After you interrupt a coaching cycle like this, immediately rehearse the problematic part by going back to your last Coaching Kata question and restarting there, or even back to the beginning of the coaching cycle. This "let's start over" technique from music practice helps internalize desired thinking patterns. However, pausing and interrupting a coaching cycle can be overdone, so pick your priorities. Note also that pausing and starting over should in no way seem punitive. You should give it a friendly, caring, and simple "Oh, let's fix this now" feeling.

2. Feedback for the learner's next step.

This is the main feedback and adjustment in a coaching cycle, which is often done at the threshold of knowledge. Once you and the learner recognize the current threshold of knowledge, regardless of where you are in the coaching cycle you'll often go right to question 4 and discuss the next step that the learner proposes, to help see beyond that point. Don't overload the learner with comments and activities here, either. Just focus on their next step and what you want them to practice. You'll be back tomorrow.

An interesting alternative strategy is to sometimes not correct the learner's planning for the next step, even though it contains an error that you see, and instead allow the learner to make the mistake and let the experience be the teacher. This works best when the learner's next step is cheap, small, relatively harmless, and quick. You'll have to decide on a case-by-case basis on what occasions to use this approach.

In giving feedback be sure to (a) first describe specifically and clearly what you observe—what the learner is doing or not doing—and then (b) provide a specific and purposeful instruction about how the learner could or should proceed differently. Don't withhold the rationale for your feedback and just give corrective feedback, but also raise the issue you see that is leading to that particular feedback.

Feedback Too Vague	Good, Specific Feedback
"You should be more detailed in grasping the current condition."	*"Making a run chart based on timing 30 cycles can help you get a more detailed understanding of the current condition."*
"You need to give that more thought."	*"How could you be sure this pattern holds across both shifts?"*

These questions are the main
headings for your coaching cycles

The Five Coaching Kata Questions

1. What is the **Target Condition**?
2. What is the **Actual Condition** now?
   --------(Then reflect on the last step)--------
3. What **Obstacles** do you think are preventing you from reaching the target condition? Which *one* are you addressing now?
4. What is your **Next Step**? (Next experiment) What do you expect?
5. How quickly can we go and see what we **Have Learned** from taking that step?

Frame: You're framing and anchoring the coaching cycle dialogue.

Reflect: You're reviewing the learner's last step.

Focus: You're confirming the current obstacle that the learner is working on.

Next Experiment: You're helping the learner design the next step at the threshold of knowledge, based on what was learned from the last step.

Next Coaching Cycle: You're agreeing on when the next experiment will be done, the time for the next coaching cycle, and what information the learner should prepare.

QUICK TIPS

TO THE BEGINNER COACH	TO THE BEGINNER LEARNER
• Stick to the five-question sequence. • Don't skip questions. • Hold the five question card in your hand during the coaching cycle. Ask all the questions on the front and back of the card, one at a time, exactly as they are written on the card. • Listen to your learner. • Ask only simple, open-ended clarifying questions between the card questions. • Find the current knowledge threshold, and confirm the learner is conducting their next experiment there.	• You just need to answer the questions. No need to elaborate unless you are asked. • As you respond, use your storyboard . . . point and read! • A coaching cycle is actually just that simple.

AN EXAMPLE COACHING CYCLE

Data Entry in the Sales Department

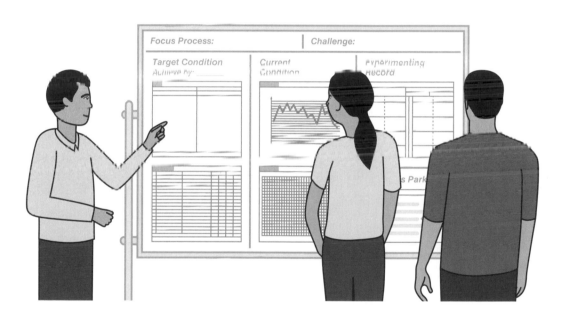

As you read this **example coaching cycle dialogue** and the subsequent debrief between the coach and second coach, notice what didn't go well in the coaching cycle.[1]

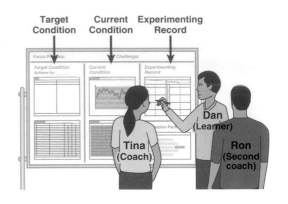

> **Learner:** Dan
>
> **Coach:** Tina (coaches the learner)
>
> **2nd Coach:** Ron (coaches the coach)

- -

Ron is heading over to the Sales Department, where he has promised to observe some of Tina's coaching cycles as her second coach. On the way, Ron thought about what he wanted to watch for. In his first few coaching cycle observations he found it difficult to watch the coach/learner dialogue and think about it at the same time. For this reason he'd made a list of observation tips for second coaches, which he was now mentally reviewing:

- Is the dialogue following the five-question pattern?
- Where is the learner's knowledge threshold in this coaching cycle?
- What is the point of weakness?
- Where is the learner's procedure not following the Improvement Kata?
- Where does the dialogue get unstructured?
- What did the coach notice and not notice?

Coach Tina greeted Ron as they met for a few minutes before the next coaching cycle, "Thank you for coming and taking the time to review my coaching practice. My next coaching cycle is with Dan, who's working on shortening the lead time for processing sales contracts." Tina and Ron headed off together to Dan's storyboard.

Tina and Dan's Coaching Cycle

> Tina: "Good morning, Dan. I've asked Ron to watch my coaching today, to give me some feedback afterward. Is that all right with you?"

---

1 The original version of this coaching cycle was written by Tilo Schwarz (www.lernzone.com) and published in *Yokoten* magazine, Issue 5, 2016 (www.yokoten.de).

Dan: "No problem. Good morning, Ron."

Tina: "Before we get going, can you remind us about your focus process and the challenge?"

Dan: "Sure. I'm currently focused on sales contract processing, and our challenge is to have processing a contract take 20 minutes or less. This is part of a larger challenge for the whole Sales value stream that we call *Sale today, closed today*."

(Tina now refers to the **Five Question Card** *she is holding.)* ⇒

Tina: "OK, **what is the target condition for this process?**"

Dan: "The target condition is that the data entry portion of handling a sales contract takes 6 minutes or less, by June 15."

Tina: "**What is the actual condition now?**"

Dan points to a run chart on his storyboard: "At the moment it takes between 32 and 41 minutes to process a sales contract. The data entry portion of that is too long."

Tina asks a clarifying question: "What does 'too long' mean in numbers?"

Dan: "The last days have been really busy, and I didn't have time to measure the data entry time for the contracts we've recently processed. But when we measured it two weeks ago and made this run chart, data entry took between 11 and 15 minutes."

(Tina now **flips over her five question card** *and asks the reflection questions on the back of the card.)* ⇒

Tina: "**What did you plan as your last step?**"

Dan: "I set up some timing for several cycles of sales contract processing."

Tina: "**What did you expect?**"

Dan: "I wanted to get a sense for the steps and times for this process."

Tina: "**What actually happened?**"

Dan (pointing): "I was able to get the basic steps and their times. As you can see in the run chart from two weeks ago, there was a lot of variability."

Tina: "**What did you learn?**"

Dan: "I learned that data entry is usually the single largest block of time in processing sales contracts."

*(Tina **flips her five question card** back over to the front side and continues with the questions there.)* ⇒

The Five Questions
① What is the **Target Condition?**
② What is the **Actual Condition** now?
————(Turn Card Over)————▸
③ What **Obstacles** do you think are preventing you from reaching the target condition? Which "one" are you addressing now?
④ What is your **Next Step?** (Next experiment) What do you expect?
⑤ How quickly can we go and see what we **Have Learned** from taking that step?

*You'll often work on the same obstacle with several experiments

COACHING KATA

Tina: "**What obstacles do you think are preventing you from reaching the target condition, and which one are you addressing now?**"

Dan reads through his entire obstacles parking lot, then goes to the current focus obstacle: "Data entry is too complex. Sometimes it takes too long to enter the list of customer items; other times it's something else."

Tina asks a clarifying question: "What exactly is the obstacle?"

Dan: "I don't know exactly. It's different each time, since every customer order is different."

Tina: "What is the reason for the data entry taking so long?"

Dan: "I think the entire manual data entry process takes a lot of time, as well as the review of the article numbers. Maybe this process could be automated if someone from IT took a look at it."

Tina: "**What is your next step?**"

Dan: "I'll talk to the guys in IT and ask them to look at it. Maybe then we can find a way to reduce the data entry time."

Tina: "What do you expect from this step?"

Dan: "To know what part of data entry can be automated."

Tina: "**How quickly can we go and see what we have learned from taking that step?**"

Dan: "If I can talk to our colleagues in IT today, then maybe tomorrow or the day after. Let's meet again in three days. By then I should have something."

Dan made a note of the agreed-on next step and date, and they ended the coaching cycle.

After Dan went back to his work area, Tina asked Ron, *"What do you think? How did the coaching cycle go?"* She was curious to hear his feedback.

What Do You Think?

Ron and Tina's discussion after the coaching cycle, as well as Ron's feedback to Tina, follows below. Before reading that, think about your answers to the following questions:

- Where is the learner Dan's threshold of knowledge in this coaching cycle?

- If you were coach Tina, what feedback would you give to Dan?

- What do you predict that Ron's feedback to Tina will be?

Feedback from Second Coach Ron to Coach Tina

Ron checked his notes, thought for a moment, and said to Tina: "I observed that you and Dan didn't really have a good grasp of the obstacles, and the next step you agreed on is pretty vague and will take a long time. Dan seems to be jumping to an automation solution."

Ron went on with a list of points: "I think it's important to agree on a specific, concrete obstacle first, and then agree on a precise next step related to that obstacle. The problems that the obstacle causes should be measurable, since otherwise the learner can't formulate a measurable expectation for their next step. I think it's also helpful to agree on significantly smaller steps. You and Dan should actually be meeting for another coaching cycle tomorrow."

Tina replied (somewhat impatiently), "Yes, I noticed that too. That was the problem. Dan didn't know the obstacles well—simply calling the data entry process 'complex.' So I wanted to get him down to at least one obstacle. And then the next step somehow got too big. But I didn't know what else to do. Honestly, your feedback here is not helping me much. What should I do differently?"

Ron noted that Tina was pushing back, so he said, "I do need to learn more about observing coaching cycles. Let's use your dialogue with Dan to think about what good feedback should look like. We now have both views on the coaching cycle—yours from inside and mine from the outside."

Tina responded. "I agree, we both noticed the same problem, but I'm not sure what to do about it."

Ron thought about it. "Generally speaking, your feedback to the learner should relate to the point of weakness in the coaching cycle, which is usually going to be the threshold of knowledge. The threshold of knowledge in your coaching cycle seemed to be at question 3, the obstacles."

Tina jumped in: "Ah, and at that point I probably should have shifted the dialogue to the next step, instead of continuing to drill down on the obstacles, which Dan doesn't yet understand well enough. If I push, he's going to come up with some answer, rather than saying, 'I don't know,' since I'm his boss."

Tina continued: "In my own Improvement Kata practice I learned that at a knowledge threshold we have to actually go and take a step in order to learn more and see further. Discussing opinions doesn't help. Sending Dan back for closer observation and investigation of the obstacles would have been a better next step, because that was the threshold of knowledge in our dialogue."

Ron added, "Exactly. And maybe the threshold of knowledge started appearing even earlier, since the data on the actual condition was not up to date. The last measurements were taken two weeks ago."

Tina agreed: "True, that was another weak point that I didn't pick up on. Hmm, now there are two potential thresholds of knowledge. So what should I have focused on?"

Ron: "Both of the issues are connected. Not having up-to-date data makes it difficult to identify true obstacles, which makes it almost impossible for the learner to formulate a measurable expectation for their next step."

"I've come to the conclusion that good coaching cycle feedback should concentrate on one sticking point in the dialogue, at the threshold of knowledge. If possible, the feedback should pertain to the first point of weakness that arises in the dialogue, since the five Coaching Kata questions nest within each other and progressively focus in, like a funnel. If one question is not answered well enough, then the answers to the following questions will be even worse."

Tina summed up: "I observed that Dan's data on the actual condition was not current. Without data to study it became difficult to identify specific obstacles. If I notice that actual condition data is not up to date and that's the knowledge threshold, then at that point I should go straight to question 4. The next step is to get and analyze current data. In fact, whenever we hit the knowledge threshold, we can pretty much go to question 4."

"I agree," replied Ron. "And since Dan would be gathering data for a run chart, you can encourage him to also make notes on his timing worksheet about obstacles he observes."

"Depending on how far into the five questions you are when you hit the knowledge threshold, there may be no need to keep going with all five questions. At that point you and the learner can plan the next step accordingly, agree on the time for the next coaching cycle, and then the coaching cycle is done. You'll be back for the next one tomorrow, or even sooner if you and the learner would like.

"Once you find the current threshold of knowledge, don't be afraid to step out of the five question sequence and discuss the learner's next step to remedy that point of weakness. And the learner should then take that step as quickly as possible!"

A COACHING CYCLE
STEP-BY-STEP

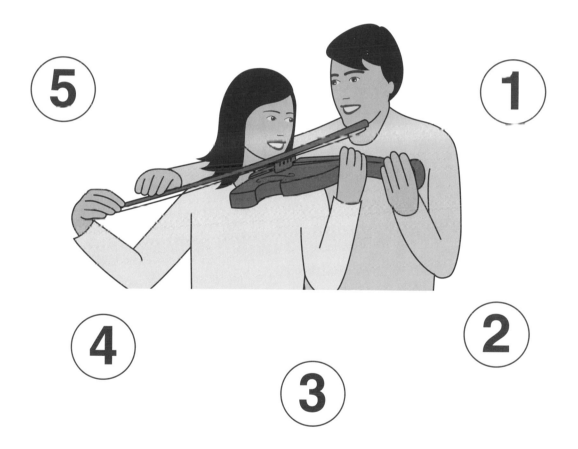

Start a Coaching Cycle by Putting the Learner at Ease

It can be uncomfortable to be a beginner. You feel unsure, lose a sense of identity, and become vulnerable. Novice learners may even perceive coaching as meaning they did something wrong. Don't start a coaching cycle by jumping right into the five questions. Start with building some trust and understanding, showing the learner that you are interested in them and their success, and enabling you to be helpful.

A coaching cycle does not judge success or failure. Both the coach and the learner should have a genuine interest in achieving the target condition, how the learner is proceeding, what is being learned, and what will be the next step. It's a dialogue, not an exercise of authority. As you get started:

- Begin by greeting one another.

   When you can in the coaching cycle, stand next to the learner, facing their storyboard, rather than facing one another head-on.

- With a new learner, briefly go over the practice and coaching approach so the learner understands what is taking place: *you're practicing skill patterns to make them a habit.* Many of us practice with more interest and motivation when we know what we're doing and why.

One key to putting the learner at ease can be to help the learner realize that it's normal to be a beginner when you're starting to learn a new skill, just like an athlete. As mentioned above, it may be a good idea to remind yourself and the learner about the purpose of a coaching cycle, which is to develop the learner's scientific thinking skills by offering procedural feedback, based on observation, on his or her Improvement Kata practice.

Your learner will naturally try to be skillful right from the start with the Improvement Kata routines, especially if you are their boss. So it helps if you create a mindset that it's OK to make mistakes—of enjoying the discovery and learning process. If you like, you can even point out that you are practicing and learning your coaching routines too.

Ask the Learner, *"What Is the Challenge?"*

Before you begin the five-question coaching dialogue at the storyboard, have the learner name their focus process and reiterate the overarching challenge or goal that he or she is working toward. This reminder connects the learner's target condition to a larger objective and helps the learner recognize how their efforts fit in with the bigger picture. The rest of the coaching cycle dialogue will be anchored by the challenge.

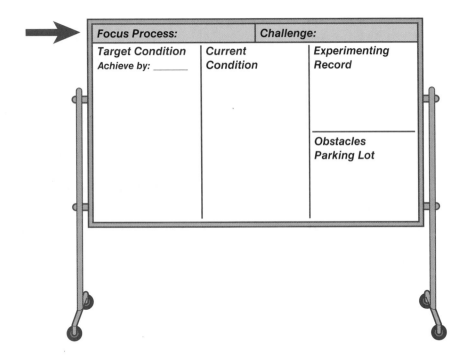

Now you can get into asking the five Coaching Kata questions ➤

QUESTION 1

FRAMING AND ANCHORING
Orienting Yourselves

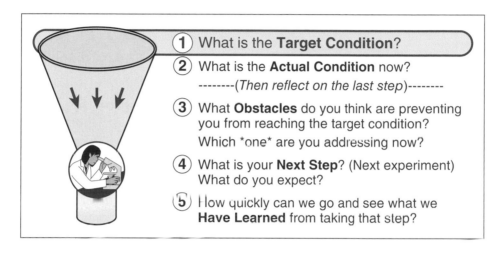

(1) What is the **Target Condition**?

(2) What is the **Actual Condition** now?

--------*(Then reflect on the last step)*--------

(3) What **Obstacles** do you think are preventing you from reaching the target condition?
Which *one* are you addressing now?

(4) What is your **Next Step**? (Next experiment)
What do you expect?

(5) How quickly can we go and see what we **Have Learned** from taking that step?

Consensus on both the target condition (Question 1) and current actual condition (Question 2) is essential for avoiding endless discussion. What is the learner trying to achieve, and where exactly are they now? The first two questions are simple and can often be answered quickly, but they are important because the other questions relate back to them.

KEY POINTS
about the
Target
Condition

- Don't skip over questions 1 and 2, even if it starts to feel a bit like play-acting. Go through all five questions in each coaching cycle, because you are framing the dialogue and trying to convey the thinking pattern inherent in the five questions. Many new coaches ask, "Do I really need to ask question 1 every coaching cycle?" The answer is yes, because the rest of the coaching cycle relates back to that question. It only takes a few seconds.

- The learner should point to their target condition form and read the target condition as it is written there.

- There should be no verbs or action items in the target condition, nor should it describe a lack of something. It should describe a measurable destination.

- If possible, the target condition should be in alignment with the challenge that's noted on the storyboard. It should be a step in that direction.

- There should be both an outcome metric and a process metric that will tell the learner when the target condition is achieved. The process metric should be directly observable at the focus process.

- Do you (the coach) understand the target condition? If it is not clear to you, or if the learner cannot explain it clearly, it is likely the learner is not clear about the target condition either.

EXAMPLE
CLARIFYING
QUESTIONS

"Please read through the target condition."

"What do you want to be happening?" "How will you know?"

"What is the pattern you're trying to achieve?"

"What are the intended process steps and sequence?"

"What is the achieve-by date?

"How do you picture the target condition?"

"Tell me about how this target condition relates mathematically to the challenge."

"Can you describe the target condition with numbers?"

"Let's run through the math on this."

"How are you measuring it?"

"What is the process metric? What value do you want it to have?"

"What is the outcome metric? What value do you want it to have?"

- The learner didn't prepare the storyboard before the coaching cycle to ensure that the required updated information is ready and in a sequence that matches the five Coaching Kata questions.

- The learner states a solution or countermeasure as the target condition, rather than describing a desired new state of the focus process.

- The learner sees the removal of an obstacle as the target condition, rather than describing a desired future condition. That is, the learner describes the target condition as something that will *not* be happening, rather than what *will* be happening.

- The target condition is only an outcome metric, without a process metric or any description of a desired operating pattern.

- The description of target condition is vague and not measurable.

QUESTION 2

FRAMING AND ANCHORING
Orienting Yourselves *(Cont.)*

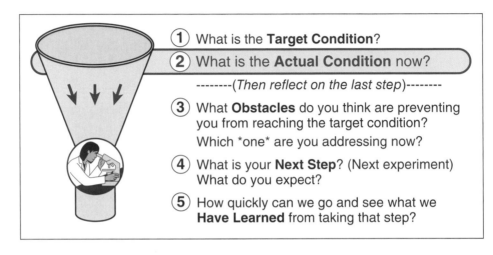

① What is the **Target Condition**?

② What is the **Actual Condition** now?

--------*(Then reflect on the last step)*--------

③ What **Obstacles** do you think are preventing you from reaching the target condition? Which *one* are you addressing now?

④ What is your **Next Step**? (Next experiment) What do you expect?

⑤ How quickly can we go and see what we **Have Learned** from taking that step?

Understanding the current condition is vitally important, both initially and ongoing. Many mistakes can arise when the learner does not measure and maintain an up-to-date understanding of the current condition as changes are made.

At question 2 be sure to review the current values for the process metric and the outcome metric. These are the minimum metrics that the learner should have updated and graphed, ideally in run charts, before each coaching cycle.

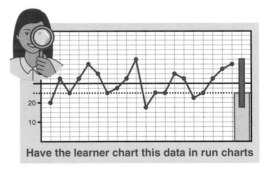

Have the learner chart this data in run charts

KEY POINTS about the Actual Condition

- After the first few coaching cycles, for question 2 the learner should no longer be referring back to the initial current condition. The learner should describe the condition now, based on recent direct observation and measurement.

- Question 2 is not a review of steps the learner has taken. The learner should simply describe how the focus work process is actually operating now, relative to the target condition.

- As always, ask the learner to physically point at the relevant supporting documents and data on their storyboard.

- Check that you can directly compare the target condition and the current condition. This is a common problem.

- Ensure there is current data for the outcome metric and process metric. Ideally they are in run charts.

- Whenever possible you should go and see what the learner is talking about. *"Show me"* and *"Tell me more about . . ."* are useful coaching phrases at any point in the coaching cycle.

**EXAMPLE
CLARIFYING
QUESTIONS**

"What are the latest facts and data for the current condition now?"

"How do you know?"

"Can you show me the data?"

"Please show me the block diagram."

"Please show me the run chart of the process metric."

"Let's go and see."

From this point forward in the coaching cycle a useful question can be: *"What do you think?"* Remember, you're asking such questions to see if the learner is thinking scientifically according to the pattern of the Improvement Kata. An answer like, *"I think we're not sure yet"* is scientific, whereas answers such as, *"I think what's going on is . . ."* may represent unscientific conjecture, unless the learner is stating that as a hypothesis that the learner plans to test.

To see if the learner's actions are based on facts and data, not assumptions, you can always ask: *"How can you tell?"*

- The actual condition on the learner's storyboard is not actual any more.

- The learner bases their description of the current condition on opinion, hearsay, and assumptions about what they think is happening.

- The description of the actual condition is not based on any data.

- Process and outcome metric run charts are missing on the storyboard.

- The learner is not actually going to the focus process to see the real current condition.

- The current condition description includes words like *no*, *none*, or *lack*, which indicates the learner already has a solution in mind.

- The learner is not directly comparing the actual condition to the target condition.

Reflect

Date & step	What do you expect + metric		What happened	What we learned
Step	**Prediction**		**Results**	**Learning**
		Do a Coaching Cycle / Conduct the Experiment		

REVIEWING THE LEARNER'S LAST STEP

Flip the card

Reflect on the Last Step Taken
Because you don't actually know
what the result of a step will be!

① What did you plan as your **Last Step**?
② What did you **Expect**?
③ What **Actually Happened**?
④ What did you **Learn**?

Return to question 3

① What is the **Target Condition**?

② What is the **Actual Condition** now?

-------*(Then reflect on the last step)*-------

③ What **Obstacles** do you think are preventing you from reaching the target condition? Which *one* are you addressing now?

④ What is your **Next Step**? (Next experiment) What do you expect?

⑤ How quickly can we go and see what we **Have Learned** from taking that step?

Now turn to and use the "reflection section" on the back of your five question card.

Reflecting on the learner's last step is where learning comes from. What is learned from taking one step helps determine the next step (the next experiment). To reflect, the learner refers to the last filled-in row on their experimenting record, while you ask the four questions on the back of your card. Those four questions correlate to the four columns in the learner's experimenting record:

Q1: What was your last step?

The learner points to and reads the description in **column 1**.

Q2: What did you expect?

The learner points to and reads their prediction in **column 2**, including how he or she proposed to measure the experiment.

Q3: What actually happened?

The learner points to and reads the resulting facts and data from the experiment, recorded in **column 3**, plus supporting documents such as new run charts. The learner should only refer to facts and data here, no interpretation yet.

Q4: What did you learn?

Before the coaching cycle, the learner has compared column 2 (expectation) and column 3 (resulting facts and data) and summarized what they learned in column 4. The learner now points to and reads the box in **column 4**. This is the place where the learner should make an interpretation of the results.

KEY POINTS
about the
Reflection

- Prediction error helps the learner find their way forward. Some of the best experiments have an unexpected result—a surprise—that helps the learner discover what will be necessary to reach the target condition. A target condition is reached through numerous small learning steps and experiments, many of which will generate "negative" (but highly useful) results.

Acknowledging and learning from prediction error can be difficult because it runs counter to our instincts. If the learner feels threatened by prediction errors they may start just laying on more countermeasures, rather than analyzing and learning from the situation.

Try to depersonalize the process of experimentation by emphasizing using experiments to learn. To function in this way your coaching cycle reflection should have a positive, we-are-detectives, no-blame feeling. To create that kind of depersonalized atmosphere, treat unexpected results not as good or bad, but simply as occurrences that can teach us something about the focus process and our improvement process. Of course, the learner should continue rapidly experimenting, in order to achieve the target condition by its set achieve-by date.

- The information in the four columns of the experimenting record should be written in by the learner *before* the coaching cycle. During the reflection portion of the coaching cycle the learner should respond to your questions by simply reading from their experimenting record.

- In **column 2** the learner should have written down what they expect from a step before they took that step. (You checked this during the last coaching cycle.)

- In **column 3** the learner should record only facts and data. No interpretation yet.

- In **column 4** the learner should record the conclusions they have drawn from the experiment. This might include new information about how the process is operating, better clarity on the nature or causes of obstacles, or even an "I don't know" statement that better defines the threshold of knowledge. Column 4 is often the most difficult of the four reflection questions.

- Whenever necessary, have the learner adjust or correct what is written in the experimenting record immediately during the coaching cycle.

- An experimenting record form should be dedicated to one obstacle. If the learner starts working on a different obstacle, they should use a new experimenting record.

EXAMPLE
CLARIFYING
QUESTIONS

Q1: What was your last step?

"What was the threshold of knowledge?"

"What did you plan to do?"

"What was being tested?"

Q2: What did you expect?

"What did you think would happen?"

"What did you want to learn?"

Q3: What actually happened?

"Can you show me the data?"

"How do you know?"

"What does the data say?"

"What specifically did you observe?"

"Is there a run chart?"

Q4: What did you learn?

If a hypothesis was being tested, was it: *"Confirmed"* / *"Refuted?"* / *"Can't tell?"*

"What was different than expected?"

"What do the data and your observations lead you to believe?"

"What are the implications for your next step?"

"Did you learn more about any obstacles?"

POTENTIAL
WEAK POINTS

- The learner reports only verbally, without a completed experimenting record.

- The learner mistakes a refuted prediction as a failure.

- Columns 3 and 4 have nearly identical entries. The learner fails to distinguish between what happened (facts and data only) and what they learned (interpretation).

- After conducting an experiment, a beginner learner continues to take more steps without first going through a coaching cycle.

QUESTION 3

CURRENT OBSTACLE
Stay Focused

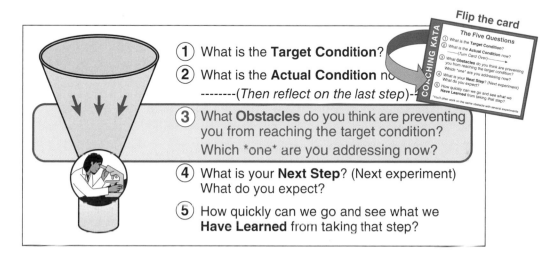

① What is the **Target Condition**?

② What is the **Actual Condition** no[w]?

--------(*Then reflect on the last step*)-[-]

③ What **Obstacles** do you think are preventing you from reaching the target condition? Which *one* are you addressing now?

④ What is your **Next Step**? (Next experiment) What do you expect?

⑤ How quickly can we go and see what we **Have Learned** from taking that step?

Turn to the front of your card and continue with the questions there

Identifying obstacles means focusing in. Obstacles are what the learner experiments against as they strive for the target condition.

Have the learner answer the first part of question 3 by pointing at their obstacle parking lot (OPL) and quickly reading through all of the obstacles currently listed there. This represents the learner's current impression about what the obstacles are. The second part of question 3, "Which *one* are you addressing now?" then usually defines the focus for the rest of this coaching cycle.

The learner should have updated the OPL before the coaching cycle, adding obstacles that have been discovered and crossing off obstacles that are no longer an issue. An arrow should indicate the one obstacle that's currently being worked on. That obstacle should also be written on the learner's experimenting record.

The obstacles parking lot is merely a place to record and hold perceived and encountered obstacles. It is not an action-item list, and the learner will usually not end up working on all the listed obstacles. This helps the learner realize how flawed initial perceptions and predictions can be, which is a key aspect of thinking scientifically. The OPL also helps the learner relax by acknowledging problems while keeping the learner from working on too many at once. The goal is to narrow down the scope of what the learner works on to reach the target condition, not to eliminate all potential obstacles.

Obstacles should be specific and measurable. If the target condition was vaguely stated, then the obstacles will probably be vague too. With a clearly defined target condition and a directly measurable process metric, obstacles should be easily recognized and measured.

Watch out for an obstacle recorded as a "lack of . . ." or a to-do item, which is incorrect. Lack of a countermeasure that the learner already has in mind is not an obstacle. "Lack of training" is not an obstacle, but "Some persons do the work incorrectly" is. When the learner's description of an obstacle begins with words like "need to . . . ," it suggests that the learner is already jumping to a solution.

KEY POINTS
about the
Current
Obstacle

- Obstacles are good to have because they tell you that you are on the move.

- The learner should generally work on one obstacle at a time, though there are exceptions.

- The learner is free to work on any obstacle. Don't worry about starting with the biggest or most important one, especially if the learner is a beginner. Just have the learner pick one and get going. Working on one obstacle will often lead the learner to other obstacles, and in that manner the obstacles that need to be addressed will reveal themselves sooner or later.

- It is perfectly legitimate for an obstacle to simply be something the learner needs to investigate, measure, and learn more about. This kind of obstacle might be noted on the OPL as, "We don't yet understand . . . ."

- Action items and potential solutions are not the same as obstacles or problems. Here's some Improvement Kata terminology: What the learner does to overcome an **obstacle** or **problem** on the way to the target condition is called

steps or **experiments**. When the learner overcomes an obstacle, it means they've developed a **solution** to that problem.

- It almost always takes more than one step to break through an obstacle, and often many more. The learner may work on one obstacle for some time, going through a series of experiments related to that obstacle. That's normal.

- Sometimes the effort to overcome one obstacle also eliminates other obstacles or makes them irrelevant.

- Each experimenting record is normally dedicated to one obstacle. If the learner is switching to a different obstacle, they should start a new experimenting record.

- Sometimes it is OK for the learner to drop the focus on an obstacle and, instead, shift to another obstacle, based on something that has been learned.

- Sometimes the learner will identify legitimate problems that may relate to the challenge, but not the next target condition. Start a separate list—off the storyboard—so the learner knows their concerns have been acknowledged and that they just aren't working on those issues now.

EXAMPLE
CLARIFYING
QUESTIONS

"What exactly is the obstacle?"

"What exactly is the problem?"

"What problem does that obstacle cause?"

"How will you measure that?"

"Are there new obstacles you have identified?"

"Should any obstacles get crossed off the list?"

If lack of a perceived solution is being stated as an obstacle, ask: *"What problem would that solve?"* in order to get at the actual obstacle.

If only one obstacle is identified, you can ask, *"If that one problem is addressed, will you be at the target condition?"* Sometimes this leads the learner to more obstacles.

- The obstacles parking lot is treated as an action-item list.

- The obstacle is stated as a solution or to-do item.

- The obstacle is too vague, not measurable. If the learner can't be specific about an obstacle they may not understand the situation at the focus process enough or may be unaccustomed to being specific.

- The obstacles parking lot is outdated—failure to cross off obstacles or add newly discovered obstacles.

- The obstacles parking lot contains entries not connected to the target condition.

QUESTION 4

PLANNING THE NEXT EXPERIMENT

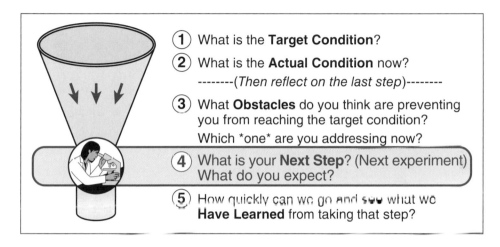

(1) What is the **Target Condition**?

(2) What is the **Actual Condition** now?

--------*(Then reflect on the last step)*--------

(3) What **Obstacles** do you think are preventing you from reaching the target condition? Which *one* are you addressing now?

(4) What is your **Next Step**? (Next experiment) What do you expect?

(5) How quickly can we go and see what we **Have Learned** from taking that step?

The entire coaching cycle focuses down to this point, the threshold of knowledge and the learner's next step.

Your task here is to ensure that the learner has planned a well-designed experiment to tell you what you need to know next, and, if not, to give corrective input. Remember, the plan for the next step is discussed in the coaching cycle, but the learner takes the step *after* the coaching cycle—ideally as soon as possible.

EXPERIMENTING RECORD	*(Each row = one experiment)*				
Obstacle:		Process:			
		Learner:		Coach:	
Date & step	What do you expect + metric			What happened	What we learned
Last Experiment					
Next Experiment					

Prediction Side

First have the learner tell you what they see as the current knowledge threshold. Ask, *"What is the threshold of knowledge now?"* or *"What do we need to learn next?"*

Then have the learner tell you, *"This is what I intend to do next and why,"* while you listen. Do this by having the learner simply read (and point to) their latest entries in columns 1 and 2 of their experimenting record. Based on learnings from the last step (discussed in the *Reflection* you just did) but before this coaching cycle, the learner should have written their proposed next step and a corresponding expectation on the left (prediction) side of their experimenting record.

Note that at question 4 you *do* want the learner to go beyond the threshold of knowledge and make a prediction. Here it is OK for the learner to say things like, "I think . . . ," because in order to be scientific the learner must state in advance, and write down, what he or she predicts will be the result of the next step. Comparing the actual results with this prediction is where useful surprise and learning come from.

After the learner has read from columns 1 and 2 of the experimenting record, then you can go into more depth in your dialogue with the learner, about details and how they plan to carry out the next step, and so on. The coach should either accept the learner's proposed next step (the next experiment) or give feedback to help improve the design of the next step. Use the "Coach's Checklist for Planning the Next Experiment" in the following pages to help you either validate the learner's proposed next step or get the learner to fine-tune their proposed step. If you think the learner needs to do more analysis and preparation before taking the next step, which is not unusual, then that should be the learner's next step.

As you discuss the learner's plan for the next experiment, you can have the learner immediately adjust or correct things that are written in column 1 and 2 of their experimenting record. You're not changing data, you're adjusting a plan. Or, if you like, you can opt to let the learner go forward with making a small mistake as a learning experience.

As soon as the next step (not a list of steps) is clear, the coaching cycle is near its end. There's no need to try to look further ahead or for long discussion at this point. It's time for the learner to take the next step as quickly as possible, so they can see further based on that.

KEY POINTS
about the
Next Step

- The coach and learner should have identified and discussed the current knowledge threshold before the next step is determined. The current knowledge threshold typically defines what will be the next experiment. This will often send you back to further investigate something you thought you already knew.

- Help the learner understand that any step they take is an experiment.

- Get the learner to think about the desired result, not about something to be implemented. It helps to have the learner first state what they need to learn, and then describe their plan for learning it.

- Designing and conducting the next experiment toward the target condition is a great place for the learner to involve other persons in the focus process and get their ideas.

- The learner should set up experiments so that mistakes and unexpected results will not create an unsafe condition or harm the customer process. (Sometimes this is humorously referred to as *limiting the blast radius*.)

- If the next step can be taken right away, then by all means do that. How about right after this coaching cycle?

- Experiments do not have to be big or long, even though we may think that. Asking the learner, *"What can we learn today?"* can help to narrow the scope.

At the beginning learners will often try to make the next step bigger than it needs to be, which can overshoot the knowledge threshold and hamper learning. Guide the learner into experiments that are as small and as rapid as possible for the situation. You're not looking for big leaps. You're looking for a good experiment. Caution: if your coaching cycles are not daily, the learner's steps may tend to get too big, because the learner will naturally want to do lots of things before you finally meet again.

- "Go and get more information" can be a next step. That's normal. There are different kinds of experiments, as described in the following table.

Types of Experiments	
All of these qualify as a type of experiment, since you don't know in advance what the outcome will be.	**What the learner can expect from this type of experiment.**
Go and See Observation and data collection, without changing anything, to learn more about a process or situation.	The learner should expect to get information about how something is currently functioning.
Exploratory Experiment Introducing a change in a process simply to see, via direct observation, how the process reacts.	The learner should expect to gain more information about the focus process in general, beyond what can be learned from passive observation.
Testing a Hypothesis Introducing a change, ideally in only a single factor, with a quantitative prediction of what will happen.	The learner should expect to learn about the effect(s) of a specific change.

Coach's Checklist for Planning the Next Experiment

❏   Is the experiment being done at the current threshold of knowledge?

❏   Is the learner's prediction about the effect of the next step written down?

❏   Is the next step something that actually addresses the current obstacle?

❏   Does it have something to do with the current obstacle?

❏   Is the experiment a single-factor experiment? (This is not always possible.)

❏   Does the learner have a plan to test their prediction soon, quickly, and inexpensively?

❏   If the prediction fails, will no one be harmed?

❏   Is the step measurable? Will the learner be able to use facts and data to tell if the prediction was correct or not?

❏   Does the learner plan to collect enough data points about the outcome of the experiment?

> ❑ Is the next step/experiment part of a chain of learning? Does it build on what was learned in the previous step?
>
> ❑ Don't say, "Let's try it and see if it works," since this makes an experiment a matter of success versus failure. Say, "Let's try it and see what we learn."

EXAMPLE CLARIFYING QUESTIONS

1. About the threshold of knowledge:

"What is the threshold of knowledge now?"

"What do we need to learn next?"

2. About the design of the next experiment:

"How will the test be done?"

"How will you measure it?"

"How will you collect the data?"

"What is the process metric?"

"How many data points do you want?"

"What is the outcome metric?"

"What happens if the outcome is not as expected?"

"Can you test this today?

"Could we test it right now?"

"What can we learn today?"

3. About the learner's prediction—you can ask two slightly different questions here:

"What do you expect to happen?"

"What do you expect to learn?"

Other questions are:

"What do you want to happen?"

"How will you know?"

POTENTIAL
WEAK POINTS

- Failure to identify the current threshold of knowledge before designing the next experiment.

- Definition of the next step is too vague (and thus an equally vague "What do you expect?").

- Coach doesn't ask the learner how they will measure the effect of an experiment.

- Coach fails to have the learner write down the details of the next experiment, including what the learner expects to happen and to learn.

- Instead of stating an expectation, the learner just restates the next step in past tense.

- Next step is an action item, not an experiment. Learner wants to implement an idea without testing it.

- Learner overlooks "Go and see" as a legitimate experiment.

- The experiment is too risky.

- The next step is too large.

READY TO GO

PREPARING FOR THE NEXT COACHING CYCLE

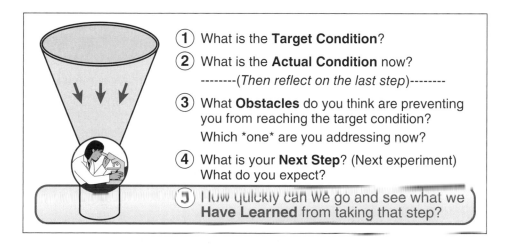

1. What is the **Target Condition**?
2. What is the **Actual Condition** now?
   --------(*Then reflect on the last step*)--------
3. What **Obstacles** do you think are preventing you from reaching the target condition?
   Which *one* are you addressing now?
4. What is your **Next Step**? (Next experiment)
   What do you expect?
5. How quickly can we go and see what we **Have Learned** from taking that step?

With question 5 you are looking for a fast turnaround. The purpose here is to get the learner to do the next experiment as quickly as possible, because both of you can't see further toward the target condition until that happens.

When the learner's next step is clear and written on the experimenting record, a coaching cycle is essentially done. All that's left is confirming the time for the next coaching cycle. There is no need to discuss further, because both coach and learner are at the current knowledge threshold at least until they get the results from the next experiment.

The next coaching cycle will often be the next regularly scheduled one, but you can also add a coaching cycle any time you would like. For example, to give a beginner learner closer coaching and less chance to acquire poor habits, you can schedule a coaching cycle for right after the learner has taken their next step. Sometimes you may even decide to accompany or check in on the learner as they carry out their next step.

Having only a single action item may feel uncomfortable if you are accustomed to full action-item lists. You may soon discover, however, that experimenting every day is faster and more effective than trying to lay out the exact path of steps in advance.

And you're done

KEY POINTS
about the
Next Coaching
Cycle

- Question 5 can be tricky. New coaches and learners often incorrectly think it means, *"When will you have it done?"* but question 5 is more about seeing, *"What are we learning?"* Caution! Even when you ask question 5 with the correct intention, the learner may still actually be hearing you say, "When will you have it done?"

- Agree on a specific date and time for the next coaching cycle.

- Agree on what data and information the learner should obtain, prepare, and have recorded on their storyboard before the next coaching cycle.

- The first response to, *"When can we see?"* is often something like, "Next week." Challenge this! If necessary, accompany the learner to show him or her how to experiment cheaply and quickly, to get new information and see further as swiftly as possible. How to run rapid experiments is one of the skills you are teaching.

**EXAMPLE
CLARIFYING
QUESTIONS**

"How could we do this experiment sooner?"

"How could we do this experiment today?"

"How about we do the experiment right now, together?"

POTENTIAL
WEAK POINTS

- A common error is having a task orientation instead of a learning orientation. For example, if the coach incorrectly asks, *"When can we go see what has been accomplished?"* rather than, *"When can we go see what we have learned from taking that step?"*

- Coach and learner keep on discussing even though the coaching cycle should now end, for instance speculating about what will happen with the next step. A coaching cycle should stay focused on the next step and then stop.

- The next coaching cycle is too far in the future. Coaching cycles are too infrequent, resulting in more than one step getting discussed in the coaching cycle.

- No specific place and time are agreed upon for the next coaching cycle before ending this coaching cycle.

SUMMARY

> *See you at the next coaching cycle*

Coaching cycles will seem stiff and awkward at first, for both the coach and the learner. In time the format will flesh out with your own clarifying questions and style, and a certain, "Wow, look at the obstacles we are overcoming!" dynamic should appear. That's when energy and self-efficacy are created.

Practice Protocol:
What the Learner Should Do During a Coaching Cycle

	COACH'S QUESTION	LEARNER'S RESPONSE
	What is the challenge?	Learner explains what he or she understands the overarching challenge to be, which comes from the level above the learner.
1	**What is the target condition?**	Learner reads through the description of the target condition that's on the storyboard, pointing to the items as he or she reads.
2	**What is the actual condition now?**	The learner reads through the facts, data, and diagrams on the storyboard that describe the current condition as it is *now* (not the initial current condition). The learner should point while reading.
REFLECTION	**What was your last step?**	Learner reads from the first column of their experimenting record.
	What did you expect?	Learner reads from the second column of their experimenting record.
	What actually happened?	Learner reads from the third column of their experimenting record.
	What did you learn?	Learner reads from the fourth column of their experimenting record.
3	**What obstacles do you think are preventing you from reaching the target condition?** **Which *one* are you addressing now?**	Learner reads through the items on the obstacles parking lot and then points to the obstacle he or she is currently working on. The learner should have an arrow next to this obstacle. The learner may work on one obstacle for several experiments.
4	**What is your next step? (The next experiment) What do you expect?**	Learner proposes the next step, reading from the first and second columns in the next row of the experimenting record. Ensure the learner is designing a good next experiment before you approve it.
5	**How quickly can we go and see what we have learned from taking that step?**	Learner proposes the date and time for the next coaching cycle. Ensure that the learner is doing the experiment as soon, quickly, and cheaply as possible. Agree on facts and data to bring to the next coaching cycle, and you're done.

On the Achieve-by Date the Four-Step Improvement Kata Pattern Repeats

When the learner reaches their target condition or its achieve-by date, the four-step Improvement Kata pattern repeats. However, before that the coach and learner should do a summary reflection over the entire process. This can lead to learnings that can be applied in the next cycle through the four steps of the Improvement Kata pattern. See the short "Summary Reflection" chapter at the end of Part II. Have the learner reflect on how they worked by asking questions such as:

"Why are we using the Improvement Kata pattern?"

"What did we gain by doing that?"

"What went well?"

"What could be better?"

"What aspects of the Improvement Kata should we work on next time?"

CONCLUSION

An education isn't how much you have committed to memory,
or even how much you know. It's being able to differentiate
between what you know and what you don't.

—Anatole France

The scientific thinking patterns of the Improvement Kata and Coaching Kata are universal and applicable in all sorts of organizations. It's about a different way of managing ourselves in order to better utilize our astonishing human capabilities.

Here's a little secret. A way of thinking is not something you use only at work and then turn off. The principles and practice routines presented here shape a mindset that you end up taking into the rest of your life, too. The Improvement Kata is a routine of thinking and acting that gives us a systematic and constructive way of dealing with problems, uncertainty, and change. In other words, how we can work—and work together—to achieve beyond what we can see. People in business, education, government, and daily living can learn and benefit from practicing the fundamental Starter Kata patterns presented in *The Toyota Kata Practice Guide*. Practicing these routines:

- Defuses the tension around a problem and allows us to work together.

- Reframes how we look at the world and react to it, helping us recognize that everything is to some degree uncertain and every step we take is an experiment.

I invite you to actively share with others what you are learning from your Toyota Kata practice.

Levels of Proficiency

Practicing the Starter Kata is likely to quickly make you better at problem solving, and it grows from there. How much do you need to practice in order to acquire scientific thinking skill, and how do you gauge success in practicing the Improvement Kata and Coaching Kata?

Ultimately the yardstick for success is the degree to which scientific thinking imbues the interactions and way of working in your organization. You should notice the language in your organization gravitating away from rushing to solutions and more toward a scientific process of developing solutions. You should notice subtle changes in your meetings—toward the systematic pattern of the five Coaching Kata questions and greater ease with leaving some uncertainty in the room as you head to your next experiment. You should discover yourselves talking about things in a different way, becoming less willing to jump to conclusions and more excited about testing your ideas. You may find yourself more eager to take on challenges. When you hear people referring to the "threshold of knowledge" and saying things like, *"There may be an even better idea behind this one,"* you know you are doing a better job of utilizing our human capabilities.

Suggestions for the minimum amount of practice necessary to reach basic skill levels for the Improvement Kata and Coaching Kata were mentioned in the body of this book, which I'll repeat here. As a general guideline, and that's all, you might look at it roughly as follows. Your mileage may vary.

> **Basic competency with the Improvement Kata pattern:** Three successive target conditions on the same focus process and 30 cycles of experimenting.

> **On top of that, for basic Coaching Kata competency:** Conducting 60 coaching cycles, with at least 20 of those including observation and feedback from a second coach.

An interesting attempt to describe levels of skill development is the five-stage model of skill acquisition proposed in 1980 by Stuart and Hubert Dreyfus. The stages of the Dreyfus model are only theoretical landmarks, but they provide a useful sense of skill progression. If nothing else, the Dreyfus model helps you understand how skill building usually works. Here are two tables that describe Dreyfus levels for an Improvement Kata learner and an Improvement Kata coach. Over time you can populate the descriptions in these tables with observable behaviors that match your world. Note, however, that gauging skill level is not a self-judgment. Until you become proficient in the skill you are practicing you can't assess skill level, because to judge expertise you need expertise.[1]

---

1   Research is clear: the less skill we have, the more we tend to overestimate our ability.

AN IMPROVEMENT KATA SKILL LEVEL SCALE

Skill Level	Description	Degree of Autonomy
Expert (Not everyone reaches this level)	• No longer relies on rules/guidelines/maxims. • Grasp of situations & decision making are intuitive. • Has vision of what is possible.	Able to take responsibility for going beyond existing standards and creating own interpretations.
Proficient	• Has unconscious understanding and applies the Improvement Kata pattern more on "autopilot." • Deviates from the strict Kata to fit the situation. • Sees what is most important in a situation. **High self-efficacy in applying the IK pattern**	Able to take full responsibility for own work and coach others.
Competent	• Has standardized and routinized procedures. • Sees actions partially in terms of long-term goals. • Can prioritize.	Able to achieve most tasks using own judgment.
Advanced Beginner	• Actions are based on the Kata. • Situational perception still limited. • All aspects are given equal importance.	Able to achieve some steps using own judgment, but coaching is needed for overall task.
Novice	• Strict adherence to the Kata. • Little situational perception & discretionary judgement. • Has to purposely concentrate on Starter Kata routines. *Low self-efficacy in applying the IK pattern*	Needs close coaching and instruction.

Adapted from the Dreyfus Model of Skill Acquisition. Dreyfus, Stuart E., *Formal Models vs. Human Situational Understanding: Inherent Limitations on the Modelling of Business Expertise*, Berkeley, 1981.

A COACHING KATA SKILL LEVEL SCALE

Skill Level	Description	Autonomy
Expert (Not everyone reaches this level)	• Intuitive grasp of coaching based on deep, practiced understanding. • Direct, yet supportive. • Coaching conversations are natural; learner doesn't notice being coached. • Sought after for coaching advice.	Second coach needed occasionally.
Proficient	• Clear perception of learner's gaps or weaknesses. • Uses coaching to guide: adapts to the situation, asks meaningful questions. • Ability to assess learner's preferred learning style. • Has second coach capability.	Second coach needed periodically.
Competent	• Can sense learner's uncertainty level and knowledge threshold. • Consistently coaches learner with a repeatable pattern. • Coaching is a normal part of coach's daily work.	
Advanced Beginner	• Recognizes need for second coach. • Becoming comfortable providing feedback to learner. • Beginning to observe and listen more (versus talk and advise). • Asks some clarifying questions to gain insight into learner's thinking.	Should have a second coach observe each coaching cycle.
Novice	• Rigidity in asking questions. Uses closed-ended questions. • Lack of discipline to follow a pattern and recognize its importance. • Focuses on results rather than the process for achieving results. • Not able to identify when learner has hit a threshold of knowledge.	

Adapted from the Dreyfus Model of Skill Acquisition by Jennifer Ayers, Yvonne Muir, and Julie Simmons.

You can be said to have mastered something when you have great command of it, and, in the case of scientific thinking, it even becomes a way you view the world. At some level of mastery you'll see all the steps of the Improvement Kata at once, and be able to flow naturally and easily between them to suit almost any situation. We build buildings in linear, discrete steps, just like the way you first practice the Improvement Kata. The concrete contractors come in, then the framers, then the electrician, then the plumber, and so on. But in a practiced mind all the Improvement Kata steps are there all the time. If you happen upon a brick, then you'll put it in the wall, even if the foundation is not yet done and you may have to adjust later. It becomes automatic.

Since the Improvement Kata is a meta skill, the patterns embedded in its Starter Kata are a basis upon which all sorts of creativity and initiative can proliferate. Sure, there's the learner's level of scientific thinking skill development as measured by the linear Dreyfus scale, but from the meta perspective there is also how well the learner is doing in reaching whatever challenging goals they may have, by smoothly applying those skills in a situation-appropriate mix.

Everyone does not need to reach "expert" level in scientific thinking. It is enough to become proficient. Notice how in sports there are top athletes and there are people playing in the park on the weekend, but all are playing, enjoying, and trying to get better at the same sport. Scientific thinking is like that too. Perhaps the best level of skill development to reach for with scientific thinking is not that of *expert*, but of perpetual learner.

Common Ground

There have been many calls for applying greater scientific thinking in business, government, education, and daily life. However, concepts that don't come with some concrete practice routines for beginners are by themselves unlikely to lead to change. They may be good ideas, but they lack a way of operationalizing them, which makes them *concepts without a Kata*.

I invite proponents of other scientific thinking models, in business and education, to go further than just making models and presenting inventories of principles and characteristics. That's great, but alone is not likely to change us. We also need some Kata—some starter practice routines—to help us transition to the behavior and thought patterns those models depict. I like to encourage other Improvement Kata / Coaching Kata colleagues and communities, who may have their own views. Together we're creating a more experiential dynamic, to help humans everywhere practice more scientific ways of thinking and acting, and developing ourselves toward the best we can imagine and more.

Perhaps every organization should ultimately have its own set of Starter Kata for developing essential scientific thinking skills, to suit its particular circumstances and culture. However, organizations should not develop their own Kata while they are still beginners. They're not ready for that. A more promising approach is to begin with established practice routines like those in *The Toyota Kata Practice Guide*, and then evolve those routines as a critical mass of persons developing scientific thinking knowledge and skill. The practice routines of the Improvement Kata and Coaching Kata are a great starting point.

What remains constant? I'll conclude with what we call the *Toyota Kata Code*, which defines what doesn't really change as you keep moving ahead and find your own way:

The Toyota Kata Code

1. Conditions are unpredictable.

2. Enjoy the learning zone.

3. Understand the direction, grasp the current condition, establish a target condition, experiment toward the target condition.

4. Beginners practice Starter Kata exactly.

5. Be a coach, have a coach.

And with that, my best wishes to you!

FORMS AND TEMPLATES

THE IMPROVEMENT KATA
A SCIENTIFIC PATTERN FOR EVERYONE

Let's face it—we have a natural tendency to jump to conclusions without realizing that our unconscious predispositions are influencing what we see, think, and do. You can make scientific, creative working a habit and get more comfortable with uncertainty by practicing the repeatable, four-step pattern called the *Improvement Kata.*

A **Kata** is a routine you practice to make its pattern a habit.

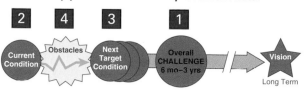

START HERE 1

Describe the overall challenge you're reaching for, in a meaningful way.

What new situation do you want to have six months to three years from now?

Future-state mapping is a useful tool here.

USE THE OVERARCHING CHALLENGE AS A FRAME FOR THE FOLLOWING STEPS

2 **Current Condition:** Study the facts and data of where you are now. You're trying to see, sketch, measure, and understand the current pattern, as an input to Step 3.

3 **Next Target Condition:** Now describe where you want to be *next* on the way to your challenge. It will usually take a series of target conditions to reach your challenge goal. Be sure the target condition is measurable in some way and has a specified achieve-by date between one week and three months out.

4 **Experiment Toward the Target Condition:** You can't foresee the exact path to the target condition. The obstacles you encounter show you what you *need* to work on to get there. Find the path by conducting experiments daily, using the *experimenting record* and asking the *five Coaching Kata questions* after each experiment.

The point at which you have no facts and data is the *threshold of knowledge.* There's always a threshold of knowledge.

To see further, conduct your next experiment there.

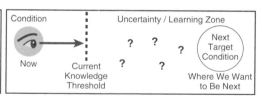

Learner's Storyboard

Focus Process:		Challenge:
Target Condition Achieve by: _____	**Current Condition**	**Experimenting Record**
		Obstacles Parking Lot

Coaching Kata Five Question Card

COACHING KATA

The Five Questions

① What is the **Target Condition**?

② What is the **Actual Condition** now?

--------(*Turn Card Over*)------------→

③ What **Obstacles** do you think are preventing you from reaching the target condition?
Which *one* are you addressing now?

④ What is your **Next Step**? (Next experiment)
What do you expect?

⑤ How quickly can we go and see what we Have Learned from taking that step?

*You'll often work on the same obstacle with several experiments

Reflect on the Last Step Taken

Because you don't actually know
what the result of a step will be!

① What did you plan as your **Last Step?**

② What did you **Expect?**

③ What **Actually Happened?**

④ What did you **Learn?**

-----------------------------→
Return to question 3

Current Condition / Target Condition Form

CURRENT CONDITION / TARGET CONDITION			Outcome Metric	
Learner:	Coach:	Focus Process	Process Metric	
		Current Condition Date	Target Condition Achieve-by Date	
1 Outcome Performance	Actual output			
	Operating time			
	Is there overtime?			
2 Customer Demand & Planned Cycle	Requirement			
	Takt time			
	Planned cycle time			
3 Operating Patterns	Process steps and sequence			
	Variation			
	Observations about the current operating patterns			
4 Equipment Capacity	Automated equipment constraints?			
5 Core Work	Calculated number of operators			

Steps of Process Analysis

STEP 1:
Process
Outcomes

STEPS 2–5:
Pattern of
Working

1 **GRAPH PROCESS OUTCOME PERFORMANCE**
How is the process performing over time?

2 **CALCULATE THE CUSTOMER DEMAND RATE
AND PLANNED CYCLE TIME**
How frequently should the process do what it does?

3 **STUDY THE PROCESS'S OPERATING PATTERNS**
☐ Draw a block diagram of the process steps and sequence.
☐ Time exit cycles and draw run charts, to make variation visible.
☐ Record your observations about the current operating patterns.

4 **CHECK EQUIPMENT CAPACITY**
Are there any equipment constraints? What are they?
(This step is only for processes that include automated equipment.)

5 **CALCULATE THE CORE WORK CONTENT**
How many operators would be necessary
if the process had no variation?

Timing Form

TIMING WORKSHEET	Process		Metric	
	Date		Operator	☐
Cycle	Observed Times (Data)		Observations about the current operating pattern (Facts)	
1				
2				
3				
4				
5				
6				
7				
8				
9				
10				
11				
12				
13				
14				
15				
16				
17				
18				
19				
20				
21				
22				
23				
24				
25				

Check box if this is process output

Experimenting Record

EXPERIMENTING RECORD *(Each row = one experiment)*						
Obstacle:		**Process:**				
		Learner:		**Coach:**		
Date & step	**What do you expect + metric**	**What happened**	**What we learned**			

Conduct the Experiment

Do a Coaching Cycle

Second Coach Observation Form

COACHING CYCLE OBSERVATIONS		Process:
		Date:
Coach:	Learner:	Start/End:

Question	COACH	LEARNER
Review Challenge		
Q1: *Target condition?*		
Q2: *Actual condition now?*		
Reflect: *Experim. Record*		
Q3: *Obstacles? Which one?*		
Q4: *Next step? Experim. Record*		
Q5: *When see what learned?*		

What is the knowledge threshold?	Impressions:
Key point(s) for this coach to practice next:	Next coaching cycle:

INDEX

ABOUT THE AUTHOR

Mike Rother is an engineer, researcher, and teacher who works to develop scientific thinking in individuals, teams, and organizations. He shares his findings widely and is in the Association for Manufacturing Excellence Hall of Fame.

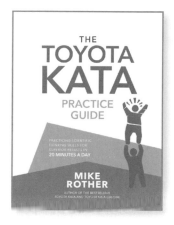
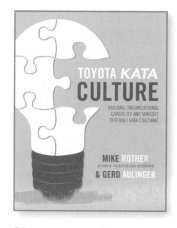